Using Video Games to Level Up Collaboration for Students

Using Video Games to Level Up Collaboration for Students provides a research-informed, systematic approach for using cooperative multiplayer video games as tools for teaching collaborative social skills and building social connections. Video games have become an ingrained part of our culture, and many teachers, school leaders and allied health professionals are exploring ways to harness digital games–based learning in their schools and settings. At the same time, collaborative skills and social inclusion have never been more important for our children and young adults.

Taking a practical approach to supporting a range of learners, this book provides a three-stage system that guides professionals with all levels of gaming experience through skill instruction, supported play and guided reflection. A range of scaffolds and resources support the implementation of this program in primary and secondary classrooms and private clinics. Complementing this intervention design are a set of principles of game design that assist in the selection of games for use with this program, which assists with the selection of existing games or the design of future games for use with this program.

Whether you are a novice or an experienced gamer, *Using Video Games to Level Up Collaboration for Students* provides educators with an innovative approach to ensuring that children and young adults can develop the collaborative social skills essential for thriving in their communities. By using an area of interest and strength for many individuals experiencing challenges with developing friendships and collaborative social skills, this intervention program will help your school or setting to level up social outcomes for all participants.

Matthew Harrison is an experienced educator and researcher with a passion for utilising technology to enhance social learning and inclusion. He has taught in Australia, South Korea and the United Kingdom at primary, secondary and tertiary levels. Matthew is currently lecturing in Learning Intervention at the University of Melbourne.

Using Video Games to Level Up Collaboration for Students

A Fun, Practical Way to Support Social-emotional Skills Development

Matthew Harrison

Routledge
Taylor & Francis Group
LONDON AND NEW YORK

Cover image: © Getty Images

First published 2023
by Routledge
4 Park Square, Milton Park, Abingdon, Oxon OX14 4RN

and by Routledge
605 Third Avenue, New York, NY 10158

Routledge is an imprint of the Taylor & Francis Group, an informa business

British Library Cataloguing-in-Publication Data
A catalogue record for this book is available from the British Library

Library of Congress Cataloging-in-Publication Data
A catalog record has been requested for this book

ISBN: 9780367458805 (hbk)
ISBN: 9780367458829 (pbk)
ISBN: 9781003025917 (ebk)

DOI: 10.4324/9781003025917

Typeset in Bembo
by Deanta Global Publishing Services, Chennai, India

This book is dedicated to my partner Sarah and my parents Brian and Helen who have shown great belief, good humour and much patience in supporting me to keep playing.

Contents

Figures

Tables

Foreword

Matthew Harrison's *Level Up Collaboration: Using Video Games to Develop Collaborative Social Skills* is a remarkable research-based book that will influence the practice of interventionists and game designers around the world. This book is based on Matt's rigorous PhD study and on his life history as an avid gamer and a dedicated teacher. As a teacher, and now academic, Matt has, I believe, always had a keen eye for what works, and what matters, to his students.

Making friends, providing and taking constructive feedback, developing the skills necessary for working in a group and managing the complexity that comes with different perspective on a single experience are all aspects of human connectedness that matter. These ways of interacting can also be extraordinarily challenging for some students to master. Moving towards success for some requires skilful explicit teaching, modelling and the provision of extensive and interesting opportunities to practice the who, what, how, when and why of social skills. *Level Up Collaboration* provides educators, school leaders and allied health professionals with the system and structure they need to support the implementation of a games-based program focused on building collaborative skills.

In this time of the COVID-19 pandemic, something else that we have learned really matters is that all students are supported, whether face to face or online, so they have successful experiences during their school years. As a teacher, academic and researcher for the last four decades, I have focused my career on developing strategies, interventions and frameworks that support those students who do not find learning, or school, easy. In my role as professor within the Melbourne Graduate School of Education, Matthew and I work together as members of the Learning Intervention (LI) team. Our LI team comprises teachers, allied health professionals and academics who are passionate about supporting the learning and well-being of all students.

As a group, we are interested in how to orchestrate the best possible classroom learning experiences and, when necessary, in knowing how to 'intervene' for students who require extra support. We aspire to equip all pre-service, classroom and specialist educators with the knowledge and skills necessary to access, implement and evaluate practices that research indicates should have a positive impact on student learning and well-being. With the addition of

Level Up Collaboration to the professional literature, Matthew has added another audience to the list of those the Learning Intervention team seeks to influence – game developers. Specifically and importantly, Matthew's book offers insights to game developers from an expert educator about how to design cooperative games that support students with a disability. This is timely knowledge to make available, particularly as gaming is important to the identity of many children and young adults with or without a disability, and because the estimated number of gamers worldwide is set to grow from 2.69 billion in 2020 to 3.07 billion in 2023.

It is clear that broadening the reach and understanding of interventions is an aspect of educational practice that also really matters. It is vitally important to ensure that programs targeting students who need to develop social skills are as effective as possible – these students and their teachers do not have time to waste on ineffective interventions. *Level Up Collaboration* is carefully researched and informed by key findings from education, cognitive psychology and the science of learning. It is a research-based, interest-oriented and strength-focussed program that offers interventionists and game developers an exciting way to harness the talents of students with diverse needs. It is the future.

When asked about the impetus for his research and this book, Matthew acknowledges that the story of *Level Up Collaboration* began long before he was a teacher. It is linked to both Matthew's childhood experiences of trying to make sense of the social world through cooperative gaming and his later experiences teaching students with neurological differences in a variety of settings in Australia and overseas. As a child of the 1980s and 1990s, Matthew was a fan of the Nintendo Legend of Zelda series. And, a relevant quote, that reinforces the importance of *Level Up Collaboration* to the students it supports, comes from the first screens of this game. When giving players a sword, the Old Man says, 'It's dangerous to go alone, take this!' I agree that in this world, it is dangerous – and lonely and unnecessary – for anyone, especially our students with disabilities, to 'go alone'. All children and young people can learn to make friends, work in cooperative groups and gain confidence in their abilities. To do so, they need pre-service teachers, classroom practitioners, specialist educators, interventionists and game developers who have equipped themselves with the power, courage and wisdom of *Level Up Collaboration: Using Video Games to Develop Collaborative Social Skills*. For all the readers of this book, the quest is about to begin!

Lorraine Graham
Professor of Learning Intervention
Melbourne Graduate School of Education
University of Melbourne

Acknowledgements

It is important to me to acknowledge my support network of individuals who have had a significant impact on my thinking and have tirelessly sustained me throughout the endeavour of writing this book. I would first like to thank my three doctoral supervisors and mentors who guided the research that inform *Level Up Collaboration*: Dr Natasha Ziebell, Dr Anthony (Tony) Jones and Vale Professor David Clarke. I would particularly like to acknowledge their generosity and positivity and I hope in the future I can provide the same high quality of supervision for my research students. The passing of David was difficult for all of us, but it was a great privilege to have had the opportunity to learn from him over the last four years. This journey began with my original supervisor, Dr Nick Reynolds, who provided much of the early guidance for the research project. Following his retirement, Nick has remained both a friend and a mentor.

I would also like to acknowledge the care, consideration and wisdom offered to me by my mentor and professional supervisor, Professor Lorraine Graham, and my colleagues in the Learning Intervention team. They have done so much to enable me to finish this book, and I recognise that I am exceptionally fortunate to work with these people.

This project would not have been possible without my partner Sarah and my parents Brian and Helen. I have heard many times that completing a doctorate is an emotional roller coaster. Sarah has offered unwavering support and patience as well as an endless supply of coffee to ensure that I persevered in challenging times. My parents have always been a source of sound counsel and inspiration, and I owe so much of my success to them. I would like to acknowledge the creative work of Megan McLennan and the professional expertise of Jess Rowlings. Finally, I would like to thank my neurodiverse friends, colleagues and students from whom I have learnt so much. I truly believe that the world is moving in the right direction as we work towards a more inclusive society.

1 Setting the scene for digital games–based intervention

Harnessing the educational power of gaming

As a gamer and a teacher, I have always had an emphatic belief in the power of gaming as a vehicle for learning and building connections. Through a rather indirect path that sometimes frustrated my parents, this belief steered me on a journey of pedagogical experimentation that resulted in me completing a PhD on using cooperative video games to support social skills development. Ultimately, this led to the creation of the intervention that is the focus of this book: Level Up Collaboration.

As a teacher-researcher, I developed an intense interest in reconciling the practice of using games as teaching tools with the extensive research into cognitive psychology that clearly shows us the conditions in which children learn best. This interest has served me well in my current role as researcher and teacher trainer and motivated me to write this book for my fellow interventionists (whether teachers, teacher assistants or allied health professionals), as well as game designers.

But the story of Level Up Collaboration really begins long before I started teaching. My understanding of gaming as an inherently social activity stems from my own childhood, and my experiences trying to make sense of the social world through cooperative gaming. Woven into this introductory chapter are also my experiences of working with students with neurological differences in mainstream and specialist settings, and how I came to recognise the potential of video games as particularly powerful tools for inclusive education. Through sharing my own story, I hope to convince interventionists that games can have a place within their setting when positioned in a way that builds from the evidence and harnesses the strengths and interests of the children in their care. And for game designers reading this book, I hope to share the significant impact design components can have on developing the social skills of children.

When I first considered writing this book, the thought was slightly overwhelming. Nevertheless, I felt that it had to be written. I am certainly not the first person to use video games as tools for teaching, and I am not the first person to use video games to support children and young adults with social-emotional challenges. But relatively speaking, digital games–based learning is still

DOI: 10.4324/9781003025917-1

in its infancy as a pedagogical approach. And, quite simply, a limited amount of evidence-based practical information is available to interventionists wanting to use video games with children and young adults with social differences. Hopefully, you will find that this book not only provides the requisite practical advice and structure that you need to implement a successful intervention in your setting, but also equips with you with an understanding of the underpinning research evidence.

Developing a keen interest in gaming from a young age

Gaming has always been part of my life and it most likely always will be. My interest in video games was the primary vehicle through which I bonded with my younger brother Josh. While we were never allowed to have the 'holy grail' of gaming – a Nintendo Entertainment System (NES) – we did have a then state-of-the-art 286 IBM compatible personal computer, complete with a 256 colour monitor, a keyboard and even a mouse (with a track ball in the bottom that we had to clean every three or four days). Josh and I spent hours upon hours playing whatever games we could get our hands on through our friends, through extended family or through the local market.

Shareware titles were all the rage, with this model of distribution providing extended demos of games that could be shared legally via the lunchtime exchange of floppy disks. If you are of a certain generation and had or continue to have an interest in gaming, you will surely remember Commander Keen. Created by Texan game developer ID Software, this two-dimensional platform game was the closest (legally available) thing to Super Mario Bros. on a computer. In this game, players moved largely from left to right of the screen, navigating their way past terrifying aliens, collecting tokens to increase their score (represented in this game as candy bars) and trying to find the key cards to open the exit for the level. Although this was officially a single-player game, we transformed it into a cooperative multiplayer experience. Josh, myself and other friends who lived in our neighbourhood would take turns controlling the protagonist, Keen, with the non-players offering advice and providing feedback on the player's performance. We also developed systems for ensuring fairness, such as changing players at every level or life lost, with caveats for new players or when attempting more challenging levels. That said, it was not always a harmonious affair. When we encountered sections that were particularly challenging, the collective group would often discuss nominating a more skilled player to skip ahead and to navigate the group past this particular point. As expected, this could be controversial, especially for the player forgoing their turn. But this led to the development of systems for dispute resolution, including a last resort appeal to the higher court of my parents.

These discussions and debates centred around the game, often referred to in game studies as the 'meta game', formed as much of my experiences of

Commander Keen as actually playing the game. Through engaging in interactions around this and other games, we utilised a raft of technical vocabulary, we called on our knowledge of what other conversationists likely knew and did not know to explain our theories, and, without realising it, we were using rich persuasive language to implore our friends to believe our version of events in describing epic sessions of play. These are communication skills that I still call on today, and I have these discussions partly to thank for providing a space for practising and refining them at a young age. Josh and I eventually got our own gaming devices, and I feel like something was lost in this transition. I still believe that the best multiplayer gaming experiences are those shared in both the virtual and physical environments, and, for the purposes of teaching, this means everyone sharing one screen and one experience.

Learning to connect and teach through gaming

In my first months of teaching, I was apprehensive about leaning too heavily into gaming. However, I soon found it to be asset in connecting with many of my students. In my second year I had a large cohort of students on individual learning plans for academic, social-emotional and behavioural reasons. After initially figuring each other out, these students were some of my favourite people to teach. I loved their off-kilter senses of humour, their different ways of seeing our world and their genuine love for their special areas of interest. Within the staff room these students became known as my 'celebrities', as every teacher in the school had heard of them even if they had never met them in person. It is with this group of children that I first experimented with using multiplayer gaming as a tool for teaching collaborative social skills.

The advent of the Friday lunchtime gaming club started as a reward for demonstrating positive behaviour at lunchtimes during the week, but it soon became apparent that this club could become something more than casual play (which is important in and of itself). When I began to run these Friday lunchtime sessions, I started to notice that some of the players were acting in ways that were more conducive to collaborative play than I would have expected. As gaming served as an area of strength for these students, they had a lexicon for sharing information with their fellow players. More than this, I observed some individuals demonstrating behaviours in this context that they would not display when playing cricket in physical education or outside at lunchtimes. In one memorable instance, an experienced player waived his turn playing New Super Mario Bros. Wii because he wanted a less skilled player to have another turn at practising using the Ice Flower power up. He declared that he would provide coaching to help this player improve. For him, it appeared to be a calculated long-term investment in the collective skill base of the team. As a teacher and gamer, this display of strategic generosity sparked my curiosity.

It was these early experiences of running the games club that led me to the pursuit of further study and eventually the completion of my PhD. By this time, I had worked in South Korea teaching in a high school for gifted students, been a leading teacher in the United Kingdom and returned home to Australia to teach students with complex needs in what we term a Special Development School. With the enthusiastic support of my principal, this specialised setting provided fertile ground for developing a more structured approach to digital games–based intervention. It was the culmination of my experiences working within these schools and researching my own social skills groups as well as those run by other teachers that served as the foundation for the intervention that you are about to explore in this book.

Who can the Level Up Collaboration intervention help?

As an intervention program, Level Up Collaboration can help children and young adults with a range of functional needs. Some examples of populations that I have supported through this program include:

- children who find it difficult to make friends;
- individuals who need assistance with knowing how to provide constructive feedback in a way that minimises hurting the feelings of others;
- students who communicate using augmented and alternative communication (AAC) and require a social context to practice using it;
- young adults who lack the confidence to take on leadership positions within group tasks.

You might notice that I have avoided using diagnostic language. Since I began teaching, much has changed in how we discuss disability and education. Some intervention participants have had formal diagnostic labels, such as attention deficit hyperactivity disorder (ADHD), obsessive-compulsive disorder (OCD) and autism spectrum disorder (ASD). Other children have come to join my interventions having been described lovingly by their teachers as 'just a bit different'. What all these children have had in common is that they required support to establish sustainable friendships and to develop the collaborative social skills required for effectively working within a group. My job was never to diagnose or to seek funding support, but rather to focus on the individual areas of strength and need for each of these children. This approach reflects a broader shift experienced by many Australian teachers and, as I understand it, by other systems around the world. Medical labels of disability can be particularly problematic when used to categorise individuals who share a common 'label' but have very different functional needs (Berman & Graham, 2018; Rohmer & Louvet, 2018).

It is through the lens of 'functional needs' that I will frame most of the discussions of difference in this book. When thinking about functional needs, I ask 'What are the specific challenges an individual experiences, and how can we support them?' By considering individual areas of strength and challenge, we can sidestep the stereotypes that often accompany labels of disability. While a label can be one way of beginning to understand what a child or young adult requires, we need to get to know them in all their complexities before we can truly recognise and prioritise our efforts.

Considering the language of neurodiversity

As evident from the discussion above, labels have been of little concern to me. Since I began teaching in 2008 I have had the good fortune of becoming close friends with many people in the Australian autistic community. Some of these people have been, and continue to be, colleagues at the University of Melbourne. Others have been people who have heard me speak on the radio or on television and who have reached out to me. After many long hours of conversation and learning from these individuals, I have come to see the pride with which the autistic community has taken in reclaiming ownership of being 'autistic'. These people have changed the way in which I use this word and have implored me to adopt the lens of neurodiversity.

Throughout this book, I have deliberately used the terms 'autistic' or 'on the autism spectrum' interchangeably to acknowledge and respect the various preferences of individuals in the autism community with whom I work. This is consistent with a diversity model approach (Donaldson et al., 2017; Dunn & Andrews, 2015; Sarrett, 2016). I also want to be very clear in discussing how I use the term 'intervention' to describe targeted teaching, and I do want not to suggest that autistic individuals need to change who they are as people. The differences of autism are something to celebrate and, where possible, our school systems should adjust to be more inclusive of these differences.

Two audiences, one book

Although many readers may be engaging with this book out of curiosity derived from an interest in either gaming or strength-based social skills programs, the two targeted audiences for this book are **interventionists** and **game designers** (but everyone is welcome!).

⬇⬇⬆ CHEAT CODE *(KEY VOCABULARY + DEFINITION)*

Interventionist: an individual who supports children by planning, implementing, monitoring and evaluating an educational intervention or program designed to address a targeted area of need (such as the social skills required for effective collaboration). Teachers, teaching assistants and allied health professionals can all be interventionists.

⬇⬇⬆ CHEAT CODE *(KEY VOCABULARY + DEFINITION)*

Game designer: an individual who plans and/or programs elements of video games, designing interactions between the player and the game world, systems or rules (Salen & Zimmerman, 2004). This can include aesthetic (visual and sound) and gameplay components of a video game. Although some game designers work independently, most commercially developed games are created by teams of game designers.

These two distinct audiences might seem an odd coupling, but what became apparent through my research is that in digital games–based interventions, each of these two groups can better fulfil their role when they understand the role of the other. Effective interventionists and game designers are both experts in creating situations that encourage interactions between players. Central to this is the notion of designed 'positive interdependence'.

⬇⬇⬆ CHEAT CODE *(KEY VOCABULARY + DEFINITION)*

Positive interdependence: designing situations or problems that require the coordinated actions of multiple players, which, in turn, encourages or enforces interaction between the players (González-González & Blanco-Izquierdo, 2012; Voulgari & Komis, 2010; Zea et al., 2009).

The teachers, teaching assistants or allied health professionals conducting digital games–based interventions have an important role to play in creating a sense of positive interdependence. They need to be able to predict and react to the social interactions of their participants in a way that is likely to promote and reinforce the performance of targeted social skills. For game designers, positive interdependence is achieved through the careful design of the rules of play and the creation of levels that create the conditions for social interactions. This might sound simple but, in reality, it requires an expert understanding of behaviour.

The complexities in teaching targeted social skills are compounded further when the environmental conditions are not ideal. If you are a teacher or teaching assistant, think back to a time when you had to work with children when the acoustics were not ideal, such as when your classroom was next to the school gymnasium. As you can probably guess from this very specific example, I had the joy of experiencing this first hand in my second year of teaching, when my spelling lessons were regularly competing with the dulcet tones of 26 bouncing basketballs. Although frustrating at the time, this provides a useful analogy. Effective game design can create a focused virtual environment that allows children to centre their attention on practising the targeted social skills. Alternatively, poor game design can create the environmental equivalent of pairing literacy instruction with the not-so-joyful sounds of basketball. It might be fun for the children, but the learning ultimately suffers. When interventionists understand game design, they can identify and evaluate which virtual environments are more likely to support the individual learning needs of their children. Therefore, while this book has distinct sections discussing the steps in implementing Level Up Collaboration and the ideal virtual environments in which participants can practise the use of collaborative social skills, both interventionists and game designers will benefit from reading this book in its entirety.

Optimising learning: Using this book as a guide for implementing an effective digital games–based intervention

> The establishment of precise but flexible interventions likely requires developing manuals that specify the key components of the intervention... Manuals standardise interventions by giving step-by-step instructions for each stage of the intervention, along with problems that the user is likely to encounter and possible solutions to these problems.
>
> —Kasari and Smith (2013, p. 258)

As Kasari and Smith (2013) contend in the above quote, there is value for interventionists in having a documented series of steps to follow. It is my hope that interventionists, regardless of their level of familiarity with digital games–based interventions, benefit from a structured system to plan, implement and evaluate their social skills programs. This begins with Chapter 3, which provides an overview of a research-informed three-stage system for use in a range of contexts. You can follow this system to explicitly teach the meaning and contexts of key social skills, to support learners in practising the performance of these skills through cooperative gameplay and to guide reflection at a team and individual level following play. Chapters 4, 5 and 6 explore each of the three stages in-depth, providing concrete steps as well as supporting practical strategies and advice on how to overcome common areas of challenge.

When I first began sharing this system with other interventionists, often I was asked which social skills should be prioritised and the order in which these skills should be taught. Chapter 7 provides a list of 15 high priority collaborative social skills, although when reviewing these, you also need to give careful consideration to your school context and the cultural ecology of your children. Throughout this book, I refer to these 15 skills as the **Target Skills**. Alongside these skills, I also offer strategies that I have found to be effective in helping my children acquire and utilise these skills.

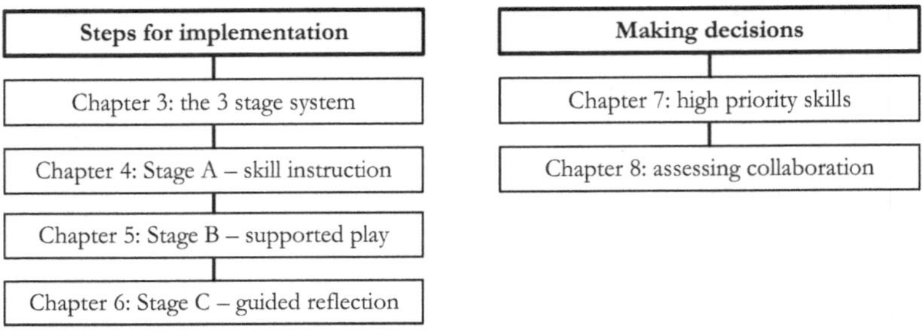

Figure 1.1 Key chapters for planning your intervention.

Another popular request, particularly from the teachers with which I have worked, is for assessment instruments for measuring child progress. All interventionists should be generating data on their children and their growth, but this can often be confusing or difficult to put into practice in a busy environment. Chapter 8 provides an evidence-based assessment instrument alongside advice on how to monitor data and use this to inform the direction of your instruction, as well as how to provide feedback to your children.

Optimising game design: Creating the ideal virtual environment for collaboration

While interventionists can discuss, shape and reinforce behaviours in the physical environment, it is largely the game developers who pull the strings in the virtual environment. Their decisions enable or present barriers to collaboration through the styles of play they choose to promote within their games. Chapter 10 provides 39 specific game design recommendations for selecting or designing multiplayer games that create the ideal conditions for collaboration.

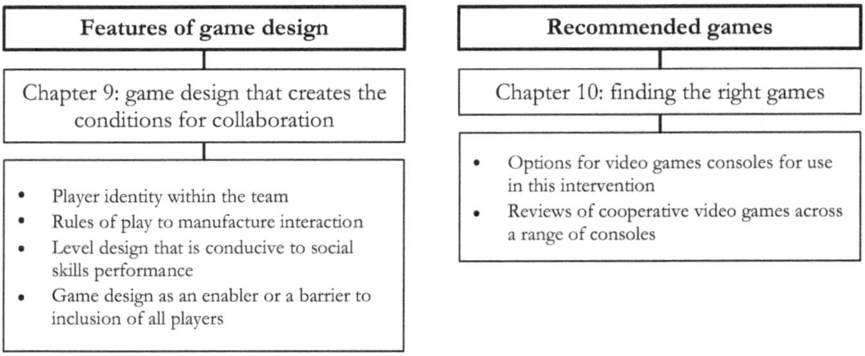

Figure 1.2 Key chapters for understanding how game design can create the optimal conditions.

I illustrate each recommendation with examples drawn from both my research and the broader game design literature, where available. Understanding these recommendations is important, whether you are an interventionist selecting a game to use in this intervention or if you are designing a new game to facilitate collaborative play.

Of course, evaluating which games align with the 39 recommendations is a time-intensive (although also fun) exercise. I am often asked by interested individuals which games in particular I think are well designed for facilitating collaborative play. There are so many games and gaming systems available on the market, and who has time to play them all? To save you this burden, I have taken on this task, and I share the fruits of my labour in Chapter 10. I include 17 recommended games in this final chapter, reviewing each game's alignment with the recommendations and offering anecdotes from my experiences in testing each respective title. In this section, I have purposely selected a variety of games across multiple platforms. You can pick up some of the older titles fairly cheaply in second-hand stores or from online shops. Other titles are more recent releases, allowing you to ride the wave of 'what's hot right now'.

Summary of key ideas in Chapter 1

- Gaming and gaming culture can be a powerful vehicle for connecting with our children and young adults. It often presents a space of mutual interest and relative strength for many individuals requiring support with social capacity building.
- The Level Up Collaboration intervention focuses on developing the collaborative social skills that every child and young adult requires, rather than trying to culturally homogenise individuals with disabilities and differences.
- Interventionists (teachers, teaching assistants and allied health professionals) have an important role to play in optimising the acquisition and supporting the performance of these collaborative social skills (referred to as the Target Skills and detailed in Chapter 7).
- Game designers can help to ensure that the conditions for collaborative play are optimal through designing rules and systems that create a sense of positive interdependence between the players.

References

Berman, J., & Graham, L. (2018). *Learning intervention: Educational casework and responsive teaching for sustainable learning*. Routledge.

Donaldson, A. L., Krejcha, K., & McMillin, A. (2017). A strengths-based approach to autism: Neurodiversity and partnering with the autism community. *Perspectives of the ASHA Special Interest Groups*, *2*(1), 56–68.

Dunn, D. S., & Andrews, E. E. (2015). Person-first and identity-first language: Developing psychologists' cultural competence using disability language. *American Psychologist, 70*(3), 255–264.

González-González, C., & Blanco-Izquierdo, F. (2012). Designing social videogames for educational uses. *Computers & Education, 58*(1), 250–262.

Kasari, C., & Smith, T. (2013). Interventions in schools for children with autism spectrum disorder: Methods and recommendations. *Autism, 17*(3), 254–267.

Rohmer, O., & Louvet, E. (2018). Implicit stereotyping against people with disability. *Group Processes and Intergroup Relations, 21*(1), 127–140.

Salen, K., & Zimmerman, E. (2004). *Rules of play: Game design fundamentals*. MIT Press.

Sarrett, J. C. (2016). Biocertification and neurodiversity: The role and implications of self-diagnosis in autistic communities. *Neuroethics, 9*, 23–36.

Voulgari, I., & Komis, V. (2010). 'Elven Elder LVL59 LFP/RB. Please PM me': Immersion, collaborative tasks and problem-solving in massively multiplayer online games. *Learning, Media and Technology, 35*(2), 171–202.

Zea, N. P., Sánchez, J. L. G., Gutiérrez, F. L., Cabrera, M. J., & Paderewski, P. (2009). Design of educational multiplayer videogames: A vision from collaborative learning. *Advances in Engineering Software, 40*(12), 1251–1260.

2 Research informing Level Up Collaboration

Introduction

Level Up Collaboration is built on the foundations of high-quality research into how children learn most effectively, and this chapter serves as the starting point in understanding that research. To help you understand and be able to communicate the importance of certain components of the intervention design and the underlying structure, you need to understand the theories that underpin it. But rather than providing all of the minute details or controversies surrounding each of the theories, I provide concise summaries of the 'big ideas' that you need to know to be able to implement this intervention. I also provide you with the language to help explain these theories, principles and strategies to your colleagues, parents and, ideally, the children themselves. Included within each discussion is a series of 'cheat codes', which are concise (but not comprehensive) definitions you can use to communicate these concepts and strategies succinctly with these audiences. Each section also points you to further reading that will allow you to investigate the theory and underpinning research in far more detail than is possible in this single chapter.

Theories to understand the processes and barriers for learning

To be able to explain why particular components of Level Up Collaboration are important in supporting effective learning, you will need to be able to clearly communicate the guiding principles drawn from the science of learning that informed the design of this intervention program. An overview of these principles is explored in the following sections of this chapter and then put into action in the subsequent chapters.

What are biologically primary and biologically secondary skills?

When I was in Year 7, I attended Herman E Utley Middle School in Rockwall, Texas. My favourite subject at school that year was Life Science, which provided a comprehensive introduction to Biology. Central to the content of this subject was the politicised teaching of evolution, and the impact evolution has

DOI: 10.4324/9781003025917-2

had on the development of the human race. It was only much later when I was reading the work of Sweller, Ayers and Kalyuga (2011) that I considered the role of evolution in children developing the knowledge and skills required for effective social communication and interaction. Sweller, Kalyuga and Ayers point to the seminal work of Geary (as helpfully synthesised in Sweller, 2008) to explain a distinction between **biologically primary** and **biologically secondary** knowledge and skills. When I learnt of this theory, it fundamentally changed the way I conceptualised the processes of learning. More importantly, it shifted my understanding of my role as a teacher in supporting my students, and for viewing the needs of children participating in my interventions.

As we have evolved over hundreds of thousands of years, we have been genetically programmed to more easily learn knowledge and skills that have become essential for our survival as a species. Geary refers to these as biologically primary knowledge and skills. As humans are predispositioned to develop biologically primary knowledge and skills, most children can learn to pick up objects, to walk or to develop the oral language of their environment through modelling and observation of older children and adults.

⬇⬇⬆ CHEAT CODE *(KEY VOCABULARY + DEFINITION)*

Biologically primary knowledge and skills: the knowledge and skills humans have evolved to be genetically predispositioned to learn (Sweller, 2008).

By contrast, biologically secondary knowledge and skills consist of those things that have become important for us as a species only relatively recently, such as the ability to read written text (Sweller, 2008; Sweller, Ayers and Kalyuga, 2011). Continuing with the example of learning to read, the notion of aspiring to universal literacy has also only relatively recently entered the mainstream of consciousness. As such, as a species we have not evolved to learn to read naturally, as we have not had enough time. We have also not evolved to learn how to complete algebraic problems through mere observation, and thus most people require this to be explicitly taught to them.

⬇⬇⬆ CHEAT CODE *(KEY VOCABULARY + DEFINITION)*

Biologically secondary knowledge and skills: the knowledge and skills that have only relatively recently become important for us as a species, so humans have not evolved to learn these naturally (Sweller, 2008).

So, what about the knowledge and skills required for effective social interaction and communication? For most children these come naturally. Despite the popular labelling of collaboration as a so-called 21st Century Skill, learning to work together has been key to the survival of humans since the Stone Age. However, for some children these skills appear not to come naturally. As an example, many of the neurodiverse children I have taught have required explicit instruction in the language used to label individual social skills, the steps in performing these skills and the underlying rationale as to why these skills are important for interacting with others. A range of complex reasons can be cited for why our children might not have developed these skills through natural observation, including histories of childhood trauma and lack of opportunities for observing modelled use of the skills. What is important is that when children require intensive support, educators and therapists should view these skills as biologically secondary for these children. They should, as a consequence, provide the explicit teaching required to ensure that these children have the best possible chance to develop these collaborative social skills.

SUGGESTED FURTHER READING:

- Sweller, J. (2008). Instructional implications of David C. Geary's evolutionary educational psychology. *Educational Psychologist, 43*(4), 214–216.

What is Social Learning Theory and what are the implications for learning new skills?

Social Learning Theory is an integration of behaviourist stimulus-response or reinforcement theories and cognitive models of learning, focusing on the role of the environment (Bandura, 1977; Kretchmar, 2008; Rotter, 1982). That is, behaviour is learnt through reinforcement and consequences in the social environment. In describing his model of Social Learning Theory, Bandura (1977) built on the established behaviourist learning theories that focused on classical and operant conditioning. Classical conditioning involves learning through *involuntary* psychological or emotional responses, such as fear, while operant conditioning describes learning through which *voluntary* behaviour is either strengthened or weakened by the consequences of antecedents (Bandura, 1977; Bitterman, 2006). Importantly, positive reinforcement will have little impact if the consequence does not align with an individual's needs (Duchesne & McMaugh, 2016).

Rumjaun and Narod (2020) contend that Bandura, using these theoretical assumptions as his starting point, contributed two important ideas that result in this theory remaining valid to this day. First, that mediating processes occur between stimuli and responses; that is, the internal cognitive processes occurring between an input in the environment and a responding behaviour. Bandura (1968; 1977) suggested four mediating internal processes: the attention paid to a particular environmental input; the retention or recall of a particular behaviour that can be used as a response to the input; the ability to reproduce the behaviour; and the motivation to perform a behaviour. These mediating processes all contribute to whether a learner produces a certain behaviour in response to an input.

Bandura (1968; 1977) also suggested that these stimuli and responses are provided in the social environment through the process of 'observational learning'. In descripting observational learning, Bandura (1968; 1977) emphasised the processes through which an individual observes and imitates the behaviours or skills of models (either adults or peers), leading to a natural acquisition of these behaviours or skills. This has important implications for the use of video modelling, which is explored later in this chapter.

SUGGESTED FURTHER READING:

- Rumjaun, A., & Narod, F. (2020). Social learning theory—Albert Bandura. In *Science education in theory and practice* (pp. 85–99). Springer, Cham.

Schema theory: What are the differences between novices and experts?

To understand the differences between a novice, or someone with very little understanding and experience, and an expert, it is important to understand schema theory. A schema is a way of organising knowledge or information, like a database system we use for storing and recalling what has already been learnt, that can be drawn on when learning new information (Kirschner & Hendrick, 2020). Using this conceptual model, we possess a schema for everything we have learnt, including our knowledge of socially expected behaviours and the conditions in which we should use these behaviours. Social experts, or people with a high degree of social sophistication, possess schemata for a wide range of social skills that they can draw on in a variety of contexts. These are combined with other skills and performed with very little effort as the performance of these skills is largely automated. Social experts can build on their existing schemata to learn related skills or to apply existing skills in new contexts. Novices do not have these schemata on which to build, so they are starting from the very beginning. In other words, they will most likely not recognise the conditions in which unfamiliar social skills should be used, and they do not have an understanding of the steps required when using an expected social skill. Recognising the importance of when and how to 'take turns' is a common area of challenge for many children. When considering taking turns, most (but not all) adults have developed sufficient schemas so they can recognise contexts when other people want to use a limited resource, such as the lone photocopier in the staff room or the same vending machine in the cafeteria. Once we understand that we need to take turns using this resource, we draw on our knowledge of previous situations that are identical or similar to the current context. We then identify the conventions and steps that we need to take to ensure that we can access the resource in a timely manner while minimising the inconvenience or frustration to the other parties. Of course, emotional self-regulation plays an important role in our ability to take turns successfully, but our children first need to acquire knowledge of what they are looking for, and how they can perform the skills successfully before we can increase independent skill performance.

SUGGESTED FURTHER READING:

- Kirschner, P. A., & Hendrick, C. (2020). *How learning happens: Seminal works in educational psychology and what they mean in practice*. Routledge, Taylor & Francis Group.

Theories of instruction to optimise learning

Using these theoretical understandings of learning as a starting point, it is important to consider the role of the interventionist and the instructional strategies they can use to optimise the learning within this intervention.

What is explicit instruction and why is it important when learning new social skills?

Although there is an abundance of ambiguity around what constitutes explicit instruction, personally, I am partial to understanding it from the perspective of the 'I do, we do, you do' model. Ashman (2019) and Rosenshine (1986) share a set of core principles for explicit instruction that emphasise the degree to which the interventionist guides the learner depending on their level of expertise in certain targeted content or skills. For the novice, the importance is placed on breaking down new content or skills into their composite parts so that they can be learnt more easily. At this stage, the interventionist takes the lead, modelling how to solve a problem or perform each step in completing a process. As the learner demonstrates increasing understanding of the content or proficiency in performing a skill, the interventionist increases transitions to a supporting role as the learner works towards mastery. The goal is for the learner to develop independence in their ability to recall the targeted knowledge or to perform a skill without the support of the interventionist.

⬇⬇⬆ CHEAT CODE *(KEY VOCABULARY + DEFINITION)*

Explicit instruction: chunking new content or skills into small components, guiding initial attempts at working with the content or skills in a controlled context and then gradually releasing control in more open activities as the learners gain mastery (Ashman, 2019).

Applying these characteristics to the context of Level Up Collaboration, explicit instruction is vital for the acquisition of the Target Skills. As you will find in the following chapters, this intervention focuses on a structured approach in which the interventionist assesses what a child is ready to learn. They then chunk the skill into the discrete steps required for performance. The interventionist models how to perform each of these steps and then demonstrates to the child or young adult how to put these steps together to use a social skill (using video modelling, explored in the next section). Based on my extensive experience working with neurodiverse students, participants often report that they thrive when their teachers or allied health professionals use explicit instruction, as it clarifies for them exactly what they are being asked to do. I see explicit instruction as a fundamental principle for inclusive education. This is not to discount the value of other instructional approaches such as inquiry-based learning, but rather a recognition that novices require some foundational knowledge before feeling secure enough to engage in more free-form learning experiences.

SUGGESTED FURTHER READING:

- Boxer, A. (ed). (2019). *The researchED guide to explicit & direct instruction: An evidence-informed guide for teachers*. John Catt Educational.

What is video modelling and video review?

Video modelling is an explicit teaching strategy using selected footage of someone performing the incremental steps for displaying a desirable behaviour or performing a skill (Delano, 2007). Like alternative social skills interventions, a number of authors have used the theoretical lens of Social Learning Theory to explain the processes of learning that occur through the observation of video models (Bellini & Akullian, 2007; Naylor et al., 2019; Mason et al., 2016). Naylor et al. (2019) suggest that observational learning is a central tenet underpinning the effectiveness of this mode of intervention. Pointing to an assumption of observation leading to imitation, Reagon et al. (2006) argue that video modelling is effective because it allows for the systematic repetition of the identical footage, affording multiple observations of the same desired behaviour and positive consequence. Children often require repeated exposure to new ideas and multiple opportunities to practise and receive feedback upon their performance of a new skill for this information to be consolidated (Mitchell, 2014; Yates & Hattie, 2014). 'Spaced practice', sometimes referred to as 'distributed practice', operates on the principle that shorter but more frequent sessions of instruction are more effective than a single, larger block of time of teaching as learners need time to process and consider the fundamentals of what they are learning.

Adopting the assumptions of observational learning, the interventionist takes on the role of a director, guiding attention to what they want the viewer to see and not see. In other words, directors of a video model aim to remove the barriers for understanding what is required through carefully collating selected footage to model each sequential step. As the learner is observing the steps, reinforcement can be provided through complementary voiceovers, labelling each step, and providing praise in the video for the performance of the desired or targeted behaviours (Delano, 2007; Mason et al., 2016; Reagon et al., 2006). Through strategic editing of video footage, video models feature either the targeted individual (self-video modelling) or another individual as a model (peer-video modelling) appearing to perform the desired skill (Shepherd et al., 2014). As video modelling is highly visual in the way that key information is presented, it can be a particularly effective instructional tool for many neurodiverse children (Naylor et al., 2019).

⬇⬇⬆ CHEAT CODE *(KEY VOCABULARY + DEFINITION)*

Video modelling: an explicit teaching strategy using selected footage of someone performing the incremental steps for displaying a desirable behaviour or performing a skill (Delano, 2007).

Rather than editing the footage to show only desirable performance of a targeted skill or behaviour, **video review**, or video coaching, provides learners with access to an entire record of events (Barlow et al., 2014). By adopting many of the assumptions of 'social constructivism', the contexts in which children learn that skill performance is appropriate are discussed and debated through collective analysis of the video footage (Maione & Mirenda, 2006). While educators facilitate conversations around the cognitive mediation, or 'thinking processes' used in deciding when to perform a skill, the learner can also share their perspectives on the appropriateness or utility of the skill (Maione & Mirenda, 2006; Qarabash et al., 2018).

⬇⬇⬆ CHEAT CODE *(KEY VOCABULARY + DEFINITION)*

Video review: reviewing unedited footage of the child interacting with peers, with the educator guiding the child to discuss their use of skills and the actions and reactions of their peers (Maione & Mirenda, 2006).

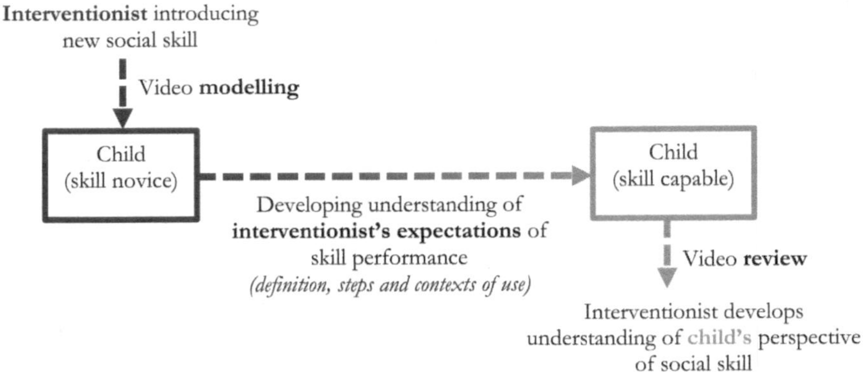

Figure 2.1 Conceptualising the relationship between video modelling and video review.

While video modelling helps teach the steps needed to perform social skills, video review facilitates a conversation around the cultural norms that inform the use of the skill. Relating this back to the concept of novices and more proficient performers of targeted skills, the diagram below conceptualises the relationship between video modelling and video review.

The diagram highlights how video modelling can help everyone understand the interventionist's expectations of a skill. Video review can then 'feed back' to the interventionist the participant's perceptions of this skill, including the cultural relevance and perceived value. Inclusive education needs to be a dialogue, and the importance of participant voice is explored later in this chapter.

SUGGESTED FURTHER READING:

- Naylor, A., Spence, S. E., & Poed, S. (2019). Using video modelling to teach expected behaviours to primary students. *Support for Learning*, *34*(4), 389–403.

Prioritising which collaborative social skills we teach

Beyond being able to articulate the underlying principles of learning and an evidence-informed narrative of how we can best teach to align with these principles, it is also important to consider what we are teaching. *Chapter* 7 details the deliberations that went into deciding on the 15 Target Skills that are the focus of this intervention, but it is important that interventionists have a broader philosophical understanding of the relationship between universal social pragmatic skills, cultural inclusion and participant voice.

What are social pragmatic skills and when are they important?

Speech and language pathologists will often refer to receptive language (comprehension or understanding), expressive language (being able to express ideas, thoughts, or questions in a meaningful way) and social pragmatic skills (that often serve as a precursor to receptive and expressive language) (Gleason & Ratner, 2009; Leonard et al., 2011). Social pragmatic skills refer to the ability to use language flexibility to fulfil a range of functions in a dynamic social context (Gleason & Ratner, 2009; Grundy, 2019). Inherently informed by cultural norms and shared understandings, I think of these skills as the social practicalities that bind expressive and receptive language to a context and make our interactions meaningful. This is more than speech; it includes skills pertaining to verbal and non-verbal interactions. Frequently mentioned examples of social pragmatic skills include the use of gestures, tone of voice and, unfortunately, eye contact (I use the word 'unfortunately' deliberately to highlight the difficulty many neurodiverse learners have in making eye contact).

Assessing and teaching social pragmatic skills can be a contentious space. As already noted in Chapter 1, the neurodiversity movement has repositioned the social skills 'deficits' that are often associated with neurological conditions, such as autism and ADHD, as social skills 'differences' that should be accommodated. Despite this advocacy, many of the instruments we use to assess social pragmatic language still privilege neurotypical norms. But that is not to say that these checklists have no value. To illustrate this point, here are some examples of items from the McGinnis Pragmatic Skills Checklist (McGinnis, 2018) that I would contend are universally important in engaging socially and expressing ourselves:

- initiates conversation (e.g., points to a sore, indicates a bug, says 'know what?');
- indicates agreement or disagreement (e.g., shakes head or nods, says 'yes' or 'no'); and
- expresses feelings/needs/problems (e.g., taps nappy to indicate it needs to be changed, says 'I'm hungry' or 'He hit me').

It is pleasing to see in these items a recognition that these skills can be performed verbally and non-verbally, with no preference given to one form over the other. These items help to ensure that everyone is able to interact in a way that helps them to feel listened to, that keeps everyone safe and that facilitates effective but flexible communication. This final point, effective but flexible, means that a child or young adult can communicate an idea, an opinion or a request in a way that is not only understood but is also comfortable to them and their social differences. Unfortunately, a number of items on this checklist do not meet this standard, as they require people to communicate in a way that is often unnatural and uncomfortable:

- maintains appropriate eye contact (e.g., initiates/maintains eye contact during interactions and conversations);
- uses appropriate physical posturing (e.g., faces speaker, makes appropriate facial expression and faces conversational partner when speaking).

These two items are about the child or young adult 'fitting in' to the expectations of society with very little practical benefit in terms of communication functionality. The inferred messages that we interpret through eye contact or facial expressions can easily be ascertained via alternative means. Forcing children or young adults to communicate in a way that causes discomfort can lead to increased levels of anxiety with little (or no) improvement in the quality of their communication (Trevisan et al., 2017). From my own professional experiences, limiting how people can communicate can discourage them from engaging in social interactions in the first place. The key is to judiciously evaluate such checklists and prioritise those pragmatic language skills that are most meaningful and inclusive of the participants in our intervention groups. The 15 Target Skills presented in Chapter 7 have all been selected strategically to align with these priorities.

What about participant voice?

Since I began my teaching career, I have witnessed many shifts in what is valued in education. Some of these shifts have been subtle but symbolically important, such as the language we use to discuss disability. Other shifts have been more pronounced and profound. The increased value placed on hearing the voices of children with disabilities and differences has had a profound effect on the way that I conceptualise my role as an interventionist. When we take the time and find the means to hear the perspectives of our children, when determining the balance between acceptance and intervention, we stop intervening *on* our children and instead start intervening *with* them. Holdsworth (2007) describes the existence of a spectrum of definitions between consultation and empowerment in student voice policies for Australian schools. In considering how you balance acceptance of differences and the need for intervention, it is useful to consider the degree to which your participants will control what is occurring during intervention.

> ⬇⬇⬆ CHEAT CODE *(KEY VOCABULARY + DEFINITION)*
>
> **Participant voice:** existing on a spectrum from minimalist consultation, when participants can inform decision making by others, to empowerment through participants taking action and responsibility for decision making over their lives (Holdsworth, 2007).

Voice can take many forms, and this is not as simple as children simply determining which skills are important for them and which skills are irrelevant. It is important that children are able to discuss their interpretation of skills, as noted during the discussion of video review. Given the complex communication challenges your participants may have, this is not always easy to do, but we know now that sustainable and ethical intervention requires our children to have a sense of agency in their learning and development (Lynch & Irvine, 2009; Saggers et al., 2011).

Listening to the voices of participants and their support networks is also vital in ensuring that the suggested impact of an intervention can be replicated in your context. While large-scale randomised control trials can highlight patterns of effectiveness across many settings, what really matters is what is likely to work in the local context, in your school or in settings (Donmoyer & Galloway, 2010; Eacott, 2017). Due to the established heterogeneity of individual differences, we know that this is especially important if you are supporting individuals on the autism spectrum (Lynch & Irvine, 2009). Arguably no one knows the needs and preferences of the participants better than the child or young adult themselves. While they might not be an expert in the science of learning, every child I have worked with has certainly known when they enjoy or detest something. Understanding the needs and preferences of your participants is of course vital in the successful implementation of any intervention.

Introducing the Response to Intervention model: Who needs which level of support?

Response to Intervention provides interventionists with a systemised, structured approach for planning. Everyone receives the level of assistance they require to develop the targeted social skills, and the approach provides a pathway when interventions fail to have the desired impact. It accomplishes this by avoiding the use of assumptions, using ongoing assessment instead to make data-informed decisions. As shown below, this framework conceptualises intervention as occurring at three tiers or levels.

Every child begins at **Tier 1**, or the universal tier. Within Tier 1 all children should receive high-quality evidence-based social skills instruction. As already noted, the overwhelming evidence is that all children benefit from the explicit teaching of social skills. Most children will respond to this instruction and can be expected to develop the targeted skills, but ongoing assessment will identify that some learners may not be acquiring the skills at the expected rate. These learners require more intensive small group intervention, which is referred to as **Tier 2** support. As these children begin to respond to the additional instruction and support, at a certain point they will no longer require small group intervention and can return to Tier 1, having developed the targeted skills. Children who do not make satisfactory progress, even when receiving Tier 2 support, will require intensive individual programs with specialised staff, such as speech and language pathologists and psychologists. This is known as

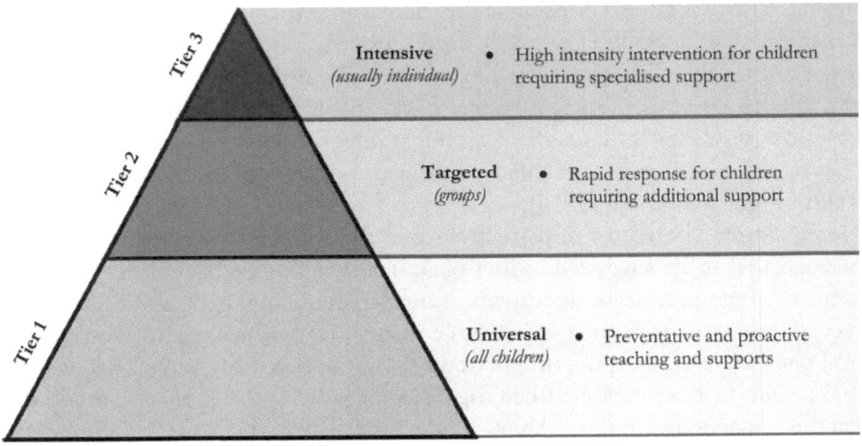

Figure 2.2 The Response to Intervention framework.

receiving **Tier 3** support, the most intensive level. As shown in the figure below, the goal should always be for children and young adults to return to receiving the universal Tier 1 supports, and no longer require Tier 2 and Tier 3 interventions.

There are three key points that every interventionist should know about using the Response to Intervention framework:

- Children need to be assessed regularly and returned to Tier 1 as soon as they demonstrate that the intervention has been effective. Chapter 8 details a number of assessment instruments that you can use to generate these data at regular points of the intervention. These can inform which level of support a child requires.
- We want to reduce the number of children receiving Tier 2 and Tier 3 support, so we need to ensure that we are building on strong foundations in Tier 1. In most contexts for most areas of learning, if you have more than 20% requiring Tier 2 support, then the Tier 1 instruction can be deemed ineffective.
- The tiers describe the levels of support a child requires at this time in this specific area of learning. Children should not be labelled as 'Tier 1', 'Tier 2' or 'Tier 3', but rather as children currently receiving Tier 1 support, Tier 2 support or Tier 3 support. Some children might be receiving Tier 1 support in most areas of Mathematics but Tier 3 support for collaborative social skills. Personally, I have had several children with autism who have, at times, been in this exact situation. Everyone has areas of strength and challenge, and individualised learning requires recognition of this variability (Berman & Graham, 2018).

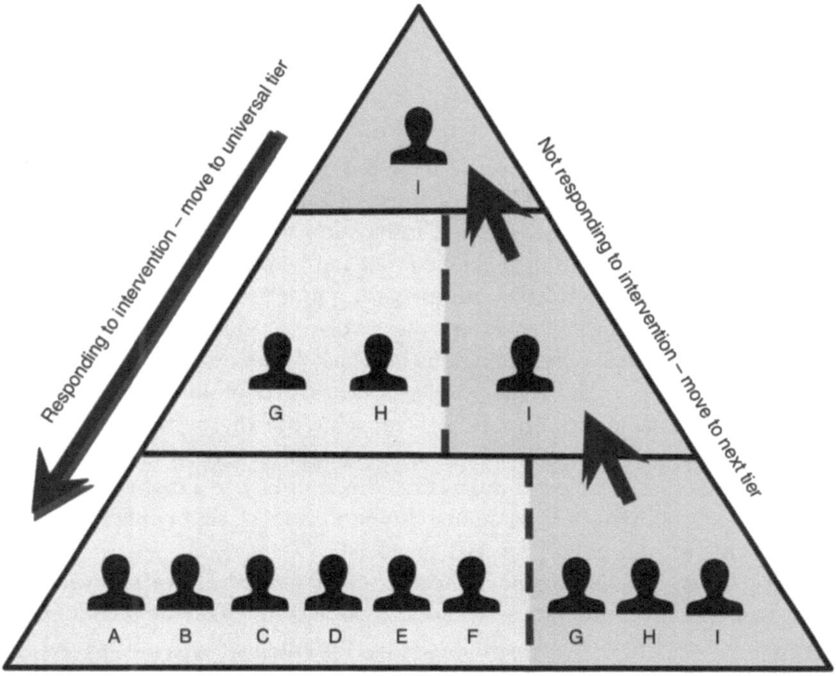

Figure 2.3 Moving between tiers in the Response to Intervention.

Thinking about the Level Up Collaboration, I have implemented this intervention largely as a small group support, building on skills taught at the universal level. Using the language of Response to Intervention, Level Up Collaboration could be considered a Tier 2 support if participants were only those children with identified social challenges. That said, there is no reason why you could not open up this intervention to all children on a rotational basis and use it as a lunchtime Tier 1 program supporting all children in developing and refining social interactions. An important part of inclusion is a sense of belonging to your community.

Summary of keys ideas in Chapter 2

- Interventionists need to be able to clearly communicate the underpinning theories of learning and instruction that inform the design of Level Up Collaboration with a wide range of audiences.
- We can make an important distinction between knowledge and skills that are biologically primary and biologically secondary, with the latter category requiring effective instruction to facilitate development. For some individuals, collaborative social skills can be conceptualised as being biologically secondary, thus requiring structured support.

- Social Learning Theory positions behaviour as learnt through reinforcement and consequences in the social environment. Often it is used to explain the effectiveness of video modelling in helping learners acquire and perform new skills.
- Experts in a particular area or domain possess schemas, or organised knowledge, about a topic or a skill that they can draw on when processing new information. Novices do not have this advantage, and therefore they cannot operate at the same level of sophistication as an expert.
- It is important that we use explicit instruction to guide novices in learning new knowledge and new skills so that can be supported in developing schemas that they can utilise with increasing independence.
- One strategy for explicit instruction is the use of video modelling, with selected footage used to display the conditions in which a skill can be used, the steps for performing the skill and the positive consequences of skill performance.
- Video review facilitates important feedback from the participants to the interventionist on their understandings of the skill and the value they place on it being used in different situations. This is similar to a discussion of the 'game tape' following a football match, with perspectives being exchanged and cognitive (thinking) processes explored.
- Participant voice is important in creating culturally responsive interventions that meet the needs and preferences of the participants. Such interventions are far more likely to be effective in developing meaningful social interactions.

References

Ashman, G. (2019). Explicit teaching. In A. Boxer (Ed.), *The researchED guide to explicit & direct instruction: An evidence-informed guide for teachers* (pp. 29–35). John Catt Educational.

Bandura, A. (1968). Social learning theory of identification processes. In D. A. Glass (Ed.), *Handbook of socialization theory and research* (pp. 213–263). Rand McNally.

Bandura, A. (1977). *Social learning theory*. Prentice Hall.

Barlow, A. T., Burroughs, E. A., Harmon, S. E., Sutton, J. T., & Yopp, D. A. (2014). Assessing views of coaching via a video-based tool. *ZDM*, *46*(2), 227–238.

Bellini, S., & Akullian, J. (2007). A meta-analysis of video modeling and video self-modeling interventions for children and adolescents with autism spectrum disorders. *Exceptional Children*, *73*(3), 264–287.

Berman, J., & Graham, L. (2018). *Learning intervention: Educational casework and responsive teaching for sustainable learning*. Routledge.

Bitterman, M. E. (2006). Classical conditioning since Pavlov. *Review of General Psychology*, *10*(4), 365–376.

Delano, M. E. (2007). Video modeling interventions for individuals with autism. *Remedial and Special Education*, *28*(1), 33–42.

Donmoyer, R., & Galloway, F. (2010). Reconsidering the utility of case study designs for researching school reform in a neo-scientific era: Insights from a multiyear, mixed-methods study. *Educational Administration Quarterly*, *46*(1), 3–30.

Duchesne, S., & McMaugh, A. (2016). *Educational psychology for learning and teaching* (5th ed.). Cengage Learning Australia.

Eacott, S. (2017). School leadership and the cult of the guru: The neo-Taylorism of Hattie. *School Leadership & Management, 37*(4), 413–426.

Gleason, J. B., & Ratner, N. B. (2009). *The development of language* (7th ed.). Pearson Allyn and Bacon.

Grundy, P. (2019). *Doing pragmatics* [Electronic resource] (4th ed.). Routledge.

Holdsworth, R. (2007). Student voice: A historical perspective and new directions. *Connect, 166*, 33.

Kirschner, P. A., & Hendrick, C. (2020). *How learning happens: Seminal works in educational psychology and what they mean in practice.* Routledge, Taylor & Francis Group.

Kretchmar, J. (2008). *Social learning theory (research starters).* Great Neck Publishing.

Leonard, M. A., Milich, R., & Lorch, E. P. (2011). The role of pragmatic language use in mediating the relation between hyperactivity and inattention and social skills problems. *Journal of Speech, Language, and Hearing Research, 54*(2), 567–579. https://doi.org/10.1044/1092-4388(2010/10-0058

Lynch, S. L., & Irvine, A. N. (2009). Inclusive education and best practice for children with autism spectrum disorder: An integrated approach. *International Journal of Inclusive Education, 13*, 845–859. https://doi.org/10.1080/13603110802475518

Maione, L., & Mirenda, P. (2006). Effects of video modeling and video feedback on peer-directed social language skills of a child with autism. *Journal of Positive Behavior Interventions, 8*(2), 106–118.

Mason, R. A., Davis, H. S., Ayres, K. M., Davis, J. L., & Mason, B. A. (2016). Video self-modeling for individuals with disabilities: A best-evidence, single case meta-analysis. *Journal of Developmental and Physical Disabilities, 28*(4), 623–642.

McGinnis, M. (2018). The McGinnis *pragmatic skills checklist.* Retrieved from https://www.jtc.org/wp-content/uploads/2018/05/McGinnis-Pragmatic-Skills-Checklist-2018-English-1.pdf

Mitchell, D. (2014). *What really works in special and inclusive education: Using evidence-based teaching strategies.* Routledge.

Naylor, A., Spence, S. E., & Poed, S. (2019). Using video modelling to teach expected behaviours to primary students. *Support for Learning, 34*(4), 389–403.

Qarabash, H., Heslop, P., Kharrufa, A., Balaam, M., & Devlin, M. (2018). Group tagging: Using video tagging to facilitate reflection on small group activities. *British Journal of Educational Technology, 1*, 1–17.

Reagon, K. A., Higbee, T. S., & Endicott, K. (2006). Teaching pretend play skills to a student with autism using video modeling with a sibling as model and play partner. *Education and Treatment of Children, 29*(3), 517–528.

Rosenshine, B. (1986). Synthesis of research on explicit teaching. *Educational Leadership, 43*(7), 60–69.

Rotter, J. B. (1982). *The development and application of social learning theory: Selected papers.* Praeger.

Rumjaun, A., & Narod, F. (2020). Social learning theory—Albert Bandura. In B. Akpan & T. J. Kennedy (Eds.) *Science education in theory and practice* (pp. 85–99). Springer.

Saggers, B., Hwang, Y. S., & Mercer, K. L. (2011). Your voice counts: Listening to the voice of high school students with autism spectrum disorder. *Australasian Journal of Special Education, 35*(2), 173–190.

Shepherd, A., Hoban, G., & Dixon, R. (2014). Using slowmation to develop the social skills of primary school students with mild intellectual disabilities: Four case studies. *Australasian Journal of Special Education, 38*(2), 150–168.

Sweller, J., Ayres, P., & Kalyuga, S. (2011). *Cognitive load theory.* Springer.

Sweller, J. (2008). Instructional implications of David C. Geary's evolutionary educational psychology. *Educational Psychologist*, *43*(4), 214–216.

Trevisan, D. A., Roberts, N., Lin, C., & Birmingham, E. (2017). How do adults and teens with self-declared autism spectrum disorder experience eye contact? A qualitative analysis of first-hand accounts. *PLOS One*, *12*(11): e0188446.

Yates, G. C., & Hattie, J. (2014). *Visible learning and the science of how we learn*. Routledge.

3 Getting started with the Level Up Collaboration intervention

> Intervention is not doing things *to* people. It is not coercive, nor is it training. Instead it is about using expertise in child development and learning to provide opportunities for learning that best meet the learnings needs of students at any particular time. It is also about using interactive, adaptive strategies that help the learner to make the most of learning opportunities.
>
> —Berman and Graham (2018, p. 1)

Introduction

In the above quote, Berman and Graham draw attention to our central role as interventionists in facilitating and optimising learning opportunities for the children with whom we work. As you read in the previous chapter, creating the optimal conditions for learning requires the use of many components. But to help put theory into practice, interventionists require a system for structured intervention that is predictable and routine-building for the children with whom we work. It must also be flexible enough to respond to the individual needs of each participant. The Level Up Collaboration intervention offers both predictability and flexibility. It is a system that I have used in a range of contexts and builds on both research and professional expertise.

Consider this chapter a form of intervention manual. To provide an overview of what you will be doing, first I outline the function of each of the three key intervention stages. I also draw your attention to a number of considerations that you need to make some decisions about before getting started, including staffing and the space you will use to implement your sessions. The following chapters in this book explore the 'nuts and bolts' of implementation for each stage in depth, providing you with the confidence to put Level Up Collaboration into action in your school or education setting.

DOI: 10.4324/9781003025917-3

The need for a consistent systematic approach to intervention

A consistent structure and a systematic approach are important both for the people implementing a social skills program and for many of the children requiring intervention. I learnt this lesson well through my own early failures as a digital games-based interventionist. My chaotic experimental experiences in the early days of my career led me to recognise the need for a predictable structure. Using a methodological process called the 'Compleat model for design-based research' (Middleton et al., 2008), I restarted with my program by going back to the very fundamentals. I then used the data I generated through analysing videos of each session to make incremental improvements to the program. I narrowed my focus to the components that I identified as making a real difference. One of the keys to success was creating predictability. Everyone involved in the intervention knew that we would be working through three key stages, as shown in the below figure.

As indicated in this figure, the role of interventionists shifts from stage to stage. While always looking to optimise the learning, our role changes depending on the purpose of the stage, what we are asking the participating children to do and the types of supports everyone requires to be successful throughout the session.

While we know that we need to be responsive to individual strengths and areas of need, the research is very clear that creating a consistent structure offers a number of important benefits for all involved. First of all, using these three clearly defined stages supports many of the neurodiverse children who benefit from Level Up Collaboration. For example, a common defining characteristic of autism, found within the prevalent diagnostic criteria, is a strong predisposition towards repeated patterns of behaviour. Many autism researchers and individuals with lived experiences argue that this results in a need for established structured routines for them to thrive (Clark & Adams, 2020; Makin

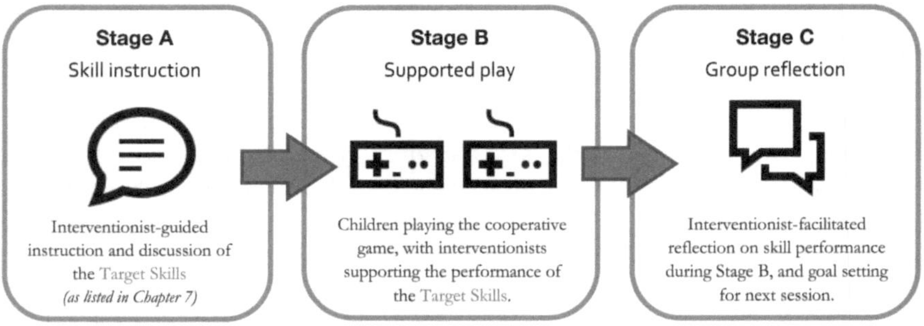

Figure 3.1 The three stages of the Level Up Collaboration intervention.

et al., 2017; Saggers et al., 2011). From my professional experiences, I would extend this not only to all neurodiverse children, but also to children with histories of trauma and social disruption. Routines help to create 'safe certainty' and a sense of calmness.

Using a consistent structure also offers practical benefits for interventionists. Safe certainty and calmness result in more time on task and focusing on learning and less need for reactive behaviour management. Planning is also easier, as you can focus on the learning goals, supports and strategies you will use within the framework. This book provides you with the tools you will need; you just need to use them to align with the needs of your children. We will now examine the function of each of the three stages and explore how these parts contribute to comprehensive intervention.

Introducing Stage A – Skill instruction

For children to develop the knowledge to perform the targeted social skills, they need to understand a number of key components about each skill:

- What can this skill look and sound like when being performed?
- Why is it considered important to be able to use this skill?
- In which contexts should they use this skill?

It is vital that each child can answer these questions about each of the skills. Once they can define the skills in isolation, interventions can then help them combine these skills in increasingly sophisticated ways so that they become more effective collaborators. Stage A addresses these foundational components through the use of **explicit instruction**, which as discussed in Chapter 2, involves the interventionist using a range of strategies to explain and model each targeted social skill directly (Kirschner & Henrick, 2020). In this stage, the interventionist is very much the leader. The interventionist uses their professional expertise to guide the teaching of the skills, using visual and written definitions and carefully selected examples as well as supporting the participants in constructing their own scenarios for use. This might be controversial for those who advocate for teaching strategies that promote minimal adult guidance. I strongly believe that voice is crucial in building the confidence and self-determination of our young learners. However, in this context, the evidence demonstrates overwhelmingly that there needs to be a strong focus on expert modelling and feedback from the interventionist (Beaumont & Sofronoff, 2013; Clark et al., 2012; Kirschner & Henrick, 2020).

Chapter 4 is dedicated to supporting interventionists in building from these principles. It provides an overview of evidence-based strategies for teaching explicitly through **video modelling** and guiding participants through discussions using **video review**. In it, I discuss technical advice and practical

Figure 3.2 Stage A focuses on the interventionist leading the group, explicitly teaching the Target Skills and facilitating group discussions.

strategies for effective video modelling and video review, in conjunction with these teaching principles. Another key component of Stage A is the setting of clear **individual and team goals** using data generated by the intervention team, including, most importantly, the voices of the children and young adults. We should always aim to intervene in partnership with participants, not intervening 'on' them.

Introducing Stage B – Supported play

For perhaps obvious reasons, my participants are always eager to get to Stage B, with the playing of cooperative games supported by the interventionists. Children are **monitored** attentively and **coached** strategically in real time, not simply left to their own devices to play a cooperative video game. They are given regular breaks to evaluate and analyse their play and progress toward their goals. A key success factor in Stage B is allowing enough uninterrupted play so that players feel they are taking the lead in decision making. At the same time, when opportune, interventionists should discreetly intervene to teach at the point of need. Utilising regular 'time out' discussions is particularly important. The game is paused temporarily so the players' focus can be redirected towards the performance of the Target Skills and the progress being made

Figure 3.3 Stage B focuses on supported play with regular breaks for reviewing the performance of Target Skills and to allow participants mental space to discuss strategies.

towards the team and individual goals. Detailed instructions and examples of how this can be done are provided in Chapter 5, which focuses on the effective implementation of Stage B.

Stage B also provides a rich source of data so that inventionists can track the progress of each child participating in the intervention. Central to this is recording video footage of the children playing together in the physical space as well as the virtual (game) space, if possible. During cooperative gameplay, the interventionists also collect informal notes of events of interest. These can serve as a form of indexing for the video review in **Stage A** (skill instruction) in the following lesson. Although this might sound like a lot to remember, this book is here to help. Chapter 5 provides some practical advice on recording this footage, and Chapter 8 illustrates how this footage can be analysed to help guide your decision making as to what each child is ready to learn.

Introducing Stage C – Group reflection

The third and final stage of each session involves the children reflecting on their application and understanding of the Target Skills. This is done in the context of the session of play in which they had just engaged, and on their team

Figure 3.4 Sessions conclude with Stage C, where participants are led through a process of structured reflection and goal setting for the following session.

and individual goals. Much like the instruction in Stage A, **Stage C** (group reflection) is guided by the interventionists, as the metacognitive processes required for the reflection are often challenging for the children participating in this intervention.

However, ample opportunities are built into the design for the children to express themselves, so your sessions can be responsive in incorporating the feedback and suggestions from those you are trying to help. By facilitating this self-expression through a structured process, children are given an avenue to help steer the intervention toward addressing their priorities. Chapter 6 details the suggested structure and supports required to optimise participant reflection, including advice for provoking a constructive dialogue around the team and individual goals.

I should note here that, although these stages operate in a linear order in each session, they are also circular. The skills used and not used in Stage B, and the reflections elicited during Stage C, inform the instruction in the following session. Each session we use data that we generated in the previous session to help map our progress and to shift our goals in accordance with what each child has shown us they are ready to learn. Processes that you can use to analyse this data and to guide your decision making are explored in Chapter 8.

Judging the length of each stage

A common question that interventionists ask is how long each stage of the intervention should be. This is one of the most important considerations to

Stage A (skill instruction)	Stage B (supported play)	Stage C (group reflection)
Approximately 35%	**Approximately 50%**	**Approximately 15%**

Figure 3.5 The optimal allocation of time across the three intervention stages.

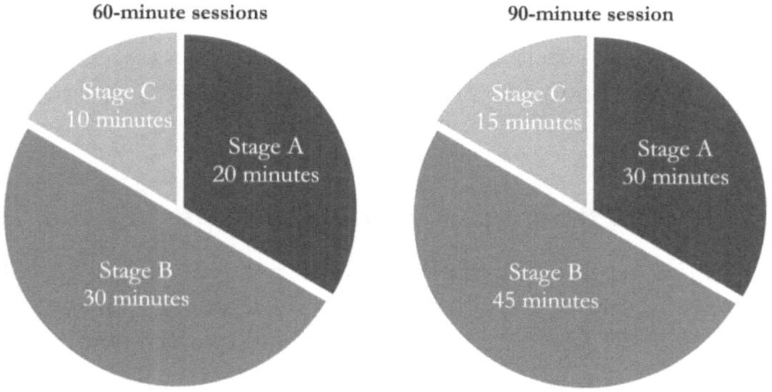

Figure 3.6 The optimal allocation of time within each stage.

get right. For a long-time, behavioural researchers suggested that for any intervention to be effective, the 'dosage' or amount of time that an intervention is implemented is a key consideration in whether the targeted outcomes are obtained (Bellini et al., 2007; Gresham et al., 2001). However, recent research by Rogers et al. (2020) has called this into question, suggesting that we do not know as much about the impact of dosage as we thought we did. This is where we need to draw on our professional experiences as educators and allied health workers. With research evidence offering conflicting findings around optimal dosage, I provide the following approach based on my professional experiences. I have found that a minimum of one Level Up Collaboration session per week for ten weeks can produce real outcomes for the participants. This is based on implementing versions of this program in both mainstream and specialist schools. Within each session, I have found that the optimal allocation of time is based on the configuration shown below.

Ideally, interventionists will have 90-minute blocks for implementing a Level Up Collaboration session, but, in reality, many educators and allied health professionals are constrained by rigid schedules. Within Australian schools, one-hour blocks of time are most common for lunchtimes or afterschool clubs. In terms of minutes allocated to each stage, this means you should be targeting the approximations shown in the graphics below.

Unfortunately, disruptions to timetabling have been a feature of most of the schools in which I have worked, so please remember that there will be times when you will not be able to align perfectly with this formula. Balancing the practicalities of timetabling pressures with an intervention implementation that allows you to do everything you need to do, and thus maintain a high degree of fidelity, can be difficult. From my observations of interventionists implementing this program, Stage A and Stage C seem to be the particular 'hotspots' because managing the length of time can become a challenge. In response to these challenges, interventionists can take a number of steps to ensure they allocate sufficient time to each stage to serve its designed function effectively, without being excessive. These steps are best discussed in context. The following three chapters focus on each respective stage, with each containing a dedicated section identifying and addressing specific challenges for that stage, including time management.

Deciding which children should participate in this intervention

Having noted in Chapter 1 the importance of avoiding stereotyping to focus instead on functional needs, I use a simple set of criteria for deciding who participates in my digital games-based interventions. I begin by asking three questions:

1 Does the child find it difficult to establish and maintain friendships with other children?

  Having taught in Australia, South Korea and the United Kingdom, some priorities for our children are culturally specific, while some are universal. In my experience, all children (and their parents) want to form meaningful bonds with their peers and feel like they belong. If a child reports that they feel like they have no friends, this is problematic. The forms of our social interactions may differ, but I believe every child wants to have friends (see Saggers et al., 2011 for heart-breaking confirmation of this). Our friendship groups represent more than just people with whom we spend our lunchtimes, they are also essential sources of emotional support, particularly for individuals with social differences (Holt et al., 2017). Friends who will stand by you are a strong defence against bullying (Rambaran et al., 2020). I would argue that it is through healthy friendships we develop a connection to our community and, in turn, develop a positive sense of identity and self-value.

2 When placed in a group of peers and assigned a goal, does this child find it difficult to co-formulate a plan of action, monitor their group performance constructively and communicate feedback in a manner that maintains a sense of collegiality?

  Increasingly we have recognised that academic knowledge and skills provide a strong foundation for learning, but to prepare our children for life beyond school we also need to teach them explicitly how to work constructively together (Griffin et al., 2012). While we work towards removing social barriers so we live can in a more inclusive society, I also believe that all children need to develop the foundational skills required for collaboration to be able to join teams and have their voices heard. Priority collaborative skills include ensuring that our learners can co-develop goals, negotiate solutions to problems and clearly communicate constructive feedback to their peers. Within these collaborative processes, there are a host of micro-skills. I interrogate these in Chapter 8.

3 Is gaming an area of strength and interest for this child?

When supporting children experiencing challenges with building friendships or developing collaborative social skills, it is important to keep in mind that these individuals are probably aware of their challenges and often have low self-esteem. If a child has a vast knowledge of gaming conventions and lore, why would we not seek to use this as a starting point? For many of the participants in the Level Up Collaboration, this is the first time they have been told that their interest and knowledge of video games is worthwhile. It is often the first time that their peers have viewed them as experts and leaders. This, in itself, is worth celebrating.

If you answer 'yes' to all three of these questions when thinking about a particular child, then I suggest that participation in Level Up Collaboration would be an ideal component of their support program. But rather than attempting to answer these questions by yourself, I suggest you work collectively with those who have the closest knowledge of the child and their experienced challenges. My first call when deciding whether to implement any supports or intervention programs is the following:

Discuss the intervention with the child, finding out their level of interest in participating, their perceived personal areas of strength and need, and their suggestions for how to implement the program.

Discuss the intervention with families or carers, they will have their own insights, developed over years of supporting their child. They will know what they like, what they find difficult and whether there are any cultural or religious considerations that the interventionists need to be mindful of when planning to support their child.

Building on information collected directly from the child and their families or carers, we can also draw on the expertise of our professional colleagues who work with the child. Working together we form the collaborative 'team around the child', with the child at the centre of everything we do as interventionists. This team might include a variety of people, as shown in the illustration below.

This team can work with the individual at the centre of the intervention to make informed decisions based on their professional expertise and body of knowledge. Each person in the team will bring their own knowledge and, perhaps, different priorities and perspectives. This type of evidence is known as 'tacit knowledge' and it is important to qualify this as distinct from beliefs, opinions or intuition (Mortier, 2020). This specialised knowledge is crucial for interpreting the other forms of evidence and is vital for:

- prioritising goals;
- analysing data and determining validity;
- deciding if an intervention such as Level Up Collaboration is practical to implement in a particular setting;
- predicting the likelihood of implementation success for an intervention with this particular cohort of individuals.

Drawing on both **stakeholder evidence** and **professional evidence** (from the team around the child) will help you make an informed decision as to whether an individual is likely to benefit from participating in Level Up Collaboration intervention.

Child's family/carers	Teachers and teaching assistants	Speech and language pathologists
School administrators and leadership	**Child** or **young adult**	Occupational therapists
Psychologists	Psychiatrists	General practitioners and paediatricians

Figure 3.7 The team around the child.

Supporting transitions between the stages

If you work regularly with children, you will have learnt that sometimes the most difficult part of the day can be transitioning between activities. While it can be difficult to fully mitigate the anxieties and anguish around transitions, through the strategic and careful use of supports we can reduce the burden on our children while still signally our expectations clearly throughout the intervention (Kasari & Smith, 2013). These supports include:

- use of visual activity schedules to establish routines and build expectations of what we will be doing and when we will be doing it;
- use of digital and non-digital timers to allow children to self-monitor the passage of time, with these resources ideally allowing for the accessibility needs of the cohort;
- the thoughtful and strategic use of space and furniture to signal where everyone should be at a particular point in the session.

It is important to consider which supports you will use and how you will use them before you implement your first session of intervention. To help you with this planning, each of the following stage-focused chapters details specific uses of these supports.

Staffing requirements and recommendations

In any intervention program, it is important to ensure that staff are well matched to the needs of the children and the running of this intervention program. Although a single adult can implement this program, optimally there should be at least two interventionists who can work as co-facilitators. Typically, this would include an intervention leader who has the overall responsibility for planning, implementing and monitoring the program, and an intervention assistant who can help with the practicalities of working with a diverse range of children. I want to make clear that teachers, teaching assistants and allied health professionals can all thrive in either of these roles. The reason I make special mention of this is that I have had some teaching assistants tell me that they do not feel like they are qualified to take on a leading role in implementing this intervention. My response to such self-doubts has always been that what really makes a difference, regardless of formal qualification, is a willingness to learn and an enthusiasm for supporting our children. Everything you need to know about planning your intervention, you can learn in this book. For your program to be successful, you need to find staff who genuinely enjoy working with this cohort and can respond to challenges in a calm and empathetic manner. It can also help if your staff share a love of gaming, although this does not mean they have to be experts in the lore and language of this medium. Interventionists just have to want to be there.

Clear communication is a key component in any collaborative pursuit. Implementing an intervention begins with a shared understanding of your purpose within the team, and the purpose of your colleague. Although the two interventionists might share many tasks, it is also important to have a clear understanding of who is primarily responsible for which component of the intervention. Although these can of course be negotiated beforehand, I have found the following role descriptions useful in helping everyone understand what they are expected to be doing.

By listing the distinct responsibilities for each facilitator explicitly, you can then draw on different areas of specialised knowledge and skills within your staff. This will ensure the right person is in the right role. When recruiting a co-facilitator, I suggest having these position descriptions on hand just to ensure that the interested party understands their role as well as your role.

Intervention leader	Intervention assistant
✓ Scheduling the time for intervention sessions (pre-intervention)	✓ Guiding children to transition to seats to begin session (Stage A)
✓ Deciding on which children require intervention (pre-intervention)	✓ Supporting participants to engage with explicit teaching and discussions (Stage A)
✓ Leading explicit teaching and guiding discussions (Stage A)	✓ Assisting with recording of skill performance (Stage B)
✓ Assisting with recording of skill performance (Stage B)	✓ Working with the children to decide on goals (Stage C)
✓ Working with the children to decide on goals (Stage C)	✓ Assisting with analysis of data following intervention sessions (post-intervention)
✓ Analysing data from intervention sessions (post-intervention)	✓ Providing feedback on timing and structure of session (post-intervention)
✓ Creating video models (post-intervention)	

Figure 3.8 Interventionist roles – leader and assistant.

Finding the right space

The goal of intervention planning is to create the optimal conditions to engage with the participants and to ensure they are tuned in and comfortable. Our choice of the physical environments in which we implement our intervention can either create or remove barriers to producing these conditions (Richmond, 2007). When identifying an appropriate space, it is important that you consider the following factors:

- **Size of the space**: As we operate in a post-COVID-19 world, we need to consider social distancing, allowing sufficient space between children and interventionists while also allowing people to be within comfortable talking distance. As I recommend a different seating arrangement for each of the stages (A, B and C), the respective chapters include a dedicated section (with illustrations) to help you plan the physical layout of your space. Refer to these diagrams when reviewing possible sites for your intervention.
- **Sensory considerations**: We know that many neurodiverse learners have sensory differences, particularly in terms of visual and sensory input (Robertson & Baron-Cohen, 2017). We need to ensure that the spaces in which we implement our interventions have minimal background noises and uncluttered walls so that the focus of the participants remains on where you are directing their attention. Sensory audits, through which your team checks to see whether a space meets the needs of your participants, should always involve the participants themselves, as they may process their sensory environment in a completely different manner to you or your team. Each of the following chapters also provides advice around how you can do this.
- **Consider using separate spaces for each stage:** To help support transitions between activities, I suggest using a different area of the room or, if possible, a different room for each of the three stages. By using a different area or room we can help to create expectations for our participants as to what they will be doing at a particular point in time. If you are trying to facilitate guided reflection, it can be challenging to hold your participants' attention if a Nintendo Switch is still in their line of sight. If you have only one space for all three stages, consider using portable dividers to create defined spaces.

THINKING ABOUT SOCIAL DISTANCING

Schools and other settings for intervention have transformed their thinking since the onset of the global COVID-19 pandemic. Everyone wants to ensure that their programs encourage safe practises around social distancing to minimise health risks to our staff and our children. While

Physical space audit checklist

	Component of the space	Yes	We can fix it	Not approp.
Safety	Is the learning space clean?	✓		
	Are there enough chairs for every participant?		✓	
	Is the entry/exit area clear?		✓	
	Are the within-class movement routes clear?	✓		
	Notes on safety considerations:			
	* Boxes storing old books need to be moved to another space to clear doorway for easy entrance/exit of the intervention room.			
Sensory environment	Is the room private and away from external noises (bouncing balls, loud talking, etc)?	✓		
	Is the lighting sufficient to see the entire room easily without being too bright? (Natural light?)	✓		
	Are there any distracting visual stimuli (LEDs on TV) or sounds (ticking clocks, dripping water) within the room?		✓	
	Are the walls free of distracting decorations (irrelevant posters, photos, etc)?	✓		
	Notes on sensory environment:			
	* We need to swap the analogue clock (ticking) for a digital clock that is silent to ensure everyone can easily concentrate during the sessions. * Put tape over LED on the TV to reduce risk of distraction.			

Figure 3.9 Example of a completed *Physical space audit checklist.*

	Components of the space	Yes	We can fix it	Not approp.
Stage specific needs	Is there a working screen to use for the explicit instruction (Stage A) large enough so everyone can view it at once?	✓		
	Is there a working screen to use for the supported play (Stage B) large enough so everyone can view it while playing?	✓		
	Are there clean walls to use to display visual supports during Stage A and B?		✓	
	Is there a table that can comfortably sit all of the participants and interventionists (Stage C)?		✓	

Notes on stage specific needs:

* Walls need to be wiped down as they are a bit dirty

* We need to get one more large table to be able to comfortably fit everyone (from Year 5/6 store room?)

Final evaluation

- Does this room meet the needs of your participants? Why or why not?

This room offers the most appropriate (available) space in the school as it meets most of the functional requirements for running the intervention. Importantly, it is close to most of the students' classrooms so it will be easy for them to find and then return to their classes when time.

Figure 3.9 (Continued)

co-located play in the same room is central to this intervention, it is important to space children apart in accordance with your local health advice. This might mean that you need to find a larger space than you would have used in a pre-COVID world, or that you can accommodate only four children in the program at once. Regulations vary from context to context, so please ensure that you are following all government guidelines in running this program in your school or setting.

To help you plan for an optimal physical environment, you can use a copy of the *Physical space audit checklist* provided to audit a space. You should complete this with the team around the child and, ideally, the children who will be participating in the intervention. Below is a completed example of this checklist. A blank version is available in the resources section at the end of this chapter.

Using the *Intervention roadmap planner*

Once you have thought about when you might run your intervention sessions, who would benefit most from participating and the ideal physical environment in your school or setting, it is time to use the *Intervention roadmap planner* sheets. This tool consists of two planning proformas:

- the *Intervention roadmap planner – participants' background information and goals* sheet; and
- the *Intervention roadmap planner – organising gaming resources* sheet.

Building a profile of your learners

As suggested by the name, the *Intervention roadmap planner – participants' background information and goals* sheet will help you to develop profiles for each of the participants, focusing on their individual interests and strengths, their specific areas of challenge and any additional notes from the child themselves. Below is a completed example of this sheet. A blank version is available in the resources section of this chapter.

Prior to the first intervention session, you should work with the child and the team around the child to complete the left-hand 'background information' column. If a child is not comfortable with this number of people in the room, then a trusted adult can work with the child first and additional information from the other members of the team can augment the child's contribution. The 'tracking session goals' section is used to record the goals that have been assigned prior to each session. As goal setting is dependent on the progress being made, these are completed over a period of time. Effective goal setting is explored further in Chapter 8, with the inclusion of a bank of goals that might be appropriate for the children with whom you are working.

Monitoring and evaluating the video games that you are using

In addition to planning for the participant in your intervention, you also need to plan which gaming resources you will use during your sessions. As explored in Chapter 10, not all cooperative multiplayer games are created equal. As you progress from session to session with your participants, it is important to track the software that you are using and to ensure it is 'fit for purpose' for the cohort with whom you are currently working. A game that is effective for one group might not be effective for another.

Intervention roadmap planner – participants' background information and goals

Participant names	Background information	Tracking session goals		
Name: *Samus*	**Interests and strengths:** *Gaming (special interest in Nintendo games), stamps, likes to sit next to new people*	Session 1 goal: *Taking turns*	Session 2 goal: *Taking turns*	Session 3 goal: *Giving verbal instructions*
	Areas of challenge: *Fine motor skills, initiating conversations with peers*	Session 4 goal: *Giving verbal instructions*	Session 5 goal: *Giving verbal instructions*	Session 6 goal: *Giving verbal instructions*
	Notes from child: *Really wants to meet friends who like the same games as they do*	Session 7 goal: *Checking for understanding*	Session 8 goal: *Giving feedback*	Session 9 goal: *Giving feedback*
Name: *Mario*	**Interests and strengths:** *Soccer, Pokémon, ice skating, Lego, reading*	Session 1 goal: *Taking turns*	Session 2 goal: *Quiet voices*	Session 3 goal: *Quiet voices*
	Areas of challenge: *Can become frustrated when playing with his friends, hates noisy spaces*	Session 4 goal: *Listening to others*	Session 5 goal: *Listening to others*	Session 6 goal: *Giving feedback*
	Notes from child: *Enjoys 2D platform games, wants to play games with the older children*	Session 7 goal: *Giving feedback*	Session 8 goal: *Giving feedback*	Session 9 goal: *Requesting feedback*
Name: *Link*	**Interests and strengths:** *Animals, particularly snails. Is known for being extremely patient with younger students*	Session 1 goal: *Offering help*	Session 2 goal: *Offering help*	Session 3 goal: *Encouraging*
	Areas of challenge: *Parents want him to spend less time alone, and instead play with peers*	Session 4 goal: *Encouraging*	Session 5 goal: *Giving feedback*	Session 6 goal: *Giving feedback*
	Notes from child: *He sometimes wants to play with peers, but is sometimes happier alone*	Session 7 goal: *Giving feedback*	Session 8 goal: *Asking for ideas to solve a problem*	Session 9 goal: *Asking for ideas to solve a problem*

Figure 3.10 Example of a completed *Intervention roadmap planner – participants' background information and goals* template.

To do your planning, you can use the *Intervention roadmap planner – organising gaming resources* sheet. Below is a completed example of this sheet. A blank version is available in the resources section of this chapter.

Prior to each session, you can record the name of the game that you plan on using, the system on which this game can be played and the maximum number of simultaneous players that the game will allow. These are three important considerations for ensuring that you are organised and understand the capabilities and requirements of the software you are planning on using in Stage B (supported play). Once you begin testing various games, you can also record your observations of the benefits and challenges of using each title. Developing your own list will complement the reviews of a range of cooperative video games that can be found in Chapter 10.

Summary of key ideas in Chapter 3

- Level Up Collaboration uses a consistent structure to provide a systematic approach to supporting children and young adults, establishing clear routines and expectations of what will happen during a session.
- Stage A focuses on interventionist-guided instruction and discussing the Target Skills.
- Stage B involves supported play, with the participants supported by the interventionists to practise the performance of the Target Skills.
- Stage C involves interventionist-facilitated reflection on the collaboration during play in Stage B, with a focus on analysing the degree to which the collective team and individuals accomplished their nominated goals.
- It is important to consider carefully which children should participate in your intervention program, focusing on children and young adults who find it difficult to form friendships, who find it challenging to collaborate with others during group tasks and who have an interest in gaming.
- Professional collaboration is a key to success, with teachers, allied health professionals, families and participants all given the opportunity to contribute to the program and the areas of focus for the child and young adults.
- Transitions into the intervention sessions, from stage to stage, and exiting the intervention need to be planned and managed carefully to ensure that the participants do not become overwhelmed with anxiety.
- When implementing these sessions with another interventionist, it is important to define roles clearly within the team.
- Also important is considering the space that you use for your sessions, as the sensory environment can represent a significant enabler or barrier for some neurodiverse participants.
- Use the provided planning templates to ensure that your intervention has the best possible chance of being effective for your children and young adults.

Intervention roadmap planner - organising gaming resources

	Game title/system	Number of players	Affordances of game	Challenges of using this game
Session 1	*Rayman Legends (Nintendo Wii U)*	*4 players*	• *Easy to learn for new players*	
Session 2	*Rayman Legends (Nintendo Wii U)*	*4 players*	• *The character 'Murfy' can be controlled using the touch screen which players with motor skills challenges found easier than the normal controller.*	
Session 3	*Rayman Legends (Nintendo Wii U)*	*4 players*		
Session 4	*Kirby and the Rainbow Paintbrush (Nintendo Wii U)*	*4 players*	• *A lot of coordination and interaction between the player controlling Kirby and the other players*	• *Some of the players found the controls difficult to learn and became frustrated.*
Session 5	*Kirby and the Rainbow Paintbrush (Nintendo Wii U)*	*4 players*		
Session 6	*Kirby and the Rainbow Paintbrush (Nintendo Wii U)*	*4 players*		
Session 7	*Kirby and the Rainbow Paintbrush (Nintendo Wii U)*	*4 players*		• *Levels are a bit repetitive so some of the participants were becoming bored of doing the same things.*
Session 8	*Super Mario 3D World (Nintendo Switch)*	*4 players*	• *Participants loved the familiar characters*	• *The 3D environment was difficult for some participants to navigate, and they quickly became lost.*
Session 9	*Super Mario 3D World (Nintendo Switch)*	*4 players*	• *Levels during this session were really varied with new ideas in every level, so participants were very excited.*	
Session 10	*Star Fox Zero (Nintendo Wii U)*	*2 players*	• *A highly requested game by some of the older participants*	• *The action was too fast for many of the participants to process what was happening.*

Figure 3.11 Example of a completed *Intervention roadmap planner – organising gaming resources* template.

References

Beaumont, R., & Sofronoff, K. (2013). Multi-modal intervention for social skills training in students with high-functioning ASD: The secret agent society. In A. Scarpa, S. W. White, & T. Attwood (Eds.), *CBT for children and adolescents with high-functioning autism spectrum disorders* (pp. 173–198). Guilford Press.

Bellini, S., Peters, J. K., Benner, L., & Hopf, A. (2007). A meta-analysis of school-based social skills interventions for children with autism spectrum disorders. *Remedial and Special Education, 28*(3), 153–162.

Berman, J., & Graham, L. (2018). *Learning intervention: Educational casework and responsive teaching for sustainable learning.* Routledge.

Clark, M., & Adams, D. (2020). Parent perspectives of what helps and hinders their child on the autism spectrum to manage their anxiety. *Clinical Psychologist, 24*(3), 315–328.

Clark, R. E., Kirschner, P. A., & Sweller, J. (2012). Putting students on the path to learning: The case for fully guided instruction. *American Educator, 36*(1), 6–11.

Gresham, F. M., Sugai, G., & Horner, R. H. (2001). Interpreting outcomes of social skills training for students with high-incidence disabilities. *Exceptional Children, 67*(3), 331–344.

Griffin, P. E., McGaw, B., & Care, E. (2012). *Assessment and teaching of 21st century skills.* Springer.

Holt, L., Bowlby, S., & Lea, J. (2017). "Everyone knows me … I sort of like move about": The friendships and encounters of young people with special educational needs in different school settings. *Environment and Planning A, 49*(6), 1361–1378.

Kasari, C., & Smith, T. (2013). Interventions in schools for children with autism spectrum disorder: Methods and recommendations. *Autism, 17*(3), 254–267.

Kirschner, P. A., & Hendrick, C. (2020). *How learning happens: Seminal works in educational psychology and what they mean in practice.* Routledge.

Makin, C., Hill, V., & Pellicano, E. (2017). The primary-to-secondary school transition for children on the autism spectrum: A multi-informant mixed-methods study. *Autism & Developmental Language Impairments, 2*, 1–17.

Middleton, J., Gorard, S., Taylor, C., & Bannan-Ritland, B. (2008). The 'compleat' design experiment: From soup to nuts. In A. Kelly, R. Lesh, & J. Baek (Eds.), *Handbook of design research methods in education: Innovations in science, technology, engineering, and mathematics learning and teaching* (pp. 21–46). Routledge.

Mortier, K. (2020). Communities of practice: A conceptual framework for inclusion of students with significant disabilities. *International Journal of Inclusive Education, 24*(3), 329–340.

Rambaran, J. A., Dijkstra, J. K., & Veenstra, R. (2020). Bullying as a group process in childhood: A longitudinal social network analysis. *Child Development, 91*(4), 1336–1352.

Richmond, C. (2007). *Teach more, manage less: A minimalist approach to behaviour management.* Scholastic.

Robertson, C. E., & Baron-Cohen, S. (2017). Sensory perception in autism. *Nature Reviews Neuroscience, 18*(11), 671–684.

Rogers, S. J., Yoder, P., Estes, A., Warren, Z., McEachin, J., Munson, J., Rocha, M., Greenson, J., Wallace, L., Gardner, E., Dawson, G., Sugar, C. A., Hellemann, G., & Whelan, F. (2020). A multisite randomized controlled trial comparing the effects of intervention intensity and intervention style on outcomes for young children with autism. *Journal of the American Academy of Child & Adolescent Psychiatry, 60*(6),710–722.

Saggers, B., Hwang, Y. S., & Mercer, K. L. (2011). Your voice counts: Listening to the voice of high school students with autism spectrum disorder. *Australasian Journal of Special Education, 35*(2), 173–190.

Resources

In this section you will find photocopiable versions of the following resources:

- the *Physical space audit checklist* template;
- the *Intervention roadmap planner – participants' background information and goals* template;
- the *Intervention roadmap planner – organising gaming resources* template.

PHYSICAL SPACE AUDIT CHECKLIST

	Component of the space	*Yes*	*We can fix it*	*Not approp.*
Safety	Is the learning space clean?			
	Are there enough chairs for every participant?			
	Is the entry/exit area clear?			
	Are the within-class movement routes clear?			
	Notes on safety considerations:			
Sensory environment	Is the room private and away from external noises (bouncing balls, loud talking, etc.)?			
	Is the lighting sufficient to see the entire room easily without being too bright? (natural light?)			
	Are there any distracting visual stimuli (LEDs on TV) or sounds (ticking clocks, dripping water) within the room?			
	Are the walls free of distracting decorations (irrelevant posters, photos, etc.)?			
	Notes on the sensory environment:			

	Components of the space	*Yes*	*We can fix it*	*Not approp.*
Stage specific needs	Is there a working screen to use for the explicit instruction (Stage A) large enough so everyone can view it at once?			
	Is there a working screen to use for the supported play (Stage B) large enough so everyone can view it while playing?			
	Are there clean walls to use to display visual supports during Stage A and Stage B?			
	Is there a table that can comfortably sit all of the participants and interventionists (Stage C)?			
	Notes on stage specific needs:			

Final evaluation

- Does this room meet the needs of your participants? Why or why not?

INTERVENTION ROADMAP PLANNER – PARTICIPANTS' BACKGROUND INFORMATION AND GOALS

		Background information	*Tracking session goals*		
Participant names	Name:	**Interests and strengths:**	Session 1 goal:	Session 2 goal:	Session 3 goal:
		Areas of challenge:	Session 4 goal:	Session 5 goal:	Session 6 goal:
		Notes from child:	Session 7 goal:	Session 8 goal:	Session 9 goal:
	Name:	**Interests and strengths:**	Session 1 goal:	Session 2 goal:	Session 3 goal:
		Areas of challenge:	Session 4 goal:	Session 5 goal:	Session 6 goal:
		Notes from child:	Session 7 goal:	Session 8 goal:	Session 9 goal:
	Name:	**Interests and strengths:**	Session 1 goal:	Session 2 goal:	Session 3 goal:
		Areas of challenge:	Session 4 goal:	Session 5 goal:	Session 6 goal:
		Notes from child:	Session 7 goal:	Session 8 goal:	Session 9 goal:

INTERVENTION ROADMAP PLANNER – ORGANISING GAMING RESOURCES

	Game title/system	*Number of players*	*Affordances of game*	*Challenges of using this game*
Session 1				
Session 2				
Session 3				
Session 4				
Session 5				
Session 6				
Session 7				
Session 8				
Session 9				
Session 10				

4 Stage A – Using explicit skill instruction and video review

Introduction

Stage A is all about teaching and learning about our participants' understandings of the focus social skills. Throughout the intervention, a significant emphasis is placed on the teacher being an instructional leader rather than a facilitator, particularly during Stage A. This is a deliberate positioning of the teacher informed by a vast body of research into the science of learning from the field of cognitive psychology (see Chapter 2). In particular, beginning with an expert-novice instructional relationship allows the teacher to manage the cognitive load on the participants carefully. Teachers can manage the speed at which they model the skills, use questioning to check for understanding and provide different forms of feedback when the participants practise performing the skills in Stage B.

An overview of the steps for implementing Stage A

As shown in the graphic below, there are eight distinct steps designed to support participants in developing their understandings of the Target Skills. These steps can be grouped together informally in four broader categories: pre-planning for the intervention session; 'checking in' to engage with the participants; 'looking back' at what has already been taught; and 'looking forward' by learning new skills and setting new goals for this session of the intervention.

Icons are included next to some of the steps, indicating that these steps use particular types of resources and supports. These icons are used throughout this chapter and the following chapters.

- When you see the document icon (📄) this indicates the use of a physical scaffold, such as a worksheet or a chart, to support the participants throughout this section.
- When you see the video icon (🎬) this indicates the use of the video footage through either video modelling or video review.
- Last but not least, the use of the computer icon (💻) indicates the use of a particular *type* of software (such as video playback software) required for implementing a core component of Stage A.

DOI: 10.4324/9781003025917-4

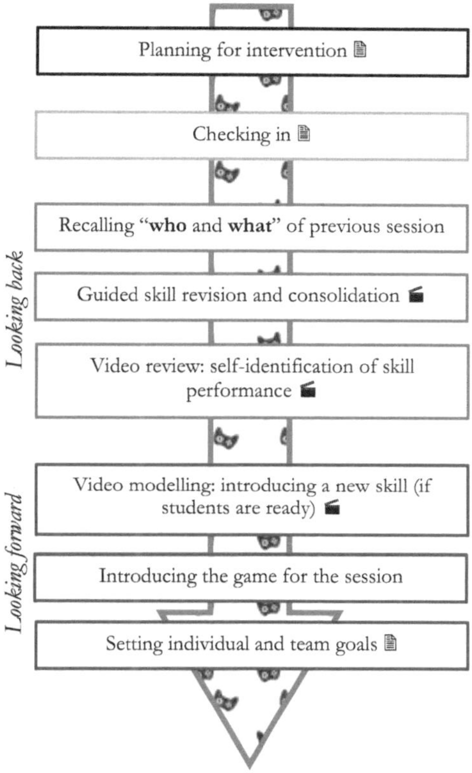

Figure 4.1 Overview of the steps for implementing Stage A.

Planning for intervention: Preparing for Stage A

Assessing what each child is ready to learn in this session

When ascertaining which skills an individual is ready to learn, it is important to use a range of data to inform these decisions rather than relying on incidental observations and assumptions. Chapter 8 discusses strategies for making data-driven decisions within this intervention, exploring how we can structure our assessments and use developmental progressions to know when a child is ready to learn a new skill.

Required and recommended instructional resources

To help you plan, the table below provides an overview of the resources requiring preparation before Stage A. Each resource is categorised as either a 'required resource' or a 'recommended resource'. When reviewing the table, you should also be aware that some of the listed resources are used in multiple stages (as listed in the 'Universal resources' column).

Setting up your *Visual activity schedule*: Many children are much less anxious when they know what task or activity is happening now, how long this task or activity will run and what they will be doing next. Using a *Visual activity schedule*, you can help to create a sense of predictability and safety in your intervention through structure and routine. The schedule will also save you constantly answering the question: 'What are we doing next?' This alone is worth the investment, creating a schedule that you can reuse through every session.

What do you need?

✓ Activity cards (see the resources section for templates)	✓ Velcro tape (the hook side)	✓ A carpet board

When creating your schedule, you do not need to invent it from scratch. Use the template provided in the resources section of this chapter as a starting point. This contains 'activity cards' for all of the core activities in Stages A, B and C, combining text and supporting visuals to communicate the purpose of each activity.

> *Practical advice on preparing your schedule*: Construct your teaching resources to last. Cut out and laminate each of the activity cards and affix a thick strip of Velcro tape to the back of each card. I personally suggest using the side of the tape with the small hooks so that you can stick your cards to a carpet board (which as the name suggests, is a piece of thick cardboard covered in carpet).

The following 'Checking in' section of this chapter provides both an example schedule as well as instructions on how to use this invaluable tool in establishing routines and expectations for your participants (and for your other interventionist!).

Target Skills icons stickers: These are written and pictorial representations of the 15 Target Skills that are prioritised within the Level Up Collaboration intervention. It is important to have these icons on hand to support verbal discussion around the meaning and use of these skills throughout the intervention. Chapter 7 explores the meaning and value of each of these skills in depth, in the context of collaborative problem-solving, and provides specific strategies for helping you to teach these skills through this intervention.

> *Practical advice on preparing your Target Skill icons* stickers: Cut out and laminate at least 10 copies of each Target Skill icon. Although this might seem excessive, you will use these icons with a number of the visual supports,

Table 4.1 Overview of required and recommended resources for Stage A

Universal resources (used in all stages)	*Resources for welcoming participants*	*Resources for video review and video modelling*
'What are we doing today?' ***Visual activity schedule*** 🗎 *(recommended resource)*: a visual schedule to help create a sense of predictability and structure for the intervention session. ***Target Skills icons*** stickers 🗎 *(required resource)*: visual representations of the 15 skills that are the focus of this intervention. ***Goal and skill performance sticker chart*** 🗎 *(required resource)*: a chart that supports participants in remembering their individual goals and for recording which of the Target Skills they have been using during cooperative play. Goals are set during Stage A. **Photos or avatars of every participant** 🗎 *(recommended resource)*: label these with their preferred names and use them to help unfamiliar participants recall who is in their team.	**'How are you feeling today?'** ***chart*** 🗎 *(recommended resource)*: a visual support that helps participants identify their emotional state during the initial check in of each session. **Fidget box** *(recommended resource)*: some of the participants may experience differences in sensory processing. Having unintrusive 'fidget toys' available can help them maintain their attention on the instruction and group discussion.	**Video playback software** 💻 **and computer/mobile device** *(required resource)*: you will need software installed on a computer or mobile device (i.e., iPad) that allows you to play back video footage during Stage A, including the video models you have created. This device will be connected to your interactive whiteboard or screen. **Video editing software** 💻 *(required resource)*: to create video models using the footage you have collected during cooperative play (Stage B), you will need editing software to ensure only positive instances of the skills being used are shown. **Interactive whiteboard or television screen** *(required resource)*: so that everyone can see the video footage, you will need a sufficiently large interactive whiteboard or television screen.

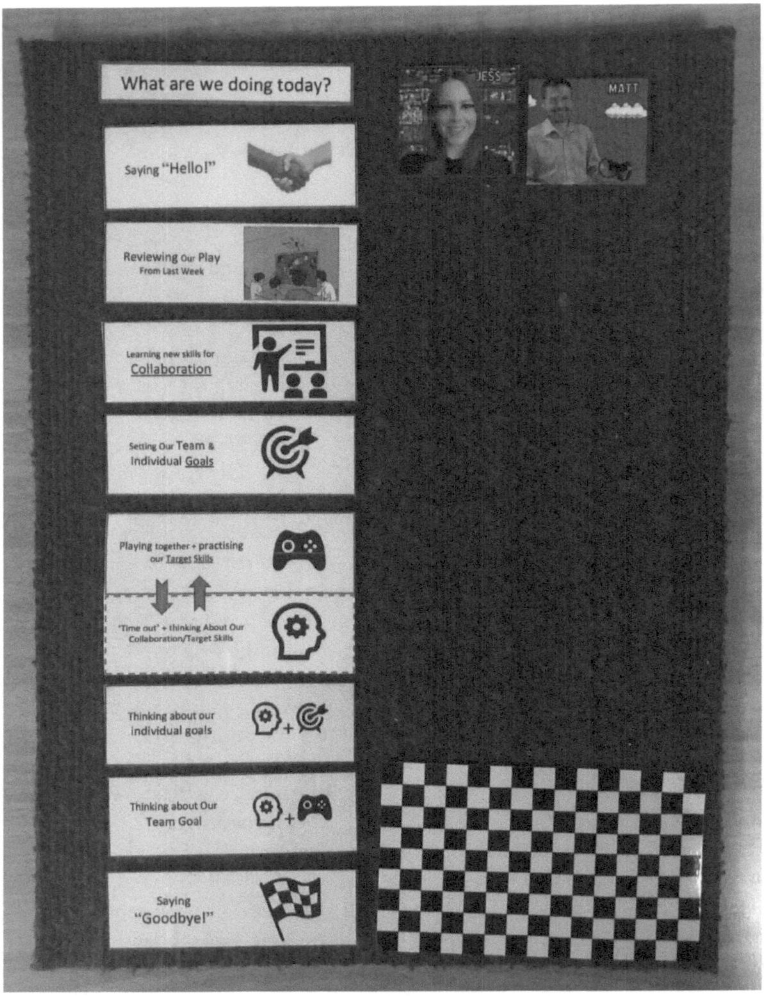

Figure 4.2 Example of a *Visual activity schedule.*

including the *Goal and skill performance sticker chart.* Affix a piece of Velcro tape to the back of each card. Again, I suggest using the side of the tape with the small hooks.

As you read through the following chapters dedicated to each of the three stages of the intervention, you will see a number of uses for these dynamic *Target Skill icons*. This includes using them in conjunction with the following charts across Stages A, B and C:

Figure 4.3 Examples of *Target Skill icons.*

- the *Goal and skill performance sticker chart* (used in Stages A, B and C);
- the *Team reflection chart* (used in Stage C);
- the *3-2-1 charts* (used in Stage B).

Goal and skill performance sticker chart: Using this multipurposed chart will help assign and remind individuals of their goals (set in Stage A), as well as help in monitoring the Target Skills that each individual is using during play. This is important as implementing this intervention can feel very 'busy', especially when working with a new group of participants or new co-interventionists. In the middle of all of the interactions and excitement occurring in the room, it is very easy for children to forget their individual Target Skill goal.

Photos or avatars of every participant: It is useful to have photos or avatars representing the participants on hand to help you and the other participants remember the names of those taking part in the program. Label these photos or pictures with the participants' preferred names and affix them to the photo frames at the bottom of each column of the *Goal and skill performance sticker chart.*

'How are you feeling today?' chart: You can use this chart to support your participants in communicating their emotional state at the beginning of each session during the 'check in'.

> *Practical advice on preparing your* 'How are you feeling today?' *chart:* Print onto larger paper (A3 size is optimal) and laminate it for durability.

Providing unintrusive fidgets and noise reducing earmuffs: By allowing children to request and use small 'fidgets', some individuals may be better able to concentrate on the instruction being provided by the interventionists or the topics being discussed by the group. I have often heard fidgets described as 'fidget toys', but I am reluctant to label them as such as I believe they are not for 'play' but rather for emotional and sensory regulation. Likewise, noise-reducing earmuffs can help participants maintain a sense of control over their auditory environment and can be an effective tool for self-regulation when paired with fidgets. The photo below shows examples of fidgets that I have found to be effective in conducting my intervention programs, as well as a pair of earmuffs.

Figure 4.4 Earmuffs and fidgets for use during interventions.

Like many learning supports, the effectiveness of these fidgets in promoting increased focus rather than another distraction will vary from child to child. My advice is, if possible, work with either an occupational therapist or an adult familiar with the child to decide whether access to these fidgets would be beneficial. Following this, have a conversation with the child before the session about the use of these supports. Their responses might surprise you; they might not like the fidgets you have available due to subtle textures, noises or a fear of looking 'different' from the other participants.

Video playback software: To be able to play back video footage as part of the video review and video modelling components of Stage A, you will need to have the software installed and ready to use before the session begins. You do not require anything too sophisticated for this, as the only features you need are full-screen viewing, the ability to pause and resume playback and file compatibility with the formats used by your camera and with the files exported from your video editing software (see below).

> *Practical advice:* Use the default software that comes pre-installed on most computers with either Windows 10 (Windows Media Player) or MacOS (QuickTime).

Video editing software: In order to create your video models, you will need software to edit your footage into positive demonstrations of the Target Skill you are trying to teach. As shown in the matrix below, a number of options are available to you, depending on your preferred platform or budget.

> *Practical advice for selecting video editing software*: You really need only three features, although some of the additional features of the more expensive packages can be fun. The required features are: (1) the ability to edit the video to show only the correct steps in performing a skill or behaviour; (2) the ability to record voiceovers; and (3) the ability to export files as either MP4 video files (all operating systems) or MOV files (most commonly used with MacOS or iOS/iPadOS). While this book cannot teach you how to use all of this software, a number of excellent tutorials are available on YouTube that can walk you through the requisite steps.

Making use of an interactive whiteboard or television screen: As this intervention has a strong reliance on digital video and digital games as teaching and learning tools, it is important that every child can access this media. Obviously, everyone needs to be able to see the video footage or game. An important consideration is ensuring that the screen is large enough so that children can sit comfortably apart and still see what they need to see. Bigger children take more space, which can mean they need a bigger screen to ensure that everyone has a decent viewing angle.

Provide comfortable chairs: In the previous chapter the physical space was discussed, but equally important is the furniture in the room. Below are photos of three types of chairs that I have found over the years to be effective for different children and young adults.

If you are unsure, it is best to consult with a qualified occupational therapist as they will have the specialised knowledge to help you make an informed choice about the benefits and potential challenges of each option. As with other choices you make in implementing this intervention, I also strongly suggest you ask the child for their preferred chair as they will be the one sitting on it!

Setting up the physical space for Stage A

When preparing for Stage A, the first things you need to consider are the 'difficult' to move objects. This involves setting up the interactive whiteboard or screen, the portable dividing wall and a device for video playback. You need to give careful consideration to the location of each of these resources so they are accessible to all the participants and interventionists who need to use them. Below is a diagram of my preferred layout.

Once you have the larger 'difficult to move' items in place, you can set up the chairs in what I term the 'community circle', which, as you can see in the diagram below, is a bit of a misnomer. Ideally, you want to ensure

Table 4.2 Matrix of video editing software

	Adobe Premiere Pro: professional video editing software that has advanced features like colour grading and allows for the use of multiple cameras.	*Final Cut Pro* (Apple): professional video editing software. Allows you to add visual overlays easily (such as the *Target Skill icons*).		
Cost ↑			*LumaFusion* (Luma Touch): a mobile video editor with a similar user interface and features to Final Cut Pro.	*Adobe Premiere Rush*: a mid-level video editing package for mobile devices that requires a monthly subscription.
	Windows Movie Maker (Microsoft): free basic software that allows you to cut and crop clips, and add voiceovers.	*iMovie* (Apple): free video editing software that allows you to 'do the basics' easily on your Mac.	*iMovie* (Apple): free video editing software that allows you to 'do the basics' easily on your mobile device.	*FilmoraGo* (Wondershare): popular free video editing software that allows for the exporting of videos without watermarks.
	Microsoft Windows (personal computer)	Apple MacOS (personal computer)	Apple iOS/ iPadOS (mobile devices)	Google Android (mobile devices)

Software platform

that everyone has comfortable leg and arm room, and a comfortable viewing angle of the screen. If you are using a touch screen, make sure you allow enough space for easy movement to and from the screen. Likewise, if you are displaying the *Goal and skill performance sticker chart* on the portable dividing wall, ensure that this is easily visible when you are setting the goals for cooperative play.

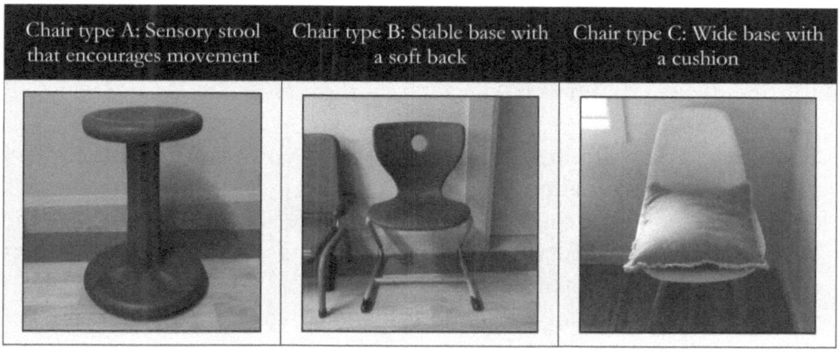

Figure 4.5 Different chair options for intervention participants.

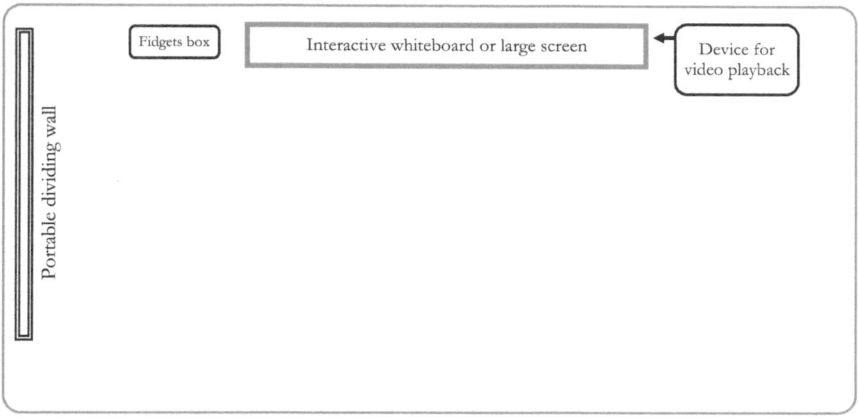

Figure 4.6 Diagram of a sample room layout for Stage A.

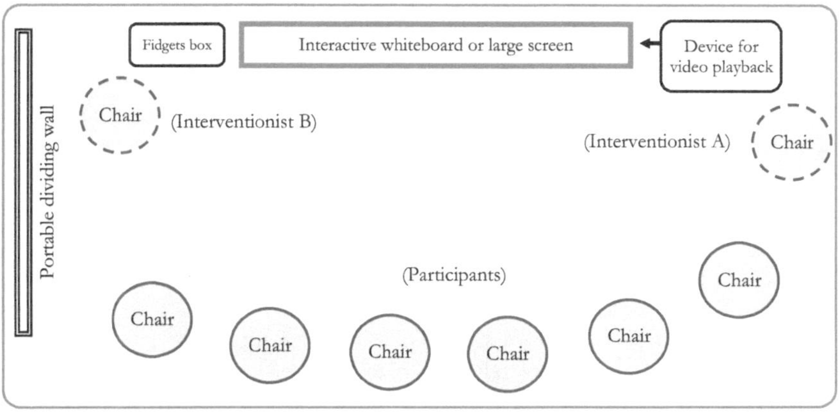

Figure 4.7 Diagram of a sample 'community circle' in Stage A.

Checking in

We know that our children will have good days and bad days, and it is important to be responsive to their emotional states when they first arrive. We can establish an effective routine for 'checking in' through the following steps:

- **Greeting each child at the door, ensuring you use their name and ask how they are feeling.** Ideally, you should greet the children one at a time as they enter the room to allow for a degree of privacy. Many of the children I have worked with are often self-conscious about sharing their emotional state with their peers.
  - 🖹 Support resource: To support this initial greeting you can use the simple 'How are you feeling today?' *chart*. Have the child point to one of the emojis (faces) to indicate how they are feeling.
  - Think about: If the child is unsure how they are feeling or which picture represents their current feelings, they might not be able to recognise their own emotional state. This needs to be taught explicitly and regularly practised. Although teaching the self-identification of emotional states is outside of the scope of this intervention, I recommend investigating complementary resources such as the *Zones of Regulation* curriculum or *The Secret Agent Society* program.
- **Support the child's transition to the community circle once they enter the room so you can continue to greet other participants as they arrive.** To help hold their interest and to ensure they continue sitting in the circle, have something for them to do. This could be an appropriate gaming video from Twitch or YouTube, ice cream containers of Lego (as long as they know that this is the only time they can play with it during the session) or a selection of books to read. The goal is a calm arrival and a predictable, orderly beginning to every session.
  - Think about: Make these expectations clear by referring the child to a *Visual activity schedule* showing them the steps they will be following. Many neurodiverse children require the building of routine and structure in order to reduce anxieties and to feel safe in their environment (Busby et al., 2012).
  - 🖹 Support resource: Use a simple timer on the interactive whiteboard or screen to allow everyone to know how much time they have left. *Online Stopwatch* (https://www.online-stopwatch.com/sensory-timers) offers a range of countdown timers that are both simple and free. What is particularly exciting is that many of these timers offer visual representations of the remaining time for children who struggle to read numerals. They can also be set up to be 'sensory friendly', avoiding loud noises when the time expires.
  - 🖹 Support resource: Use the 'What are we doing today?' *Visual activity schedule* template to help you create a predictable routine for your children, as provided in the resources section of this chapter. Put the

activities in order with the first activity at the top, working towards the final activity at the bottom of the schedule. As the group finishes each task, place the corresponding activity card in the 'finished pocket', as modelled in the photo below. If you want to make this more interactive, have the children move items from the schedule to the 'finished pocket' to indicate that the group is transitioning to the next task.

- **Begin the session with a routine group welcome in the community circle once the timer indicates it is time to start**. Beginning with a group welcome provides an opportunity for the participants to say hello to each other and reconfirm preferred names, but I always avoid overemphasising peer interaction at this stage. Many children will be nervous and will need time to 'warm up'.
  - 🗎 Resource: If required, use the 'How are you feeling today?' *chart* shown below to determine how each participant is feeling. There is a photocopiable version in the resources section of this chapter. While some days your children will find the right words very quickly, it is

Figure 4.8 Image of a 'finished pocket'.

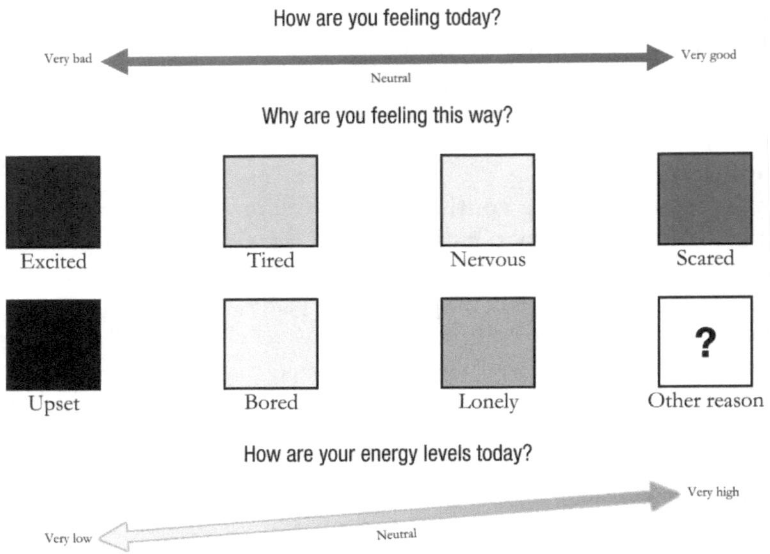

Figure 4.9 'How are you feeling today?' *chart.*

useful to have some vocabulary on hand to assist them in labelling their own emotional state.

- **Check the *Visual activity schedule* as a group, providing an overview of the sessions and timings of each component**. As an interventionist, routine is your friend, and at the heart of establishing regular and predictable practices is the use of a visual schedule that combines words and supporting icons for the major activities you will be completing throughout the session. This helps to get everyone on the same wavelength as to what you will be completing and in which order you will be doing each activity.
  - 🗎 Resource: Use the 'What are we doing today?' *Visual activity schedule* template found in the resources section of this chapter to create a schedule that you can refer to throughout your session.
  - Think about: This should be a brief component of the session as many children will be anxious to begin talking about the focus games and their collaborative play.
- **Transition to the next activity using a *Visual activity schedule*:** I have included a short reminder at the end of each activity within each stage so that you remember to guide your participants continually through each step of the intervention.

Recalling 'who and what' of previous session

It is important to see if children recall what they have learnt during the previous session so they can build from their past learnings. Not only does this provide formative feedback to the interventionist about the retention of key learnings, but it also reengages the participants with the knowledge and skills at the centre of this small group intervention. We want to make this as easy as possible for our children, given they might have had a very busy day thinking about a wide range of other topics. We can do this by following these steps:

- **Educators can help children to reflect on the last session by initially guiding them to recall the 'basic facts' of the previous intervention session.** We refer to this as recalling the '**who** and **what**' of the previous session: who was present during the session and what game did we play? Not only does this low complexity task check the children's recall of staff and peers' names, but it also draws on their presumed interest in gaming at an early stage of the session.
    - 🗎 Resource: Have *photos or avatars of every participant* available, labelled with their preferred names if possible. It is also a good idea to have artwork from the games on hand in case participants struggle to recall what they played with during the previous session. Visual prompts are important for all participants but are particularly powerful for autistic participants (Arthur-Kelly et al., 2009).
- **Transition to the next activity using a *Visual activity schedule.***

Guided skill revision and consolidation 🎬

A key part of learning is building on existing knowledge, so revision of previously taught social skills is an important part of the process. It is essential that participants have consolidated the core vocabulary used to label the skills, the steps for performing the skills and the contexts in which the skills might be useful in their long-term memories.

When determining how many Target Skills should be focused on during Stage A, it is important to consider the participants' familiarity with these skills. The table below will assist you in deciding not only how many skills to focus on during this section of the intervention, but also which skills are a good starting place in the earlier sessions of your program.

You can use the following steps to support your participants in recalling fundamental information, whether you are looking at an isolated skill or examining three skills concurrently:

1 Hold up the visual of the selected Target Skill(s) and read aloud the name(s). Have the participants tell the person sitting next to them the name of the skill. Consolidation of the vocabulary used to label each skill is key to building a common understanding between the participants of the different skills.

2 Explain and model the steps for performing the focus skill. Ensure you use examples drawn from playing a cooperative game together (see the examples provided for each Target Skill in Chapter 7). **Please note**: This

Table 4.3 Determining how many Target Skills to focus on during instruction

If this is the first or second session working with these children in this intervention: • Ask one of the children to **choose one focus Target Skill.** Limit their choices to three possible skills, selecting from *Target Skills* #1 to #5. As outlined in Chapter 7, these represent the foundational tier of skills that are the initial focus of this intervention.	If the participating children have engaged in at least two previous sessions: • Choose up **to three previously taught Target Skills**, if you believe that most of the children in the group have consolidated these skills. Analyse the data you have collected, as per Chapter 8, to help you make this decision. Otherwise, stick to one skill.

is not as effective as video modelling (Charlop-Christy et al., 2000), so we use only 'in vivo' or live modelling for the first session. To identify the steps, we use *task analysis*. We discuss the processes for analysing the steps required for each Target Skill in the section: 'Video modelling: introducing a new skill (if participants are ready)'.

3 Have the participants explain the steps to the person sitting next to them, allowing them to practise using the vocabulary used to describe each of the actions they need to perform. Not only is this another excellent opportunity for developing receptive and expressive communications skills, but it also allows the interventionist to listen in and informally check each child's understanding. The interventionist can use this time to provide feedback without drawing the attention of everyone in the group.
4 Discuss as a group the contexts of use during gameplay and external to gameplay. In the initial sessions, this will most likely require significant support, prompting and rephrasing by the interventionists. Transporting or generalising the Target Skills beyond the context of playing cooperative video games is one indicator of a successful social capacity–building intervention. Drawing from your knowledge of activities or interests beyond video games, present relevant and meaningful non-game examples along with game-based examples when discussing your focus Target Skill for this activity.
   - **Transition to the next activity using a *Visual activity schedule.***

Video review: Self-identification of skill performance

Please note: By its very nature, video review requires video footage of play from the previous session. As such, interventionists will be able to implement video review only after their first session. Using footage of previous participants is less likely to be effective if the participants do not know the players, and it also raises ethical issues surrounding the privacy of former participants.

Why is video review important?

The purpose of video review is to support participants in developing the ability to recognise independently when to perform a particular skill. Based on my experiences of running games-based interventions, 'real time' self-identification of appropriate contexts to perform a skill requires:

- knowledge of the contexts in which you can perform a skill (**When should we use this skill?**);
- an understanding of the value of the skill in constructive social interaction (**Why should we use this skill?**);
- being in an emotional state conducive to performing the skill at the point of need.

This final requirement can be the most difficult when asking participants to practise the use of unfamiliar and sometimes complex skills during an action-packed game. We use cooperative video games because they motivate many children to participate in social interactions in this context, but it can be a double-edged sword. Games-based motivation also results in an emotional investment in successfully finishing a level or reaching an objective. This can make it difficult for children to step back and review their use of the Target Skills when things have not gone their way. As explored later in this book, strategic game design can, to a certain extent, facilitate a calmer emotional environment, but the most valuable instructional tool for facilitating measured reflection and contemplation is video review.

Opportunities for participants to review their actions and their performance of the Target Skills during play allows for self-reflection of their own performance and for critical discussion among peers on how individual performance impacts the team. Crucial to this process is the guidance of interventionists in facilitating the language and tone of feedback. This will help participants in communicating the decision-making processes that led to the performance, or non-performance, of a skill. Self-reflection requires participants to consider many variables in order to evaluate events, such as the rules and goals of the game, the actions of the other players and their own emotional state at the time of play. Therefore, careful observation is also critical for monitoring participants' respective cognitive loads, supporting them to draw upon information consolidated in their long-term memories when processing new information identified in the video footage (Sweller 2016).

Successfully facilitating discussion of significant events requires strategic 'tagging' of key moments of skills performance or opportunities for performance within play. Initially, interventionists need to complete the tagging until participants learn the purpose of each target skill. Once children understand the underlying purposes of these skills, it is essential that they are involved in deciding which events should be examined collectively. Where the interventionists feel an important event has been missed, they also need to be able to tag these events to come back to at a later stage.

Steps for effective video review

Just as having a clear process for creating and using video modelling is essential for a successful implementation, having a clear set of sets for implementing video review can make all the difference. Although you are not editing the video footage, forward planning is still essential. The following figure provides an overview of the sequence of steps that I have found to be most effective in ensuring that the use of video review has the intended impact.

Preparing (during previous session)

- **Collect**: Collect footage throughout Stage B of the children playing and interacting with each other in the shared physical space.

Preparing (prior to current session)

- **Tag**: Tag events that feature either a high frequency of a focus Target Skill being used or significant amounts of social interaction between the players.

Current session

- **Initial prompting**: Prepare the participants to review the footage by asking them one of the following questions:
  - Prompting question: 'Which skills do you think you will see being used?' This predictive question helps to draw the participants' attention to the interactions shown in the footage examples of cooperative play. I refer to this as being 'skill detectives', trying to find as many of the Target Skills being used as possible.
  - Follow-up question: 'Do you remember any examples of when you used this skill last session?' This question encourages children to think back to the previous week. Even if they cannot remember,

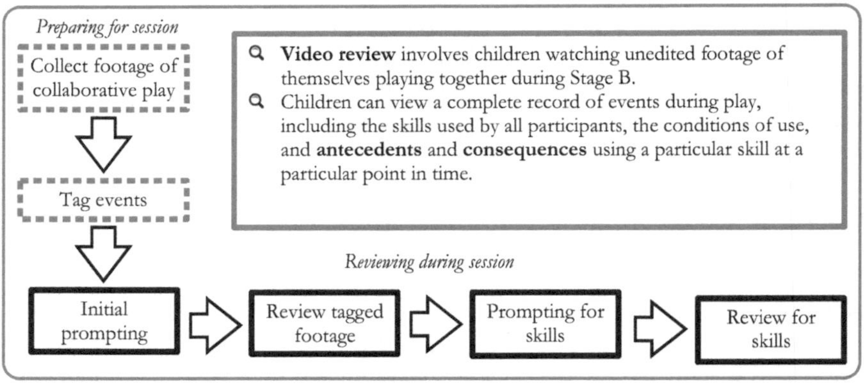

Figure 4.10 Steps for effective video review.

it will help them to tune in and engage with watching the footage of themselves.

- **Review and guide**: Review the tagged footage with the children. Either the children or the interventionists can request to pause the playback of the footage at any time to share their thoughts. During the playback, interventionists should continue to guide the participants through asking either one or more of the three review focus questions:
  - General review questions: 'Which skills did you see being used?' (name of skill) and 'How did you know they had used this skill?' (steps for performing skill). Building from the initial prompting question, children should now be able to match the name to the steps for performing a Target Skill, with concrete examples from what they have just observed in the video footage.
  - Review question relating to specific skills: 'How did using that skill help the team?' Ask them to describe what happened as a consequence of this skill being used, as this will help to reinforce the purpose of the skill. If nothing positive occurred as a result of the skill, the interventionist can suggest what ideally would have happened. For example, if someone asked for help but no one responded, this is an opportunity to teach the group how to respond to such a request. These 'missed responses' can also form part of a subsequent video modelling that teaches the group how they should respond in such a situation.
- **Continue reviewing the footage for more skills**: If you have selected your events carefully there will be a lot to discuss, but I suggest that video review should last for an absolute maximum of 10 minutes. I suggest that your footage of events should be only one or two minutes in duration so you can watch it multiple times.

- **Transition to the next activity using a *Visual activity schedule*.**

Video modelling: Introducing a new skill (if participants are ready) 🎬

Please note: Like video review, video modelling requires video footage of play from the previous session. For your first session, you can use video models of past participants, if you have permission, although this is less likely to be effective if these models are unfamiliar to your current participants (Nikopoulos & Nikopoulou-Smyrni, 2008). Alternatively, as a starting point, you can create a series of video models that feature the adult interventionists.

Why is video modelling important?

As examined in Chapter 2, the 'big idea' of video modelling is to demonstrate, or 'model', the steps in performing a target skill, some of the contexts in which the skill can be used and the positive consequences of using a skill for the individual and the player. Introducing a new skill can be difficult, but effective video models provide a high degree of clarity around what is involved in using one of the Target Skills.

Understanding task analysis

Once we know which focus social skill a child is ready to learn, we need to think about how we will teach the steps required for performing this skill so that it is useful for the child. To break down a focus social skill into smaller, more manageable steps, interventionists can use a process called **task analysis**. As indicated by its name, this involves looking at a task or a goal, in this case performing a Target Skill, identifying each individual step (also referred to as components) and thinking about the supporting language and materials you will use to teach each step (Sam, 2015). A useful strategy for identifying the requisite steps is for the interventionist to practice performing this skill in 'slow motion' with another adult before the participants arrive. While one person is performing the skill, the other can describe what they are seeing and together you can record the steps in order. Think of this as writing a recipe for performing a skill! The diagram below provides an overview of these steps, with each explored in the following sections of this chapter.

Steps for creating a video model

Preparing (prior to current session)

- **Assess your 'skill of need' for an individual child or for the collective group**: It is always important to use the data to guide you in your decision about which skills need to be your next focus for instruction. It

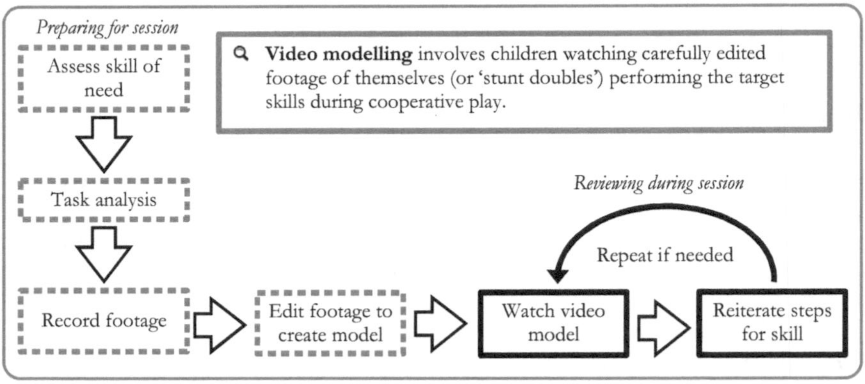

Figure 4.11 Steps for creating a video model.

could be the case that one of your participants has a particular skill that they need to focus on, but I recommend trying to identify a skill requiring attention that is relevant to the entire group.

- Chapter 8 provides a learning progression that can serve as a developmental progression, or learning map, that you can use to identify what your children can do, and which skill(s) you need to focus on next.

- **Complete a task analysis of the steps for performing the Target Skill while playing a cooperative game:** Break the Target Skill into its component steps, and check these with another member of the team by having them perform each of the steps. Ask your team member:
  - *Have you missed anything?*
  - *Have you clumped multiple steps together?*
  - *Will the child have the prerequisite skills to perform these steps?*
- 🗎 Planning resource: Using the *Video model planning* template will guide you through the steps required to ensure that the video models you create align with the research evidence and have the best possible chance of being effective for your children. The example shown is a plan for a video model for learning to ask for help using a *Help* card. Using this template will help you consider everything that needs to be pre-organised, so make sure you complete it in full before you begin filming. A photocopiable version of the *Video model planning* template is available in the resources section of this chapter.

ORDER FOR COMPLETING THE PLANNING TEMPLATE

1. Record the goal Target Skill that you want to be the focus of the video model.
2. Determine a concrete context in which you want to show the skill being used, which in this intervention will revolve around cooperative play.
3. List the sequence of steps you have determined through completing a task analysis of the Target Skills. Remember, there should be no more than five steps; otherwise, it may become too difficult for many children to commit to long-term memory.
4. Write one or more positive consequence(s) that you will show occurring after the successfully performed skill has been demonstrated. This should be something meaningful to the participants, such as someone responding positively to a request for help, and this leading to success in the game. Make sure the positive consequence connects with the context in which the skill is being used (in this case, playing cooperative video games together).
5. Determine the type of video model you think will be possible to edit: a Video Self-Model (VSM) showing the children *appearing* to perform the Target Skill without error, or a Video Peer Model (VPM) showing other children or adults performing the steps.

Video model planning template

1

Goal (Target Skill):

Asking for help (using a Help card) when Link recognises he doesn't know what to do.

3

Step # ☐ to perform skill:

(As this skills requires only 4 steps to perform you can leave this box blank)

Step # 4 to perform skill:

Footage: Link asking Samus "How do I go down the pipe?"

Voiceover: "Now that your friend knows you need help, you can tell them what the problem is so they understand."

Step # 3 to perform skill:

Footage: Link passing the Help card to Samus, and Samus taking it from him.

Voiceover: "We pass the Help card to our friend who we want to help us."

Step # 2 to perform skill:

Footage: Link picks up the Help card.

Voiceover: "We then pick up the Help card."

Step # 1 to perform skill:

Footage: Link puts his controller on the floor.

Voiceover: "When we need help we first stop what we are doing."

4

Positive consequences of skill use (to be shown):

Footage: Samus shows Link the correct button to go down the pipe in the game and the characters arrive in a bonus room. Everyone is smiling.

Voiceover: "Well done Link – you have asked for help from your friends and now you know what to do!"

5

Type of video model:

1. ✗ Video self-model (VSM)
2. Video peer model (VPM)

6

Resources required for recording video model:

1. *Help card*
2. *A friend who Link enjoys interacting with (Samus)*
3. *An unfamiliar game (Super Mario 3D World)*
4. *TV*
5. *2 controllers*
6. *Video camera (to collect the footage)*

2

Context(s) for skill use (to be shown in video model):

Footage: Link playing Super Mario 3D World with Samus, but in game characters stop moving when they arrive at a pipe (obstacle). (10 seconds of footage is enough)

Voiceover: "We like to play video games with our friends but sometimes we don't know what to do. That's okay because we can ask our friends for help using the Help card."

Figure 4.12 Example of a completed *Video model planning* template.

6. Plan the resources or props you will need for recording your footage, such as having a *Help* card on hand to use when recording a video model for 'Asking for help'.

- **Recording your footage:** Although some interventionists might be concerned about the technical skills required for recording a video model, I encourage you to keep in mind the following advice:
  1. **Keep it simple**: What really matters in terms of video modelling is clearly showing the steps in performing the skill or behaviour, and the positive consequence. You are not trying to win an Academy Award for your artistic vision!
  2. **Work as a team**: Although we strongly encourage all interventionists to develop the skills to record (and edit) video models, while you are a novice we suggest you find someone more confident to work with collaboratively to coach you through the process. Everyone has areas of strength and challenge, and we can all learn from each other.
  3. **Important to remember**: Because we want to ensure the protection of our children's privacy, always turn off cloud file sharing (i.e., iCloud) before recording and delete your footage after you have created your video model.

OPTIONS FOR DEVICES TO RECORD YOUR FOOTAGE

- Recording on a mobile phone or tablet device
- Using a GoPro
- Recording on a webcam
- Using your laptop camera

ADVICE FOR RECORDING YOUR FOOTAGE

1. Change your phone settings to high definition (this is found in 'Settings' for both iOS and Android). This will record higher quality footage that you can downsize later if you want to reduce your file size.
2. Clean your lens to ensure you are recording clear footage.
3. Mount or place your camera somewhere secure and stable to ensure that you do not get a 'shake' video. An excellent idea is to use your students, but be explicit about two things:
   - to hold the camera with two hands and to brace their elbows against their stomachs to stabilise the footage; and
   - to check that the camera is actually recording (usually indicated by a red light).

4. Always shoot holding the camera/phone horizontally (landscape) rather than vertically (portrait). If you have some students working as your film crew, you need to make this explicit as well.
5. Think about the lighting when you are recording. Key to video modelling is ensuring that the important features or steps in learning a new skill or behaviour are easy to see, while minimising everything that could be a distraction to learning.

- **Editing your footage:** Through careful editing, the video model should show the performance of the skill clearly. Earlier in this chapter, I provided a list of possible options for software that will help you to edit your footage into an effective video model.

ADVICE FOR EDITING YOUR FOOTAGE

1. Remember, a key component of video modelling is to show only the steps being performed in the way you want the children to do them. To achieve this illusion, you might need to splice together several different attempts at performing the skill, or to combine clips of the child with clips of a substitute child.
2. Depending on the software you are using, you should also be able to include an auditory narration that complements the visual illustration, but this should be kept to a minimum to avoid distraction. My advice is to avoid including music beyond a simple jingle at the beginning and end of the video.
3. Video models should ideally be between one and two minutes in length; any longer than this can cause children to disengage.

If you follow these steps, you should now have one or more video models ready for viewing during your sessions as part of Stage A (skill instruction).

Steps for viewing a video model (during Stage A)

- **Draw attention to the video model by watching it together:** During Stage A you should all watch the video models for each of the Target Skills you have prioritised as goals for children. Watching the video alongside the participants helps them to understand where their focus should be and prevents you from creating unintended distractions.
- **Reiterate the steps:** Following the viewing of each video, reiterate the key steps to help the learners consolidate their understandings of what they have just seen. This is where audio narration can be helpful, as you can just repeat what has been said in the video rather than having to 'think on your feet' as to how you will summarise the key information.

Table 4.4 Formula for an effective video model

Formula for an effective video model				
1. Explain condition(s) in which skill can be used	+	**2. Model steps to perform skill**	+	**3. Illustrate positive consequence of using skill**
Example of video footage shown ('Asking for help')				
Child looking at the screen, then their control, while their game character is not moving.	+	Student putting controller on the floor, picking up the *Help* card and passing it to their friend.	+	Friend shows the child how to move the game character, and the team makes progress in the game.
Example of complementary narration ('Asking for help')				
'Sometimes I don't know the controls for a new game. That is when I know I need to ask for help'.	+	'To ask for help I put my controller on the floor *(pause)*, I pick up the *Help* card *(pause)* and I pass it to my friend'.	+	'When I ask for help, it helps me and my team to be better at the games we play'.

- **Clarify contexts of use:** Interventionists also need to bring attention to the contexts shown in the video of where the skill was performed, such as when a participant was unsure of how to play the game and required help. Using the explicitly shown contexts in the video as a starting point, you can then ask: 'In what other situations should we use this skill?' and 'How can we recognise when this skill is useful to perform?'
- **Transition to the next activity using a *Visual activity schedule*.**

Setting individual and team goals

In the broadest sense, a goal is a desired outcome or attainment (Locke & Latham, 2002; Woolfolk & Margetts, 2016), such as finishing a level in a video game or learning how to use your voice to give instructions during play. The Level Up Collaboration intervention includes both team and individual goals. Although these goals serve different purposes within this intervention, goal setting in any context is important for effective learning. Locke and Latham (2002) identified four dimensions that highlight how goal setting can positively impact all forms of learning, including developing social capabilities:

1 goals **direct attention** to the task (such as learning the steps in 'asking for help');
2 goals **energise effort** from the learner;
3 goals **increase persistence**;
4 goals promote the **development of new knowledge** and **strategies**.

Thinking about this final dimension, the underlying purpose of this intervention is to acquire knowledge and strategies of how to work successfully with others. The other three dimensions explain how goals can help to make this learning possible. Therefore, it is vital that interventionists work with the participants to set meaningful goals, including common 'team goals' for the entire group and individual-level goals that address what each child is ready to learn.

Setting team goals

It might seem strange to consider team goals before considering individual goals in an intervention designed to develop the social capabilities of individual children, but there is a strategic purpose for this. In the context of this intervention, 'team goals' refer to the objectives of the game, such as reaching an exit point of the level or collecting a certain item. A particular advantage of using video games as the context for collaborative interaction is that participants familiar with the game genre conventions often already understand the team goal. Using the lens of cognitive load theory, Ang et al. (2007) noted that familiarity with game mechanics can allow learners to utilise their working memory capacity to address the social interactions. Contextualising each child's individual goal through the lens of achieving the team goal can make learning the Target Skills more meaningful. It provides a reason for the performance of the skills.

- **Replay footage of the game:** To prompt participants to recall and describe the common team goal, the footage shown during video review can be 'recycled' for this purpose. Often there can be a matter of days between sessions and participants might have forgotten what they were doing when they last joined the intervention. The following questions can help remind participants:
  - *How do you win in this game?*
  - *Where do you need to go in the game?*
  - *How can you help each other to do this?*

  As we are using an area of strength for many participants in this intervention, this is often the easier part of goal setting as enthusiastic gamers often already have a shared vocabulary and a set of expectations of what a team needs to be doing to make progress in the game.

Personalised individual goals

While team goals can help focus everyone on the objectives players are working towards in the game, this intervention is focused on individuals acquiring and practicing social skills in the physical environment. As each child will have their own unique needs, individual social goals are essential. Both Schunk and Ertmer (1999) and Locke and Latham (1990) suggested that achievable goals must be personalised, sufficiently challenging and attainable for the learner. Locke and Latham (2002) later added that goals also need to be understood and meaningful for the learner. Anderman and Anderman (2014) argued that for a goal to be motivating, a child must also believe the goal will be reached in the near future. Learners must also recognise what the actualisation or achievement of a goal looks like, often referred to as the 'success criteria' (Hattie, 2009; Wiliams, 2008; Yates & Hattie, 2014). Chapter 7 provides an overview of each of the 15 Target Skills that can help you find the right language for explaining these skills to your participants.

Before proceeding to Stage B (supported play), goals need to be assigned in Stage A. These goals are important as they will be reinforced regularly during play in Stage B and reflected on in Stage C. The simple process for assigning goals in Stage A is as follows:

- **Show each child their goal using the *Target Skills icons*:** Show them the icon and support them to share the name of the skill (either verbally or using an assistive communication device).
- **Ask each child to explain what this skill means to them:** Have the participant provide an example of context of use, the steps in using the skill and the positive consequences that *can* occur when this skill is used. This is also an opportune time to remind the other players about how they respond when this individual uses the Target Skill.
- **Have them place the skill on the *Goals and skill performance sticker chart*:** You will see on this instructional resource that there is a dedicated box for each participant to record the Target Skill that will be their goal. Having this clearly visible acts as an important point of reference for Stage B (supported play).

Introducing the game for the session

Please note: A key determinant of your success with implementing this intervention is selecting the right game for the right audience. Chapter 9 examines the game design principles that we know help to create the right conditions for player collaboration. I also provide a list of suggested games in Chapter 10 that adhere to these principles, which I have tested with children in my interventions.

DECIDING WHEN TO INTRODUCE A NEW GAME

One of the most common questions I am asked is when an interventionist should introduce a new game. Here are the key questions I ask myself and my intervention team to inform this decision:

- **Are all of the children still enjoying the game?** *(How do we know this? Ask them at the end of a session, but also observe them during play as their peers can influence their responses)*
- **Are the children interacting with each other during play?** *(How do we know this? See Chapter 8 for more information on assessing the frequency and sophistication of interactions)*
- **Does the section of the game that the children are currently playing align with their individual Target Skill goals?** *(How do we know this? See Chapter 8 for more information on assessing the performance of the Target Skills)*

If the answer is an emphatic yes to all of these questions, then it is fine to stay the course with the current game you are playing. If the answer is no, then I would look for an alternative title for the following week. I would often use my knowledge of the children with whom I was working and of the game to try to predict when a change might be needed and to plan for this accordingly. For some neurodiverse individuals, predictability is an important support so you will want to signpost explicitly in the prior session if you will be introducing a new game in the following session. As changes to routine can create anxieties, I would often preview the cover or printed screenshots of a new game when saying goodbye following Stage C.

For most children who choose to participate in this intervention, the primary motivator is playing video games. Children will want to know what they are playing, how many people will be playing at a time and, if the game is unfamiliar, what are the main rules and mechanics of the game. Interventionists need to transition to Stage B systematically by addressing these three questions:

- **What are we playing?** Answering this question depends on whether the participants have played the game in a previous session or whether this is a game new to most of the participants.
  - If the game is new to most of the players, introduce the game by first passing around the box or showing a trailer for the game. Ask the children if they recognise the game or whether it reminds them of another game they have played.
  - If the players have played the game before, ask one of the children to explain the name of the game and its basic premise in terms of the team goal and the rules of play. Support other children to recall the

game by passing around the game box or the printout of screenshots of the game.

- **How many players can play at once?** Regardless of whether most children have played the game before or not, always reiterate the number of players who will be simultaneously playing this session.
- **How do we play this game?** A useful structure I have developed for explaining how a game can be played begins with outlining the broad objectives of the game, dictated by the 'rules', followed by a discussion of the mechanics of how to achieve these objectives.
  - **Introduce or revise the rules of play.** This provides an overview of the game, including the genre, the types of challenges players might encounter and examples of how the game allows players to work together. This is a wonderful opportunity to draw on the expertise of the participating children, and it provides them another chance to practice verbal communication. The final section of Stage A focuses on discussing the game objectives, referred to in this intervention as the 'team goals', so try to minimise the time spent on the rules of play during this step.
  - **Introduce or revise the mechanics of how to play the game, with a particular focus on the controls.** If this is the first time playing, or it has been a while between sessions, explicitly go through the basic controls, such as moving the player's avatar and the action buttons. Watching the players test the controllers can also alert interventionists to any potential challenges with fine motor skills before play begins.

- **Transition to the next activity using a *Visual activity schedule.***

Transitioning to Stage B

Following the assignment of the team and individual goals, it is time to transition to Stage B (supported play). Depending on your physical space and the needs of your participants, you may be either using the same space for supported play as you have for instruction, or you might be transitioning to another space.

- If you are using the same space, children can remain in the seats while you produce the gaming system and game controllers. See the next chapter for more information on how to do this in a way that supports social-emotional self-regulation.
- If you are moving to another space, have the children, one at a time, move their chairs to the next space when you say their names. **Please note:** Only allow a child to move a chair by themselves if it is safe for them to do so, as we need to be mindful of their physical health.

Hotspots

- **Technical issues with video playback:** When you really need to play that video model or share video footage as part of video review, of course your device decides to 'have a moment' and to suddenly shut or freeze. I usually use a laptop as my primary device, but I also keep an iPad charged in my bag ready as a backup. Not everyone has this luxury, but it is a good idea to have a 'plan B' if feasible.
- **Taking too long to get through the welcome or the video review:** Although you do need to ensure that everyone is following along and understands what they are being asked to do, I have accidentally stretched out Stage A for 40 minutes in the past. Usually, it is either the initial welcome or the video review activity that can drag out the segment. Just be vigilant. If you have a co-interventionist, they can be a valuable timekeeper. In the past I have trialled using a participant as timekeeper, but this resulted in them losing focus on the instruction. As such, I recommend you avoid this and use a stopwatch if required. The more you implement these structured sessions, the easier it will be to know how long each activity should take in relation to the total session.

SUMMARY OF KEY IDEAS IN CHAPTER 4: CHECKLIST ☑ FOR IMPLEMENTING STAGE A

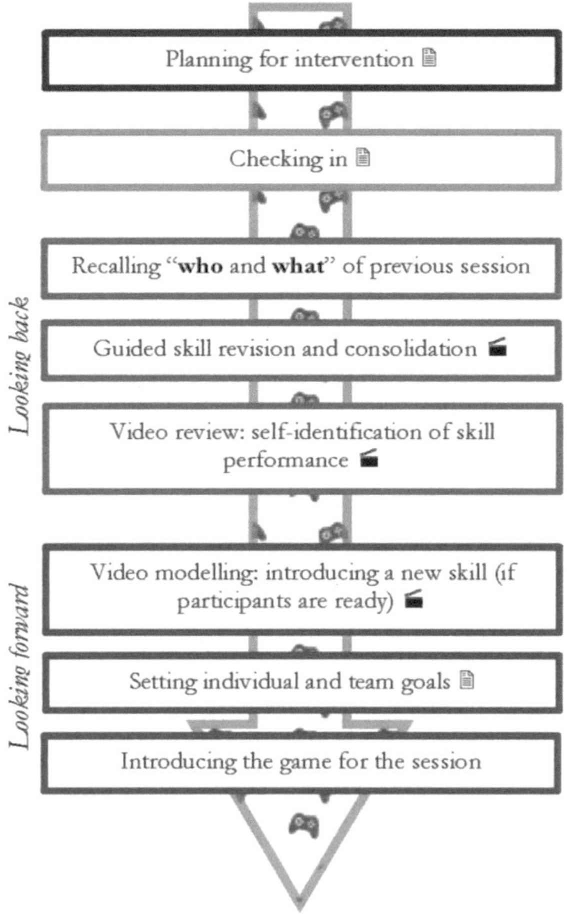

☐ Ensure that all instructional resources are on hand, device for sharing videos is working

☐ Welcome circle: Check in 'How are you feeling?', refer to the visual activity schedule

☐ Who was present during the session and what was the game that was played?

☐ Reintroduce vocabulary for focus skills, and then explain and model the steps for performing the focus skill. Support paired practice of skills and discuss contexts of use

☐ Provide initial prompting, collectively review the footage and guide the process through asking the three review questions

☐ Watch the video model together, reiterate the steps, clarify contexts of use

☐ Set team goals based around the game, and individual goals focused on the Target Skills

☐ Address these three questions: 'What are we playing?', 'How many players can play at once?' and 'How do we play this game?'

☐ Support transition to Stage B by referring to visual activity schedule, putting items in the finish pouch

References

Anderman, E. M., & Anderman, L. H. (2014). *Classroom motivation* (2nd ed.). Pearson.

Ang, C. S., Zaphiris, P., & Mahmood, S. (2007). A model of cognitive loads in massively multiplayer online role playing games. *Interacting with Computers, 19*(2), 167–179.

Arthur-Kelly, M., Sigafoos, J., Green, V., Mathisen, B., & Arthur-Kelly, R. (2009). Issues in the use of visual supports to promote communication in individuals with autism spectrum disorder. *Disability and Rehabilitation, 31*(18), 1474–1486.

Busby, R., Ingram, R., Bowron, R., Oliver, J., & Lyons, B. (2012). Teaching elementary children with autism: Addressing teacher challenges and preparation needs. *Rural Educator, 33*(2), 27–35.

Charlop-Christy, M. H., Le, L., & Freeman, K. A. (2000). A comparison of video modeling with in vivo modeling for teaching children with autism. *Journal of Autism and Developmental Disorders, 30*(6), 537–552.

Conzemius, A., & O'Neill, J. (2009). *The power of SMART goals: Using goals to improve student learning*. Solution Tree Press.

Hattie, J. (2009). *Visible learning: A synthesis of over 800 meta-analyses relating to achievement*. Routledge.

Locke, E. A., & Latham, G. P. (1990). *A theory of goal setting and task performance*. Prentice Hall.

Locke, E. A., & Latham, G. P. (2002). Building a practically useful theory of goal setting and task motivation: A 35-year odyssey. *American Psychologist, 57*(9), 705–717.

Nikopoulos, C. K., & Nikopoulou-Smyrni, P. (2008). Teaching complex social skills to children with autism; advances of video modeling. *Journal of Early and Intensive Behavior Intervention, 5*(2), 30–43.

Sam, A. (2015). *Task analysis*. National Professional Development Center on Autism Spectrum Disorder, FPG Child Development Center, University of North Carolina. http://afirm.fpg.unc.edu/task-analysis

Schunk, D. H., & Ertmer, P. A. (1999). Self-regulatory processes during computer skill acquisition: Goal and self-evaluative influences. *Journal of Educational Psychology, 91*(2), 251–260.

Sweller, J. (2016). Working memory, long-term memory, and instructional design. *Journal of Applied Research in Memory and Cognition, 5*(4), 360–367.

Wiliams, D. (2008). Changing classroom practice. *Educational Leadership, 65*(4), 36–59.

Woolfolk, A., & Margetts, K. (2016). *Educational psychology* (4th ed.). Pearson.

Yates, G. C., & Hattie, J. (2014). *Visible learning and the science of how we learn*. Routledge.

Resources for Stage A

In this section you will find photocopiable versions of the following resources:

- the *Visual activity schedule* cards templates;
- the 'How are you feeling today?' *chart* template;
- the *Goal and skill performance sticker chart* template;
- the *Video model planning* template; and
- the 15 *Target Skills icons* stickers.

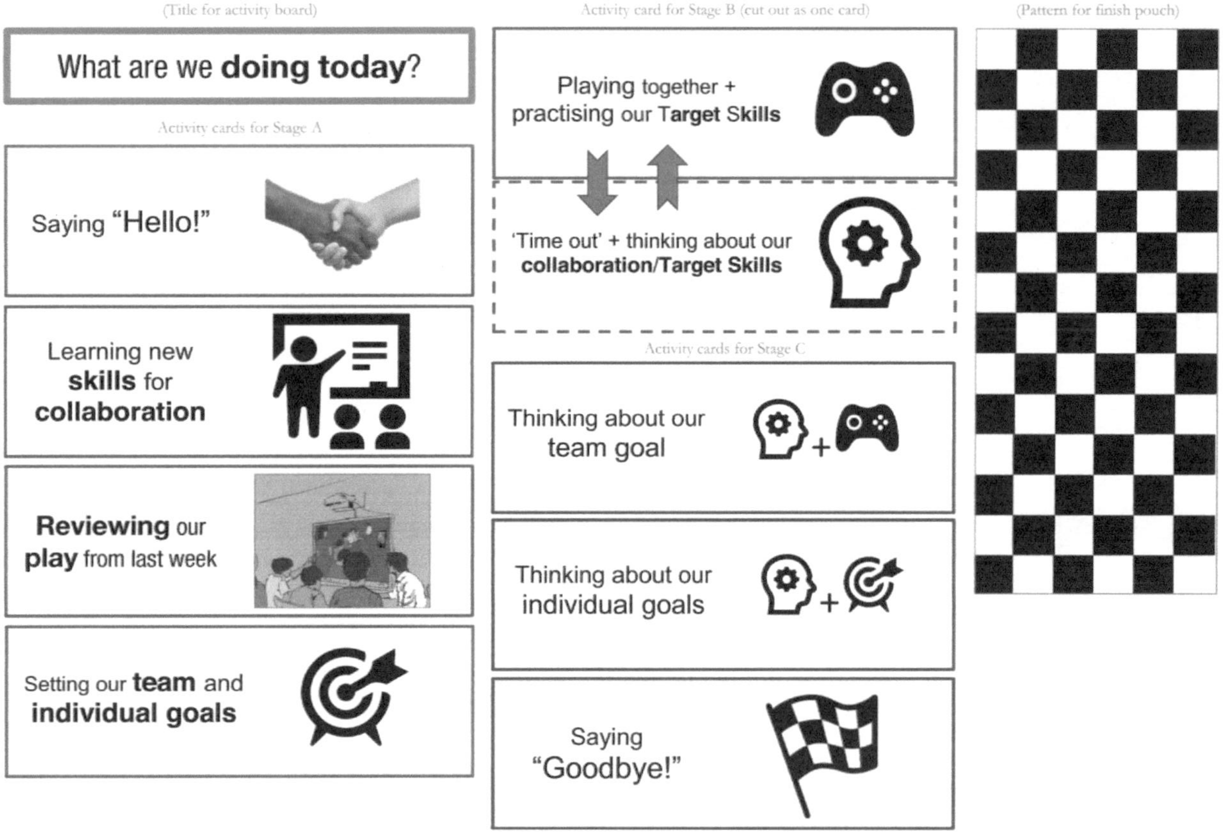
(Title for activity board)
What are we doing today?
Activity cards for Stage A
Saying "Hello!"
Learning new skills for collaboration
Reviewing our play from last week
Setting our team and individual goals
Activity card for Stage B (cut out as one card)
Playing together + practising our Target Skills
'Time out' + thinking about our collaboration/Target Skills
Activity cards for Stage C
Thinking about our team goal
Thinking about our individual goals
Saying "Goodbye!"
(Pattern for finish pouch)

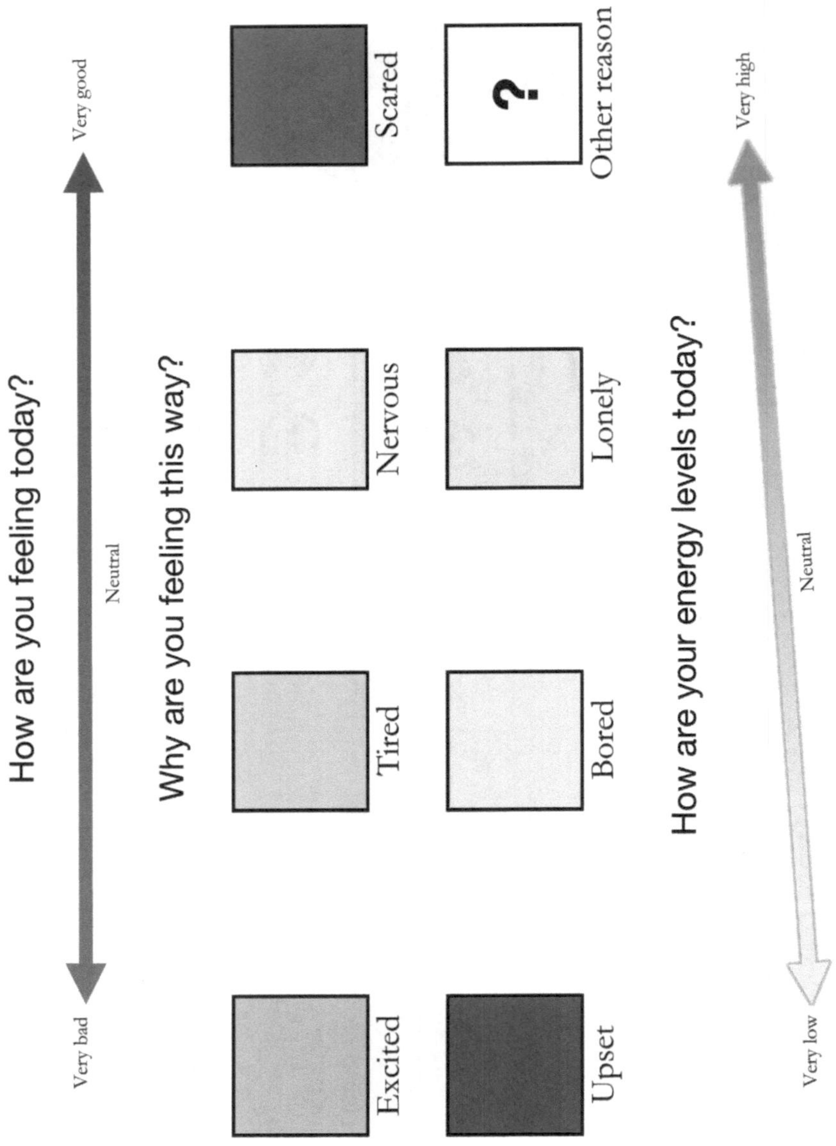
How are you feeling today?
Very bad
Neutral
Very good
Why are you feeling this way?
Excited
Tired
Nervous
Scared
Upset
Bored
Lonely
?
Other reason
How are your energy levels today?
Very low
Neutral
Very high

Goal and skill performance sticker chart

My **goal** skill	My **goal** skill	My **goal** skill
(Goal skill)	*(Goal skill)*	*(Goal skill)*
(Participant's photo/avatar)	*(Participant's photo/avatar)*	*(Participant's photo/avatar)*

Goal and skill performance sticker chart

My **goal** skill	My **goal** skill	My **goal** skill
(Goal skill)	*(Goal skill)*	*(Goal skill)*
(Participant's photo/avatar)	*(Participant's photo/avatar)*	*(Participant's photo/avatar)*

Video model planning template

1 Goal (Target Skill):

4 Positive consequences of skill use (to be shown):

3 Step # ☐ to perform skill:

Step # ☐ to perform skill:

Step # ☐ to perform skill:

Step # ☐ to perform skill:

Step # ☐ to perform skill:

5 Type of video model:

1. Video self-model (VSM)
2. Video peer model (VPM)

6 Resources required for recording video model:

2 Context(s) for skill use (to be shown in video model):

Target skills stickers (cut out)

5 Stage B – Promoting interactions during cooperative gameplay

Introduction

Gaming is at the heart of Level Up Collaboration but playing cooperative games by themselves is not enough to teach children social skills. Rather, well-designed games serve as tools that we can harness for effective teaching. The power of playing games together is in creating the right conditions for social learning. This chapter explores specific steps for monitoring interactions within simultaneous co-located gaming, rotating roles within the team, monitoring skill performance during gameplay, structuring intervention during gameplay and promoting self-regulation and social regulation. The figure below provides an overview of steps for implementing Stage B, with an emphasis on cycles of play and feedback.

Unpacking each of these steps will help you to better understand your role as a coach during this stage, with a focus on how you can best support your participants, or 'players', in performing the Target Skills and working with their peers.

Preparing for Stage B

Required and recommended resources

Just as in Stage A, it is important that interventionists have the right resources on hand to successfully implement Stage B. The table below provides an overview of all the resources you will need or that are highly recommended. These are categorised as either resources universal to all three stages, resources to be used by the participants during play or resources for recording data for the interventions.

Required equipment

- **Videogame console**: Essential to this intervention, a number of different videogame consoles are suitable for use with this intervention. See Chapter 10 for a detailed analysis of the relative strengths of common brands of videogame consoles for use in Stage B.

DOI: 10.4324/9781003025917-5

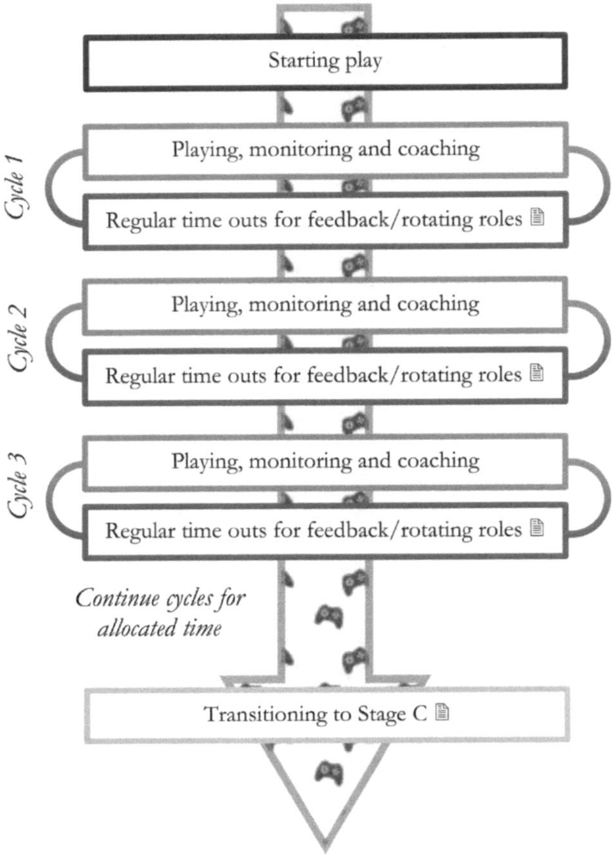

Figure 5.1 Specific steps in Stage B.

- **Game controllers**: Each respective brand of videogame console has different options for control input, with some of these options being more inclusive in accommodating a wider range of player needs. Again, Chapter 10 provides an overview of the available controller inputs for each console.
- **A shared screen** (such as a TV, interactive whiteboard or large monitor): This intervention uses local multiplayer games with players sharing a common screen. For everyone to see easily, the screen needs to be of sufficient size. This could be the same screen as used in Stage A, although many interactive whiteboards or large screens are fixed to the wall preventing easy transportation if you are moving between stages. When working out the optimal screen size, there are a number of considerations. It is important to think about how many children will be playing together at once, as greater numbers of players will require larger screens. Related to this is the comfort of the participants, particularly in relation to viewing angles.

Table 5.1 Overview of required and recommended resources

Universal resources (used in all stages)	*Resources for cooperative play*	*Resources for recording data*
'What are we doing today' ***Visual activity schedule*** 🗎 *(recommended resource)* **Photos or avatars of every participant** 🗎 *(recommended resource)* ***Target Skills icons*** 🗎 *(required resource)*: during Stage B affix these to the *Goal and skill performance sticker chart* as participants use these skills. ***Goal and skill performance sticker chart*** 🗎 *(required resource)*: supports participants during play and time-outs in remembering their individual goals, and also used for recording which of the Target Skills they have been using during play.	**Videogame console** *(required resource)*: required for playing the cooperative games. **Game controllers** *(required resource)*: you will need a sufficient number of these to enable synchronous play. **Shared screen** *(required resource)*: needs to be sized sufficiently so that everyone can easily view the video game being played. **Countdown timer** *(recommended resource)*: these can be digital or traditional timers. ***Help*** **and** ***Time-out*** **cards on Velcro boards** 🗋 *(recommended resource)*: used to communicate the need for help or a break in play. Store these on a Velcro board so they are easily found in the heat of play. **Fidgets** *(recommended resource)*: refer to Chapter 4.	**Video camera** *(required resource)*: used to record video footage of the physical environment during Stage B, including the interactions among the participants. Use the footage for creating video models and for video review, both key components of Stage A. **Screen capture device** *(recommended resource)*: used to record what is happening within the game during play.

It is also important to think about how close you want players to sit to the screen, both for the health of the players' eyes and to protect the screen from accidental damage from overly excited controller waving. In my experience, overly excited waving is a **very real risk**.

There are a number of other considerations when deciding on your screen:

- In my experience, LCD TVs provide a relatively cheap option, although many classrooms already have projectors installed as part of an interactive whiteboard.

    - The screen has to have at least one HDMI port. Almost every modern device has one, but I have encountered older devices in schools that do not have *available* ports as the only one is already in use by another device that cannot be removed.
    - If you are weighing up purchasing a projector, it is worth remembering the additional cost of replacement globes, although these have come down in price in recent years.
- **Video camera** (with stand or tripod) and **memory card**: Essential to this intervention is a camera to collect video footage of the children playing together and working towards performing the Target Skills for video modelling and video review. Consider the following when deciding on which camera to use:
    - The quality of video is dictated largely by the resolution of the camera and the lighting in the room. I recommend recording at 720p resolution as this provides a clear image of social interactions within 10 metres of the camera while also allowing for sufficient footage to be recorded to a standard memory card.
    - Audio quality is equally important to consider. Interventionists need to be able to hear the verbal utterances of the children as they play and interact with each other.
    - You will need to have a memory card, or multiple cards, with sufficient space to save your footage. I highly recommend getting a memory card that is at least 64 gigabytes (commonly written as 64GB) so you can record an entire session without interruption. Just make sure you transfer the footage to your computer and clear the card as soon as possible so you are ready for the next session.
    - In most circumstances, you will need a tripod or stand to ensure that the camera is capturing footage at the right angle. You want to ensure your footage captures all of the children, including their faces as well as their limbs. As discussed earlier, many children prefer to communicate non-verbally through gesturing, so you want to ensure that you capture this for use when creating video models or during video review in Stage A.

Recommended equipment

- **Countdown timers**: When players are taking turns at certain roles within a game, or rotating between being active players and observers, it is important that everyone knows how much time they have before roles will change again. I discuss systems for rotating roles later in this chapter, but an easy-to-use timer can be really helpful for interventionists in keeping track of the time and empowering participants in creating certainty and predictability within their environment. In my experience, the most effective timers are those that provide multiple means of representation of how much time is left, using both a numerical countdown and a support visual. Timer options include:

    - *Timer apps on mobile devices*, such as the pre-installed clock apps available on most tablet devices, can be effective if the device is 'locked' so that players can use *only* the timer function. Both iOS and Android have built-in restrictions that can be enabled to lock the devices to the timer apps. Instructions on how to manage these settings can be found easily on the Internet.
    - *Stopwatches* present another option. They are largely free from the potential distractions of timers on mobile devices. However, they lack supporting visuals. I have had children in the past also find the beeping noises of stopwatches either distracting or agitating.
    - *Sand timers* are also a wonderful low-tech solution. You will never have to recharge your sand timer and this option gives children a great visual representation of how long they have left in their current role. The main disadvantage of using a sand timer is that the amount of time is fixed (unless you find a way to add or remove sand).
- **Screen capture devices:** Recording the action occurring in the game alongside the interactions in the physical environment can be a wonderful way to highlight the relationship between what the participants are doing in the 'virtual' and the 'physical' environments. Although you can position your video camera to record both the participants and the screen, this can be cumbersome and requires careful planning. While some modern consoles come with software that allows the recording of in-game action, the use of this software during play can sometimes result in slowing down the game. If you are going to record the screen, I recommend investigating a high-definition screen capture box. I personally use an *Elgato HD60S 1080p60 Game Capture* box, but there are many options available. These external devices work as a 'bypass', with the audio-visual cable running from the video console through the video capture box and then into the TV. Everything can be saved easily to a USB memory stick with the press of a button.
- **Fidgets**: These can be the same fidgets as per Stage A. These are important tools to assist children with regulating their emotional states and can actually allow them to be more attentive to interventionists and their peers.
- **Mini whiteboards with Velcro tape:** These small whiteboards with a strip of Velcro tape serve two purposes. They help participants communicate with each other through drawing, and they also store their *Time-out, Help* and *Break* cards in an easy-to-find place when they are not in use (I will explain the purpose of these cards later in the chapter). Children often place these boards on the floor in front of them while they are playing in Stage B.

Thinking about your furniture for Stage B

Beyond the equipment, it is also important to think about your furniture. Comfortable chairs for players are essential, and I will usually have the

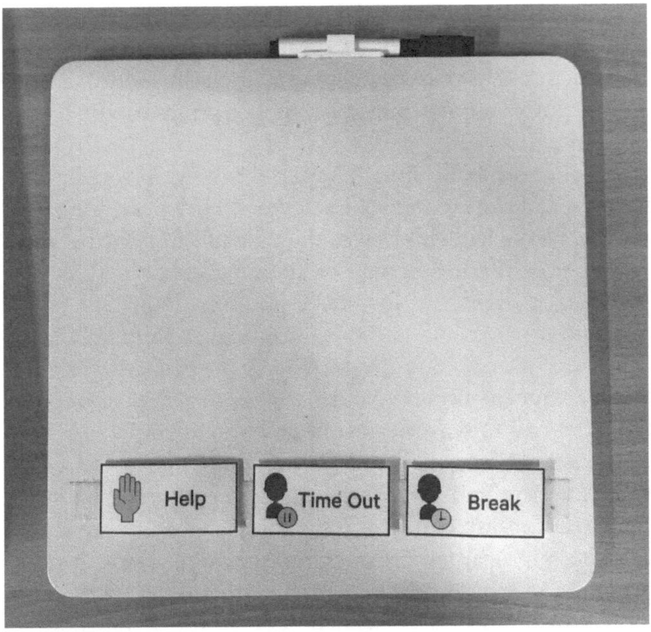

Figure 5.2 Example mini whiteboard with a strip of Velcro tape to hold the cards used in Stage B.

participants bring their chairs with them from Stage A to Stage B if we are transitioning to a separate space. If you need somewhere to display the *Goal and skill performance sticker chart*, you can also bring the portable dividing wall with you.

Setting up the space for collaborative play

Interventionists can opt to use the same space as for Stage A, or they can decide to transition to a separate space dedicated to gaming. Each option has advantages and disadvantages in terms of convenience and learning. Using the same space as Stage A is often more convenient, as the children will already be sitting in the semi-circle formation, you can use the same screen across stages and save time by not having to herd children from one location to another.

That said, there are definite benefits when using a separate space. The benefits of using a separate space include minimising distractions during instruction and establishing clear expectations for each of the three stages. Deciding whether to use a space shared between the stages or separate spaces for each stage depends on the availability of rooms and the needs of your participants. The diagram below shows how I would suggest setting up your space for Stage B for up to six children.

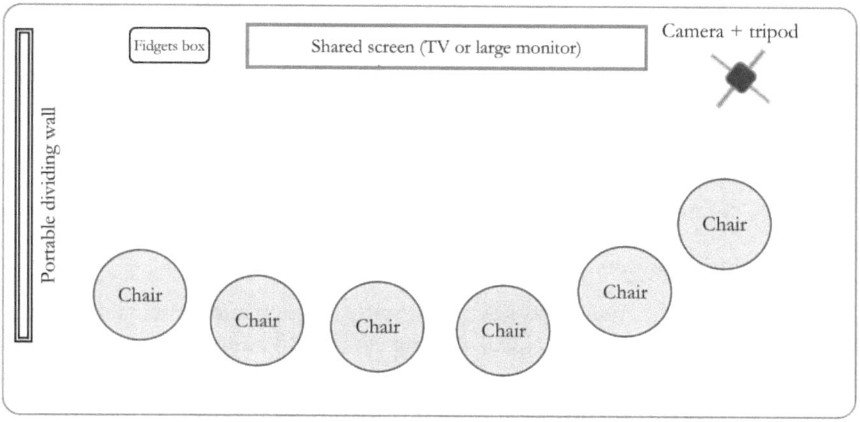

Figure 5.3 Diagram of a sample room layout for Stage B.

You can see that I have the camera and tripod angled facing the participants so that I can capture their interactions during play. It is important to check before the session begins that the camera can record all of the chairs fully in frame. I will often delegate jobs to my children when setting up but this is one job I always do myself.

It is important to think about the positioning of the chairs in terms of providing ample personal space. Playing games requires a space where all of the participating children can view the screen but with enough space between them to allow them to move their arms and feet freely and not to feel crowded by their peers. Some neurodivergent individuals need to 'stim' (stimulatory behaviour) to regulate their emotional states, such as heightened levels of anxiety or excitement. When playing games designed to build tension and excitement, this is clearly a foreseeable need. Additionally, many of the suggested games listed in Chapter 10 use motion controls. Motion controls are not only more enjoyable for some players, but they can also increase accessibility for children who experience challenges with fine motor control. Chapter 9 explores inclusive game design in more detail. This is well worth considering in the planning of your intervention, particularly in relation to how much space you afford your participants.

Defining roles for players and non-players before play

When there are more children than controllers, interventionists need to find a role for non-players to keep all participants engaged. When I ran this intervention as a 'lunchtime gaming club' it was extremely popular and ensuring that non-players had a meaningful role was a frequent challenge. Once I had defined and explicitly taught the role of non-players, most children embraced alternating between playing and advising their peers. Most interestingly, rotating roles provided some real benefits in terms of opportunities to practise many of the Target Skills. Now I always engineer Stage B so that there are more players than there are controllers. This allows all players to have a turn in verbally and non-verbally supporting their peers, to practise waiting for a turn to play and to focus on observing the actions of others both in the game and in the physical space.

Two roles within the team: 'Players' and 'Helpers'

This intervention includes two key roles, with all team members taking turns being both a 'Player' and a 'Helper'. Giving each child a printed card (as shown below) outlining these roles can help to remind them of what they should be doing to assist the team in achieving the goal. You will find photocopiable cards in the resources section of this chapter.

It is vitally important that everyone understands their roles, so it is best to keep the explanations as simple as possible.

- **Players**: These are the children with the controllers. Their role is to play the game and work with their teammates to achieve the team goal (as introduced to the children in Stage A). This includes interacting with their teammates both in the game and in the physical world. Often the challenge is getting players to stop talking and provide some thinking time for their fellow players. Using the *Time-out* card, as introduced in the following section, is one way of ensuring that everyone has time to think about their actions and use of the Target Skills.
- **Helpers**: These are the children without controllers. Their role is to help the players by drawing their attention to things (items, enemies, switches, etc.) in the game, to suggest strategies and to provide constructive feedback. Enthusiastic helping can often lead to a 'helper' wanting to take the controller from their teammate, but it must be made very clear that this is not an option.

Helper card	Player card
Suggest what the players should be doing (talking, pointing or using your communication device).	Work with the other players to achieve the team goal by **controlling** your avatar (character).
Watch what the players are doing in the game.	**Watch** what the other players are doing in the game.
Listen to the **feedback** from the players.	Listen to the **advice** of the helpers.

Figure 5.4 Player and Helper cards.

As it is likely that everyone will want to be playing the game, roles should be rotated at regular intervals. This is built into the suggested design of Stage B, as described in the 'Regular time-outs for feedback and for rotating roles' section of this chapter.

Encouraging active helpers

Looking at the diagram below, you can see that I usually seat the helpers right in the middle of the team. As players rotate through roles, they will change seats to keep the children without a controller front and centre of the screen. Putting these non-players in this position represents a small psychological step towards ensuring they feel important, close to the players and the coaching interventionist, and more than passive observers.

This diagram also depicts the lines of both direct control between the player and their characters in the game as well as the interactions between the players in the shared space and between the players' characters in the game environment. Interventionists need to be aware of where participants are focusing their attention, both in the physical and in the game environments, in order to maximise the opportunities to teach the performance of skills at the point of need. We know that differences often exist in preferred modes of communication between neurotypical and neurodiverse players, which is important to take into consideration when monitoring these interactions. Interventionists really need to know the children with whom they are working and their communication preferences.

The role of the helper changes depending on their relative knowledge of the game, their level of confidence and their relative social capital within the group. Interventionists need to explain the purpose and responsibilities of this role explicitly, including guiding the mode of delivery for feedback and also

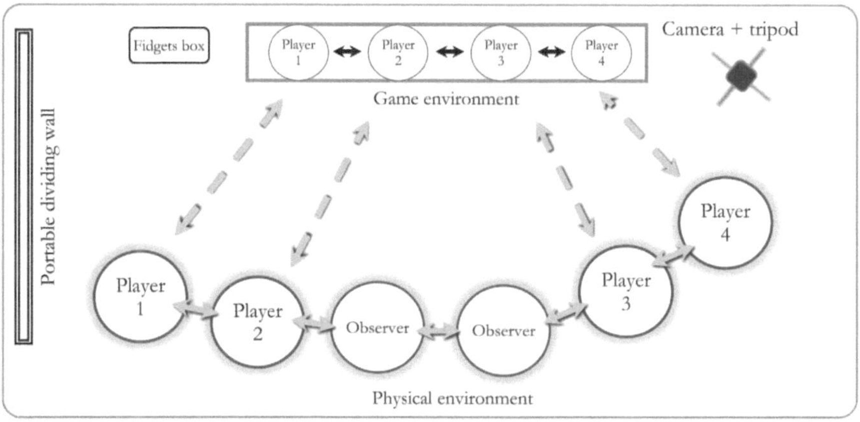

Figure 5.5 Seating arrangement for players and helpers in Stage B.

the point at which observer feedback is most useful to the players. Often overlooked is that helpers also need to recognise when it is *not* a good time to give feedback. Recognising the ideal mode and timing of feedback can be particularly challenging for participants. 'Reading the room' depends on a wide range of variables, such as recognising the emotional state of the players and predicting when there is likely to be a break in the action so that the players can shift their attention to the helpers.

Starting play

Ensuring that everything is set up and ready to go before beginning Stage B is critical, as we want to allow the children to begin playing as soon as possible. Here are some simple steps to get into the game and the skill practice as quickly as possible:

1. When I am using different spaces for Stage A and Stage B, I always transition the children into their chairs and then hand out the controllers to the individuals who will be the first set of players. If the helpers are not sitting in the middle of the semi-circle, I will quickly move them to the right spots.
2. It is always a good idea to have the game set up and ready to go prior to the session so you do not need to wait for loading screens or to navigate the console's operating system. This includes having the right mode of play selected, including all of the controllers correctly synced with the system (unless you have used these controllers in Stage A to practice the button inputs used in the game). Just make sure you have the screen turned off and the game paused.
3. Finally, just before you begin play, have the children reiterate their team goal and individual goals. Then hand out the role cards for players and helpers. Once players have established this routine in the first few sessions, this should be a very efficient and brief process.

Time-out and *Break* cards

Video games are designed to be exciting. While fast-paced action can often engage players and draw team members into interacting with each other at a high frequency, it can also overwhelm some players. For many of the children who benefit from this intervention, such a high intensity of social interaction within the pressure-filled context of playing a game can require a 'circuit breaker' when things become too intense and too high pressure. Introducing a time-out system, represented by the *Time-out* card shown below, can serve this circuit breaker function.

Sometimes a time-out is not enough, and players will require a more substantive break away from peers to regulate their emotional states. Participants can use the *Break* card shown below to request a short walk or some time to

Figure 5.6 Template for the *Time-out* card used in Stage B.

sit by themselves somewhere else in the room until they feel ready to resume play. Disagreements within the group can sometimes lead to a request for a break, but it can also be helpful when someone becomes overly excited or the auditory environment just becomes too much.

Preparing the Time-out *and* Break *cards*

In the resources section you will find a printable template for the *Time-out* and *Break* cards. Once printed, I would strongly suggest laminating these cards and affixing Velcro to the back. This allows the children to store the cards on the Velcro strip on the mini whiteboard, alongside other cards. This is convenient and minimises the organisational requirements.

Rules for using the Time-out *card*

- Anyone can play the *Time-out* card at any time, including the interventionists.
    - I have found that in the first few sessions, it is usually me calling the time-outs when I have noticed that players are either confused,

Figure 5.7 Template for the *Break* card used in Stage B.

    becoming frustrated or just need a bit of a sensory break from the enthusiastic but constant noise of the players and the game.
  - Once the players have viewed video models of the situations in which a time-out should be called and they have learnt the steps, the frequency of child-initiated time-outs will increase dramatically.
- As soon as someone picks up a *Time-out* card and holds it up, the interventionist will tell the players to pause the game.
  - The more time-outs that are used, the more this will become automatic and the number of protests will be minimised.
  - Pausing the game also ensures that no one is disadvantaged. If you have children performing the role of helper, make sure they also pause the timer being used to monitor the turns.
- The person who calls time-out can have ten seconds (very important!) to think about what they want to say and to plan their use of language.
  - Not only is this important processing time, but also it allows individuals to implement their strategies for emotional self-regulation to ensure a calm discussion. Examples of these individual 'calm down' strategies include counting down from 10, taking three deep breathes or asking to go for a walk when their emotions are very heightened.

Rules for using the **Break** *card*

- Anyone can play the *Break* card at any time, including the interventionists.
  - In my experience, the use of this card is extremely rare. When it is used, I would send the person requiring the break to work with the co-interventionist and run Stage B by myself until they return.
  - If someone requires a break and you are implementing this intervention by yourself, it is recommended that you direct the individual to a quiet area of the room with a set of earmuffs, fidgets and their whiteboard.
  - **Please note:** Ensure that you celebrate that this person has requested a break and do not position this withdrawal time as a punishment.

Help cards

While players might recognise that they need help, they also might not want to stop the game for everyone (for the reasons discussed in regard to *Luigi* and his fellow players). I have found that many of the children with whom I work do not know how to ask for help, even when they recognise they require assistance. To accommodate this particular issue, we developed the *Help* card. This card, as shown below, is a visual tool that children can use to augment or replace a verbal request for help. Recognising when we need assistance and 'Asking for help' is a fundamental skill that enables humans to learn from each other and to work effectively within a team. For this reason, 'Asking for help' is one the Target Skills explores in Chapter 7. While some interventionists might want

Figure 5.8 Template for the *Help* card used in Stage B.

their children to request help only verbally, an intermediate step might include using this card as an entry point for children struggling with the required language or who might feel anxious about showing vulnerability to others.

Preparing the Help *card*

As with the other cards that serve as supports within this intervention, the resources section of this chapter includes a printable template of the *Help* card. We know that 'Asking for help' can often occur during moments of great frustration. Using this card is a sign of self-awareness and an attempt at emotional regulation. It is exactly the behaviour we want from our children during these emotionally charged moments, as opposed to hitting the person sitting next to them or throwing the controller.

I have found this card in particular receives a fair bit of punishment as, generally, children use it during extremely tense moments of play. Lamination is your friend, but if one card requires replacement more often than the others, it is this card. Once again, I also suggest affixing Velcro on the back and storing this card on the whiteboards placed at the feet of each child.

Rules for using the Help *card*

- Any participant can use the *Help* card at any time during play or during a time-out break. Unlike the *Time-out* card, while interventionists should encourage players to use the *Help* card, they should not use it themselves. Time-outs are designed to foster a calm environment for group discussion, but the *Help* card operates on an individual-to-individual level. We want individuals to recognise they need help and then follow through the steps for asking another specific player (or interventionist) for that help. Using this card is all about working towards independence in developing positive help-seeking behaviours.
- As soon as a player picks up the card and gives it to another player, the interventionist will support the conversation. **Please note**: You might

need to call a time-out first if a child needs more substantive help. For this reason, I usually teach participants to use the *Time-out* card before the *Help* card.

- Through the creation of video models, children also need to learn what they should do when someone passes them a *Help* card. Specific steps and language need to be taught so children respond in an appropriate way. This could be to provide assistance if they are able to and are in a state of mind to do so (an important point) or to pass the child's request onto an interventionist. There will be times when the person being asked for help will themselves be frustrated, so having the 'circuit breaker' of an available interventionist on hand is important.

This final point highlights how important it is for interventionists to be active during play, always on the lookout for participants attempting to use either the *Time-out* or *Help* card. In earlier sessions, some participants might not be sure when or how they use the cards, so the interventionist needs to model this during Stage A and encourage the use of cards during Stage B. It is important for every interventionist to understand the function of these cards, and to know how best to respond when a participant first begins experimenting with using them.

The coaching role of interventionists

Interventionists often ask me what they should be doing to optimise learning while the children are playing games. I often find that when people first come to hear about my research, there is a common belief that video games by themselves can teach social skills. This is not true, as has been a constant theme within the earlier chapters of this book. While well-designed games create conditions conducive to collaboration, interventionists teach the 'when, why and how' of the Target Skills. Instruction in these skills occurs predominately in Stage A, with Stage B focusing on practising what has been taught under the careful guidance and support of interventionists.

One of the most difficult considerations when implementing Stage B is knowing when to step in and when to step back. I find it useful for interventionists to think of themselves as 'coaches' during this stage, monitoring the use of the Target Skills, reminding the children of their individual and team goals and providing guidance when there is an impasse.

We want to build independence, so we need to avoid jumping in at the first sign of confusion. Interventionists should interact with the participants strategically to ensure they remain focused on their individual goals and work with others as a way of achieving the team goal. In other words, while Stage A is interventionist-focused, Stage B is child-focused. Hattie and Timperley (2007) noted a connection between the assignment of specific goals, as you will have done in Stage A, and the ability of interventionists to provide focused and actionable feedback. In other words, if there is a shared understanding of 'where we are going', then feedback during Stage B can provide support on 'how we get there'.

Using the Goal and skill performance sticker chart

It is essential that both interventionists and players have a 'real time' record of which Target Skills each child has been using during play. The *Goal and skill performance sticker chart,* introduced in Stage A, is used to display current goals and the collection and sharing of data on which skills each player has used. Each column is allocated to a specific child, as represented by their photo. As described in the previous chapter, directly above each participant's photo is their goal Target Skill, presented as a reminder in case the child (or the interventionist!) forgets. This is a useful visual reminder to refer to during time-outs.

Collecting data using this chart is very simple. When a child attempts to perform a Target Skill, whether it is their goal skill or not, this should be recorded. Two things are very important to emphasise at this point of the discussion:

1 You might have noticed in the previous paragraph the seemingly vague use of the term 'notably' to describe the benchmark by which the performance of a skill is recorded. This vagueness is deliberate. The *Goal and skill performance sticker chart* is not intended as a 1:1 record of each child's performance of the Target Skills. Instead, it provides examples of the *types* of Target Skills they are using and, through omission, not using.
2 Related to this notion, we have deliberately limited the chart to ten available boxes for each child. This is to avoid it becoming a competition between the children. While an increased frequency of skill performance is desirable, what really matters is the sophistication of use and attempts at using new skills. If a child has a solid understanding of how and when to 'Use your voice to give instructions' there is little point in recording 20 instances of them performing this skill in the first five minutes of play.

Now that you are beginning to understand the purpose of this tool, in the following section we look at the process for using this chart during Stage B.

Positioning of interventionists to allow effective coaching during play

When coaching the players, it is important to consider how to ensure that you can monitor and interact with every child in the group while not becoming the centre of attention. As shown in the diagram below, we have found the best way is for the primary coach (interventionist), labelled as Coach 1, to stand or sit to the side of the screen facing the children. If you are fortunate enough to have a second interventionist serving as Coach 2, such as another teacher, a teaching assistant or an allied health professional, they can sit behind the children.

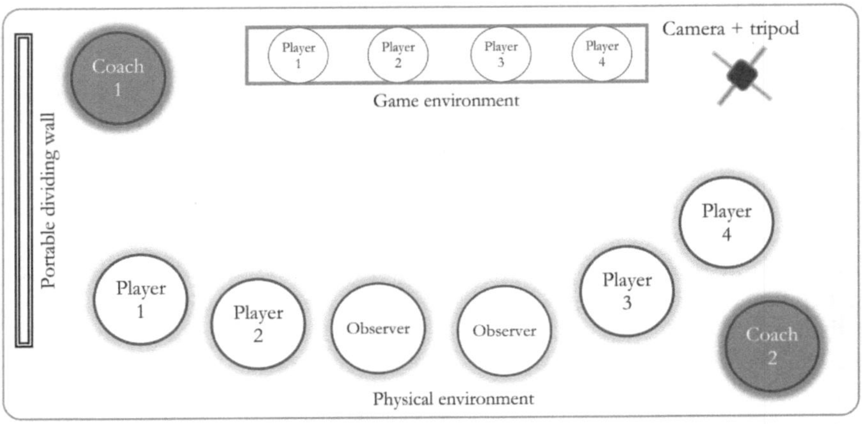

Figure 5.9 Seating arrangement for players and coaches in Stage B.

Defining the roles of each coach

Using this two-coach model, each interventionist has a slightly different role. In the event that you have only a single adult, you can combine these roles but you will be fairly busy!

- During play, Coach 1 is focused primarily on monitoring and recording skill performance data in real time using the *Goal and skill performance sticker chart*. Many children find it difficult to monitor their own use of the Target Skills, especially those with socioemotional and self-regulatory challenges. As already indicated, this chart acts as a visual reminder of each child's individual goal Target Skill, as well as a record of the skills that the interventionist has observed them using during gameplay.
  - While some research suggests that positive reinforcement external to the game should not be necessary if the game is well designed (Lee et al., 2005), my own research supports the findings of Ducheneaut and Moore (2005) that players benefit from the use of 'tangible' real-world systems such as the *Goal and skill performance sticker chart*.
  - At the time the interventionist observes the performance of a skill, they should provide 'labelled praise', with their positive feedback that includes the following three components:
    1. Commending the child for using the skill.
    2. Explaining explicitly to the group how this skill has been used in the current context.
    3. Commenting on how the performance of this skill has assisted the team in achieving the shared goal.

EXAMPLE OF LABELLED PRAISE

Well done Link for 'Asking for help' (1). I can see that you didn't know how to open the door so you asked Zelda to help you find the switch (2). This means that the team can now move to the next room in the dungeon (3).

- While Coach 1 is focused primarily on monitoring and recording data, Coach 2 focuses on supporting individual players at the point of need, moving between the children and drawing attention to opportunities for them to perform the Target Skills. It is important to strike a balance between supporting each child and allowing them the time and space to make decisions independent of the interventionist.
  - I have found Coach 2 most useful in providing subtle prompts to use the *Time-out* or *Help* cards when they detect players are becoming frustrated. Once again, to recognise this, the interventionists need to be familiar with children and know their 'warning signs'. Sometimes these may be very subtle behaviours, such as quiet self-utterances or gentle rocking, and will be interpreted only as distress by those who have experience supporting this individual. When I first implemented this intervention, I was supported by a wonderful teaching assistant. She knew the children extremely well, and together we developed this role of 'Coach 2'.
  - Beyond prompting the use of various skills, this second interventionist/coach can also support the use of oral language. Sometimes children really want to communicate about an event in the game or an idea they have, but they just struggle to find the right words to be meaningful to their peers. We want to encourage all constructive forms of communication, so when participants are trying to explain something but their message is not being understood, Coach 2 can help them to plan the right vocabulary and sentence structure to engage effectively with their peers.

Maintaining an exciting but controlled atmosphere

Cooperative gaming should be fun, but excitement can quickly turn to frustration and acrimony when things go wrong in the game, which they inevitably will. Both coaches should work together to control the atmosphere when the team experiences failure and should have a number of strategies on hand to minimise unconstructive blaming and name-calling. Ordered from the least intrusive to the most intrusive, here are some of the strategies that we found to be effective:

- **Using the *Time-out* card to halt play:** As explained earlier in this chapter, calling time-outs should be encouraged so that it becomes normalised behaviour. This can preempt the escalation of tense situations. An important effect of this is that it helps children monitor their own cognitive states and feel safe to ask for extra processing time.
- **Directing children to their 'calm down' strategies while the coach holds their controller:** In Chapter 3, we highlighted the importance of getting to know your participants before you begin working with them. This will help you learn as much as you can about their areas of strength, their interests and their challenges. Part of this process should include finding out from the child, their regular teachers or their parents which strategies are most effective in helping that particular individual calm down. Everyone is different, and although I have found the following list of simple strategies to work for most children most of the time, there may be a better option:
  - **Asking an agitated child to count along with you to ten, and then asking them to explain to you the problem they are experiencing.** This is an old strategy that my parents (both teachers) used with me to get me to regulate my emotional state by taking my mind temporarily off the problem. By counting with the child, you can lead them at the beginning and also get them to tune into what you are going to ask them to do next. This strategy is most effective if you can intervene before their emotional state becomes too heightened and there are no other players involved in causing the distress.
  - **Quietly coaching a participant to rephrase their language.** We have all said something that has been interpreted as rude or a bit sharp by someone else, when, in fact, our communication capabilities were simply limited by stress or tiredness. This strategy involves a subtle prompt to 'Say that in a different way', protecting the participant's dignity and using this as a teachable moment.
  - **Going for a 'circuit breaker' walk outside of the room.** This is the 'nuclear option' when a child can no longer be in the room with the other players due to extreme distress or there being a potential safety issue. Helping a child to calm down by encouraging them to move to another space requires two interventionists, as your team needs to be able to supervise every child directly. Different jurisdictions will have their own requirements around supervision and the isolation of children, so please check with an appropriate leader in your organisation before you begin this intervention. Although we always hope for the best for every session, having a concrete plan in place is always preferable to having to make these decisions in the heat of the moment.

CASE STUDY: SAVING A GOOD SESSION FROM *WHISPY WOODS*

Tension: One of the most popular games I have used in this intervention has been Nintendo's 2015 release Kirby and the Rainbow Paintbrush. The basic idea is for the players to guide the titular character *Kirby* safely to the exit (I provide a more detailed overview of this game in Chapter 10). This is easy enough for the first few levels, but then the team encounter their first 'boss' enemy, the wonderfully named *Whispy Woods. Whispy* is a large tree that sends out waves of wasps to try to get *Kirby*. To defeat this lumbering menace, players need to attack the trunk of the tree while keeping the wasps away from *Kirby*. If *Kirby* loses all of his health, then it is game over. This requires coordination among the players, but much like a lunchtime football game, it is rare for players to volunteer initially to play 'defence'. Everyone wants to attack *Whispy*.

This, of course, creates the potential for conflict, as was the case when two team members, Samus and Falcon, could not come to an agreement about who would hang back with *Kirby*. The result was that they both went after *Whispy* and quickly poor *Kirby* was overwhelmed by wasps. When the 'game over' screen appeared, there was a palpable sense of frustration within the team.

Solution: During Stage A we learnt about the *Time-out* card. Without prompting, Falcon recognised that now was an appropriate time for a time-out and a discussion. The interventionists helped to facilitate the negotiations but, importantly, it was the players who identified how a potential 'turn taking' system could be introduced so that everyone could have a turn at attacking *Whispy* whilst also ensuring that *Kirby* was adequately protected. They just needed the mental space and some assistance with language from the interventionists to reach an amicable agreement. Rephrasing language was a key part of ensuring that problems could be communicated clearly, but also that the focus remained on identifying the challenge for the collective team and potential solutions, rather than lingering on individual culpability for this initial failure. *Whispy* was soon defeated, and the tension soon subsided.

Regular time-outs for feedback and for rotating roles

While video games provide an excellent arena for social interaction, the high degree of engagement can also be prohibitive for children in monitoring their performance of the Target Skills during gameplay. It is therefore important to integrate regular, planned time-out breaks to discuss the skills being used through a guided review of the *Goal and skill performance sticker chart*. This guided review should focus the attention of each player back to their individual goal, including reiterating why this is important to achieving the team goal, illustrated with examples from the most recent session of play. You can embed this review time into existing systems used for allocating turns and rotating roles within the group. In fact, these planned, regular time-out breaks are also the optimal time to change roles within the team between players and helpers.

Depending on the design of the game, the avatars controlled by the players might have a designated role within the game, as further explored in Chapter 9. It is important that you rotate positions of responsibility within the playing group.

You can use the following steps to structure these regular, planned time-outs:

1 **Dictate a fixed amount of play time** prior to a planned time-out, or the **players can negotiate with each other** under the guidance of the interventionist. If I am working with older children or young adults, I will usually ask them for input but I have found that most players really do not mind how play time is decided, as long as they perceive it as fair.
2 **Start the timer for the current round of play**. I usually assign one of the non-players to keep track of the time. However, I have had some particularly engaged individuals fail to realise the timer has expired when I have the sound turned off (important for some individuals with sensory differences). If you have a second interventionist, this could be a role for them.
3 **Remember to pause the timer when a player calls a time-out**. No player wants to lose their turn, so not doing this can make the time-outs ineffective and a cause of angst.
4. **During your time-out, also monitor the duration of the break in play** so you do not spend all of your time talking rather than playing. As a general rule I limit time-outs to no more than five minutes.
5 **Review the *Goal and skill performance sticker chart* as a collective group**. Guide the group's attention using the following questions:
   a. 'What is the team goal?' As they have just been playing the game, this is usually the easiest question for the participants to answer and is a good question to start getting everyone communicating with you and each other.
   b. 'What are your Target Skills goals for today?' This draws each player's attention to the skills they should be thinking about and trying to use with an increased frequency during play.
   c. 'Which skills has everyone been using?' Having participants review the skills recorded on the chart for other players helps them become aware of the positive interactions they have been having with these individuals. As we want to focus on increasing the frequency and sophistication of interactions, this is a really good opportunity for

interventionists to illustrate some examples from the group of the combining of Target Skills and to highlight the positive consequences for achieving the team goal.

6 **At the end of each regular time-out remember to rotate roles between the players.** I usually use one of two methods to do this:
   a. either move players who are passive to the centre of the semi-circle so they are at the physical centre of conversations; or
   b. keep everyone seated in dedicated spots if space is tight.
7 **When the timer goes, regardless of whether the conversation has finished or not, you should transition back to play.** Interventionists really need to be mindful of time during these planned breaks in play.

THINKING ABOUT HYGIENE

Since the onset of the global COVID-19 pandemic, interventionists have had to consider the potential of germs spreading during their sessions. Passing controllers between players can be particularly high risk. It is important for interventionists to ensure that all controllers are cleaned with sanitiser before being passed to another player. Even if rigorous cleaning procedures are in place, some jurisdictions will require that no controllers are shared within Stage B. This means that you might have to purchase additional controllers so that there is enough for one dedicated input device for each participant. Check with an appropriate leader or health and safety officer in your school or setting, and always have a plan in place before the beginning of each session.

Transitioning to Stage C

Moving from playing exciting video games to reflecting on goal achievement and skill performance is, not surprisingly, the most difficult transition for many children. This is why using timers and establishing a set routine is so important. If our children and young adults know that they are about to change stages of the intervention and, as a result, finish their time playing the game, it can create feelings of loss and anxiety. To help combat this, we suggest communicating this transition by highlighting that cooperative play will return next session and opening the group reflection in Stage C with a discussion of the game. As we will explain in the following chapter, beginning with a discussion of the game can hold the participants' interest and segue their attention from playing to reflection. Although often not easy in the first weeks, this transition does become much easier if you maintain consistent routines in subsequent sessions of play.

Hotspots

Unsurprisingly, supported play is often the stage that is embraced by the participants most enthusiastically. That said, two particular hotspots or areas of tension can present themselves for interventionists:

- **Spending too long in time-outs and not enough time playing**: Time management is a common theme throughout the three stages. Extended discussions are an easy trap for interventionists to fall into when trying to balance teaching and play. Although we naturally want to spend time addressing the Target Skills, the recording of play means that we can return to particular scenarios or instances of skill use in the video review during Stage A in the following session. Use the timer to monitor and limit the time spent not playing and ensure that you are efficient in your communication with the participants. Like all components of this intervention, your timing and efficiency of communication will improve as you gain more experience implementing Stage B.
- **Transitioning away from play:** This aforementioned transition is typically the most difficult for many children, as they are going from the most exciting stage to the stage that is the most cognitively intense. Chapter 6 introduces strategies that interventionists can use to support moving from play to group reflection.

SUMMARY OF KEY IDEAS IN CHAPTER 5: CHECKLIST ☑ FOR IMPLEMENTING STAGE B

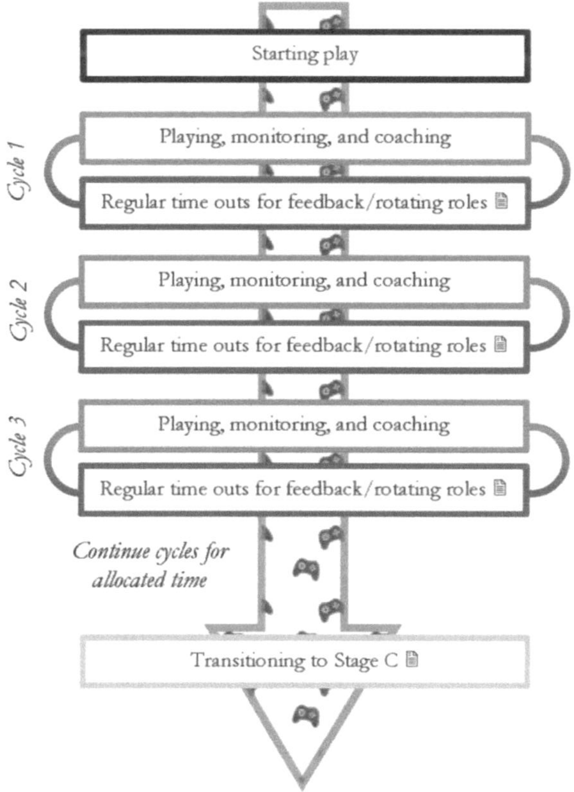

☐ Decide on a fixed amount of playtime, establish initial roles, ensure the *Time-out* cards, *Help* cards and *Break* cards are easily accessible to all participants

Actions during play (multiple cycles)

☐ Monitor and record skill performance data in real time using the Goal and Skill Performance Sticker Chart

☐ Remind participants of their individual and team goals by referring them to the Goal and Skill Performance Sticker Chart

☐ Support individual players at the point of need, moving between participants and bringing to attention opportunities for them to perform the Target Skills

Actions during regular time outs (multiple cycles)

☐ Set team goals based around the game, and individual goals focused on the Target Skills

☐ Address these three questions: 'What are we playing?', 'How many players can play at once?' and 'How do we play this game?'

☐ Support transition to Stage B by referring to visual activity schedule, putting items in the finish pouch

References

Ducheneaut, N., & Moore, R. J. (2005). More than just 'XP': Learning social skills in massively multiplayer online games. *Interactive Technology and Smart Education, 2*(2), 89–100.

Hattie, J., & Timperley, H. (2007). The power of feedback. *Review of Educational Research,* 77(1), 81–112.

Lee, M. J. W., Eustace, K., Fellows, G., Bytheway, A., & Irving, L. (2005). Rochester Castle MMORPG: Instructional gaming and collaborative learning at a Western Australian school. *Australasian Journal of Educational Technology, 21*(4), 446–469.

Resources for Stage B

In this section you will find photocopiable versions of the following resources:

- the *Roles During Play* cards template; and
- the *Help* cards, *Time-out* cards *and Break* cards template.
- **Please note:** The *Goal and skill performance sticker chart* template and *Target skills icons* stickers can be found in the resources section of Chapter 4.

Roles During Play cards template

Player card

- Work with the other players to achieve the team goal by **controlling** your avatar (character).
- **Watch** what the other players are doing in the game.
- Listen to the **advice** of the helpers.

Helper card

- **Suggest** what the players should be doing (talking, pointing or using your communication device).
- **Watch** what the players are doing in the game.
- Listen to the **feedback** from the players.

Player card

- Work with the other players to achieve the team goal by **controlling** your avatar (character).
- **Watch** what the other players are doing in the game.
- Listen to the **advice** of the helpers.

Helper card

- **Suggest** what the players should be doing (talking, pointing or using your communication device).
- **Watch** what the players are doing in the game.
- Listen to the **feedback** from the players.

Player card

- Work with the other players to achieve the team goal by **controlling** your avatar (character).
- **Watch** what the other players are doing in the game.
- Listen to the **advice** of the helpers.

Helper card

- **Suggest** what the players should be doing (talking, pointing or using your communication device).
- **Watch** what the players are doing in the game.
- Listen to the **feedback** from the players.

Player card

- Work with the other players to achieve the team goal by **controlling** your avatar (character).
- **Watch** what the other players are doing in the game.
- Listen to the **advice** of the helpers.

Helper card

- **Suggest** what the players should be doing (talking, pointing or using your communication device).
- **Watch** what the players are doing in the game.
- Listen to the **feedback** from the players.

Templates for* Help *cards,* Time-out *cards and* Break *cards

Help	Time Out	Break
Help	Time Out	Break
Help	Time Out	Break
Help	Time Out	Break

6 Stage C – Guided reflection

Introduction

Reflection is an essential part of learning. For children, it is an opportunity to reconsider events and their use of the Target Skills in the meaningful context of cooperative gameplay. Through listening and questioning children as they work through Stage C, interventionists also develop a better understanding of what each child is ready to learn when following a 'typical' learning progression.

This chapter introduces a structure for interventionists to guide their children carefully through the processes of group and individual reflection. Working within this tested structure, we provide a number of recommendations for eliciting student reflections on which skills they understood how to perform, the situations in which they recognised these skills should be used and which skills were beyond what they were ready to implement during sometime stressful gameplay.

As is shown in the figure below, Stage C is broken into a series of steps that *remind* the participants of their goals and then structures team and individual reflection on progress towards these goals through the use of supports.

Reflection helps participants consider their own growth and areas of need, the positive consequences of using the Target Skills and as a step in planning their own developmental journey. Through the steps presented in this chapter, interventionists can assist participants in analysing their use of the skills and the impact their actions have had on themselves and their team. It must be a positive and constructive process. As reflecting on social interactions during an intense session of play can be emotionally demanding, maintaining a positive approach requires the interventionist to return to a role of leading the group and guiding them through a structured process. Having the participants consider their own goals is an important component of Stage C, as the voices of those we work with should have a prominent place in deciding the direction of the goals allocated in the following session.

Guided reflection is also important in moving the conversation beyond the context of gaming. While playing cooperative games together is a meaningful context for using collaborative social skills, it is also important that participants

DOI: 10.4324/9781003025917-6

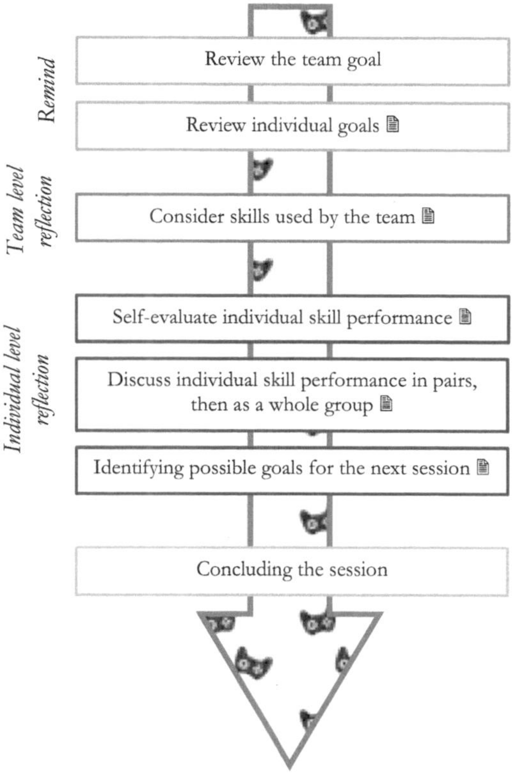

Figure 6.1 Specific steps in Stage C.

can take their learning and apply it in other team-based activities. Some people refer to this as generalising the use of these learnt skills, but I prefer the term 'transportation'. When we shift between different social scenarios, we do call on a common set of skills but we change the shape of these skills to fit within the social context. There is no 'one-size-fits-all-situations' way of performing these skills. We need to help our children and young adults to learn how to match a social context with appropriate performance of these skills so they are able to navigate social situations successfully in a neurotypically normed world. By guiding reflection on how these skills can be transported and adjusted for these different social contexts, we can help our participants better understand what is expected of them.

Preparing for Stage C

As discussed in the conclusion of the previous chapter, transitioning away from playing video games to discussing their goals and skill performance can be difficult for children. I have found that the optimal way to get the conversation on track is to establish a clear routine and start it as soon as possible following the end of Stage B. Eliciting conversations and deep reflection on their social interactions requires organisation of the resources and furniture before the session begins to ensure a smooth transition. Here are simple organisational considerations to help you move quickly into guided reflection:

- **Open the fidget box:** As noted throughout this book, cooperative play can be exhilarating but also emotionally draining, so it is always a good idea to have a fidget box on hand. I proactively offer the students a fidget as they sit down in their chair, rather than requiring them to request one.
- **Ensure that you bring the *Goal and skill performance sticker chart* with you**: I have lost count of the number of times I have forgotten to take this with me when leaving the space used for Stage B.
- **Always have the *Team reflection chart*, the *3-2-1 charts* and the *Target Skills icons*** stickers **on hand and ready to use**: The purposes and processes for using these charts to support the cognitive processes required for reflection are explained in the following sections of this chapter. Each child will need their own *3-2-1 charts* and set of *Target Skills icons* stickers.
- **Think about how you will store these resources so they are easily accessible as you need them**: I store the charts in a recycled photocopy paper cardboard box, and I keep my *Target Skills icons* stickers in zip lock sandwich bags. Another option is to have these stored on a carpeted board for easy identification and access.

Having these resources in regular and easy-to-find locations creates a sense of order for the children and allows interventionists to focus on supporting children during this vital stage.

Setting up the space for guided reflection

Having a separate space can be useful in signalling to everyone that this is the time for reflection and that playing has finished for this session. Symbolically, a new space should represent the beginning of a different routine for the children. It also means that objects of distraction, namely the gaming consoles and the games, are out of reach and, ideally, out of sight.

As shown in the diagram below, I suggest seating everyone around a circular table so that participants can easily see and reach the supporting charts in the middle.

As always, ensure the children have adequate space between themselves and their peers. Being the final stage of the session, everyone is usually a little tired following play and this needs to be taken into consideration. Forward planning of the seating arrangement can help mitigate unhelpful continuations of any disagreements that occurred during cooperative play.

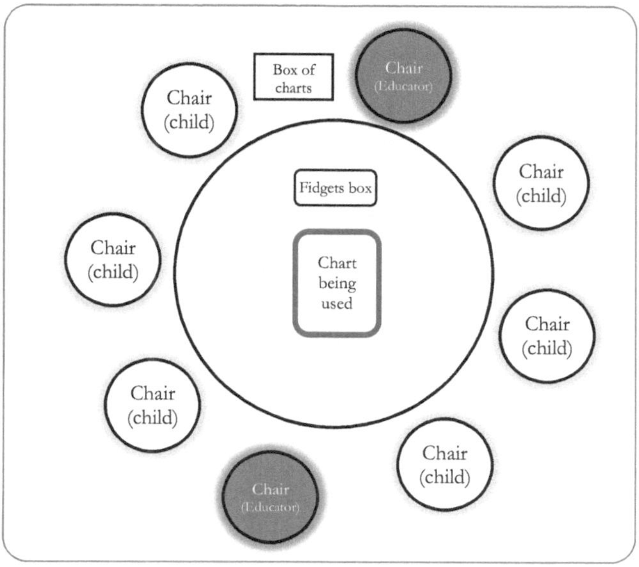

Figure 6.2 Suggested seating arrangements for Stage C.

Visual supports and organisers for prompting reflection

Structuring guided reflection so that the children understood precisely what they are expected to focus on and share in this component of the lesson can be challenging. Simplified supports can help students to organise their thoughts and respond to prompts from the interventionist. At the centre of this process is helping the children think about the skills they felt they had used during Stage B and identify skills they needed to work on in the next session.

- **Sharing the data collected during Stage B**: Providing access to the *Goal and skill performance sticker chart* allows children to review what the interventionist had recorded during Stage B, but there is a danger of them simply accepting this without any analysis or reflection.
- **Scaffolding team reflection:** Use the *Team reflection chart* as a graphic organiser for supporting students to consider and debate collectively which Target Skill they thought the entire team used effectively during play. You can also use this to support discussions about which skills they identify as needing further practice.
  - To remove the emphasis on the actions of individuals during sometimes heated reflections, this scaffolded reflection helps the team self-evaluate skill performance as a collective. It is important to avoid the 'blame game' cycle, especially when the team does not experience success.

- **Supporting individual reflection:** In conjunction with reflecting on the skills the team performed collectively, providing each child with a *3-2-1 chart* supports reflection on an individual level. This visual organiser asks each child to think of *three* skills they themselves used during play, *two* skills they could have used but did not and which *one* of these two skills they want to focus on next time.

Steps for implementing Stage C: Guided reflection

These charts will support children in thinking about their use of the Target Skills during play, but to get the most out of them, they need to be introduced carefully and sequenced in a way that allows for the building of insights. To do this, you should establish a routine that follows these steps:

1 **Review the team goal:** Once everyone is seated, begin with reviewing progress towards achieving the team (game) goal during play.

Suggested prompts for discussing the team goal
How do you 'win' in this game? What does winning look like in this game?
(factual – easier for most children to answer so a good opening prompt)
How well did the team perform in progressing through the game since the previous session?
(opinion – this could provoke disagreement within the group so 'check the temperature' of the group before asking)
Did the team make more progress or less progress than expected?
(opinion – like the previous question, if emotions are heightened following play, this question can be skipped)

- Beginning by talking about the game is important as most participants will still be thinking about specific events that have just unfolded, such as the collection of a special item or an encounter with a boss character. Leaning into these conversations provides a perfect entry point to get the children talking to the interventionist and their peers.
- It is important for interventionists to always model the use of key vocabulary in asking follow-up questions to the group, including the terms **team goal**, **collaboration** and **session**. As with the Target Skills, having a commonly understood language for discussing the intervention session is vital. Check for understanding of these words in each session, as children often forget between sessions.
- When discussing the team goals and progress made towards achieving these goals, draw attention to the connections between the collective knowledge of the team and group success. Make sure everyone remembers no one player can be solely responsible for the success or failure of the team!

2 **Review individual goals**: At this point, go around the group and check that each child recalls their assigned individual goal. This will get them thinking not just about their own goal, but about all of the other Target Skills that have been assigned to the other children.

- Place the *Goal and skill performance sticker chart* in the middle of the table as a point of reference. Although the memorisation of goals is useful, a friendly visual reminder can assist children with finding the right words after an emotionally draining session of cooperative play.

3 **Consider skills used by the team**: Beginning with team-level analysis keeps the focus on the group without singling out individuals. This step involves using the *Team reflection chart* and the group discussing which skills the team has used well and which skills require further practice.

- One by one, the interventionists introduce the Target Skills that have been explicitly taught to the group. The children then decide whether anyone in the team used this skill.
- If someone suggests they have used the skill, ask them to provide an example of **when** and **how** it was used during gameplay. At this point, it can be useful to write down these examples as interventionists can check the video footage and hopefully identify a ready-made video model for the next session!
- Obviously, in the initial sessions, this will involve fewer Target Skills as not all of the skills will have been taught. Once you have introduced all 15 Target Skills, interventionists should pick up to eight skills, prioritising those that are assigned as individual goals to the participants.

4 **Self-evaluate individual skill performance:** Have each participant 'secretly' complete the individual 3-2-1 chart, as outlined earlier (see the 'Visual supports and organisers for prompting reflection' section of this chapter). An example is shown in the image below'.

- Each child will need their own *3-2-1 chart* and a set of *Target Skill icons* stickers.
- In the first few sessions with a new group of children or young adults, interventionists will need to explicitly model how to complete this chart. A worked example of completing the *3-2-1 chart* just means that every student knows what they are expected to do and how their chart should look when it is completed. I suggest interventionists complete an example chart for the first three sessions as a whole group, and then evaluate whether this is required in later sessions.
- It is important to make clear to the child that this choice of 'focus' Target Skill might not end up being set by the interventionists as the child's goal for the next session. Interventionists need to analyse the skill performance data collected during Stage B carefully and review the learning progressions (identified in Chapter 8), but the voice of the child should be considered a vital source of data.
- Ensure that you allow enough time to process and consider each of the three steps, including encouraging them to refer to the *Goal and skill*

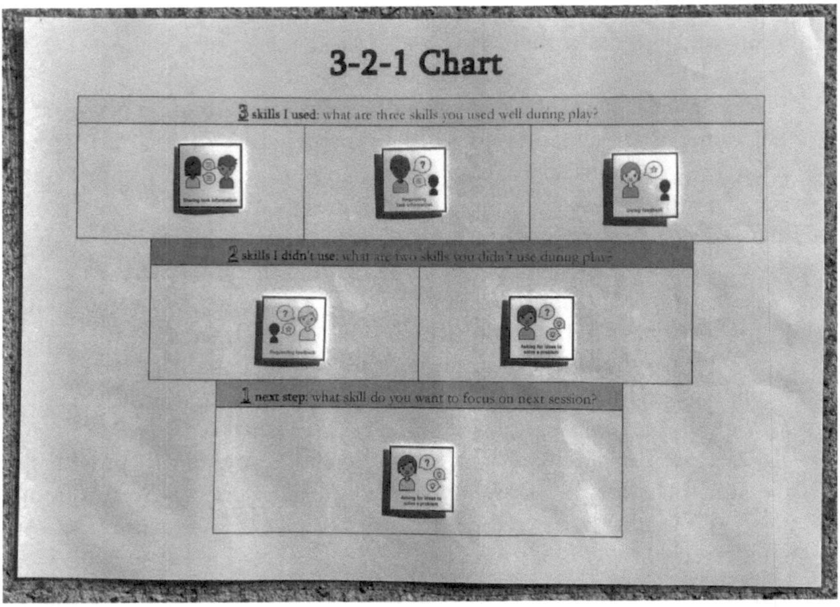

Figure 6.3 Example of a completed *3-2-1 chart.*

performance sticker chart to recall what skills the interventionist observed them performing.

5 **Discussing the *3-2-1 charts* in pairs, and then as a group**: Once every child has completed their individual *3-2-1 chart,* it is important to provide them with supported opportunities to share the product of their self-reflection and, equally important, the thinking processes that helped them to reach these conclusions. Not only is it important for children to be able to discuss their own thinking, but also this provides interventionists with an insight into how each child views their progress throughout the program.

- Many children will be nervous sharing their *3-2-1 chart* with the entire group, especially in the earlier sessions when they might not be familiar with the other children. Rehearsing what they will share with a peer makes this process much easier. As they rehearse, the monitoring interventionists can support them to find the right words and to consider what information they want to share with the entire group.
- Interventionists can help structure the syntax of the sentences required for this sharing and assist with vocabulary when necessary. In later sessions, when the children are more comfortable with speaking to their *3-2-1 charts*, the paired practice might not be necessary.
- Once each child has practised sharing their charts with a partner, they can have a short period of time to share their charts with the group. Expectations need to be carefully managed here, as this is not 'a big deal' and

should not be a cause for anxiety. The 'reflection starters' below provide a template you can use with the participants to help them with the oral language required to communicate their reflections. Of course, if they are using an alternative or augmented form of communication, such as a Picture Exchange Communication System, we want to create a template using their preferred channel. What is important is that the child or young adult is communicating their thoughts, not the mode of communication itself.

Language template ('reflection starters') for sharing 3-2-1 charts

Discussing three skills that the participant thought they had used well during play:

- 'I'm proud that I used [Target Skill] well during play. I used it when I [situation/example]'
- 'When our team [situation], I used [Target Skills] and [positive outcome]'.

Discussing two Target Skills that they did not use during play and sharing how they could use these skills next time:

- 'I didn't use [Target Skill] but I could next time when [situation]. If I use this skill it can help [positive outcome for another individual or team]'.

You might notice that I have not suggested asking why a participant thinks they did not use a certain Target Skill. This is a deliberate omission because I have found that asking some individuals to identify barriers in front of others can be embarrassing. It is important to consider the dignity of the individual and have these discussions discretely during the individual thinking time or after the session has finished. The last thing any interventionist wants is to cause embarrassment.

Discussing one Target Skill that they would like to focus on next time and why this skill is important in working together with other players to complete the team goal:

- 'The skill I want to focus on next session is [Target Skill]. This skill means [skill definition] and I can use it when [situation]. If I used this skill it can help to [positive outcome]'.

6 **Recording the possible goals for the next session**: Not only does this process for using the *3-2-1 chart* ask children to consider their role within the team, but it will also guide individuals towards setting their own goal for the next session. You should note which goals are valued by the individuals and refer to these when planning for the subsequent session. Refer to the goal-setting section in Chapter 4 for a reminder on the processes for determining the focus for your participants.

Concluding the session

Once you have completed this process for structured reflection, it is time to finish the intervention. This is not always easy to do. In my experience, the constraints of 'tight' school or parent schedules, and the very real eventuality of Stage B running overtime, often conspire to result in a very abrupt farewell. This is not a winning formula and does not provide a calm transition for tired children. Careful planning and time management throughout the session are required to ensure guaranteed time every week for a structured farewell.

Ending the session on a positive note does not need to be the intervention equivalent of an Olympic closing ceremony, but there does need to be a clear indication that the session has finished. We also want students to join the following session voluntarily, so interventionists should work to ensure that they leave in a state of mind focused on their accomplishments and the friendships they are developing through this intervention. Here is a script I use, while still sitting around the table, to signal the end of the session, celebrate achievements, model a positive reflection and ask for a positive reflection from each individual.

Ending the session

Signalling the end of the session:
'Well done everyone. It is almost the end of our time together for this session'.
[point to the visual activity schedule to show 'Saying goodbye' is the final activity.]
Celebrate an achievement of the entire team:
'I thought that the team did a wonderful job [name an achievement from the cooperative play]'.
Ask for a positive reflection from each individual:
'Link what is something that you are proud of doing during this session?'
Provide an instruction to transition:
'It is time to say goodbye and return to your class/go to your parent/wait in the waiting space out the front of the centre'.

Whether transitioning back to class, if the intervention is run as a lunchtime club, or handing children back to their parent or guardians after an out-of-school program is complete, it is important to ensure a calm and predictable conclusion. Providing a structured farewell helps to ensure that children leave as enthusiastic participants ready for their next session.

Hotspots

As with the previous stages, I have encountered several 'hotspots' when implementing Stage C.

- **Challenges with emotional recognition:** Many children with social-emotional differences can struggle with describing how they are feeling (Losh & Capps, 2006). Augmented communication devices, such as communication books and pictorial representations, can assist in bridging the 'communication gap' to help accurately report their current emotional states. However, these communication tools cannot compensate entirely for differences in emotional recognition, particularly with more subtle shades of variation, such as labelling two related but distinct feelings such as 'bored' and 'frustration'. While outside the scope of this intervention, which is focused on collaborative social skills, I suggest investigating the following complementary intervention to develop 'emotional literacy':

- Zones of Regulation: This provides both a framework and a curriculum for systematic instruction in emotional and organisational self-regulation (Kuypers, 2011). Through the categorisation of emotions and states of alertness into four symbolic coloured 'zones', students are taught to recognise their own emotional states and those of their peers. More information is available via: https://www.zonesofregulation.com

- **Keeping the focus on self-reflection**: Within the groups I have run, participants have sometimes been more interested in assessing the reflections of their peers than thinking about their own use of the Target Skills. Occasionally, a participant has shared an observation about themselves with which other members of the group disagree, and one or other members have publicly shared their diverging perspectives. At this point, interventionists must step in firmly and remind the group that each of us is reflecting on only our own actions and goals, and that the purpose of Stage C is to think about next steps rather than perceived past wrongs. I find that this is easily addressed with clear leadership and redirection back to the self, asking the aggrieved parties to consider how they could better support their peers to achieve their goals.

Summary of key ideas in Chapter 6: Checklist ☑ for implementing Stage C

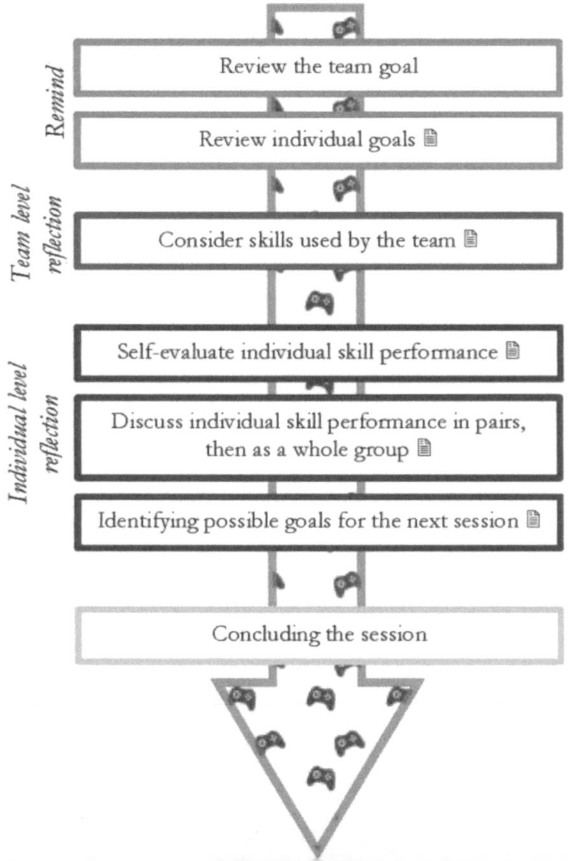

- ☐ Use the three suggested prompts to guide the participants as they review the success of the team in achieving the game goal(s)
- ☐ Use the *Goal and skill performance sticker chart* to help the participants recall which skills they used during play
- ☐ Once participants have recalled which skills they have used, use the *Team reflection chart* to identify which skills many team members used, and which skills were less frequently used
- ☐ Model the use of the *3-2-1 chart*, and then provide individuals with their own chart to map which skills they used, which skills they didn't use and a focus Target Skill for the next session
- ☐ Allow participants to share their charts with a partner to rehearse what they will share with the group, then bring everyone together to share one reflection using the 'reflection starters'
- ☐ Note which Target Skills individuals would like to focus on in the next session so that you can include their preferences when deciding on future goals
- ☐ Signal the end of the session, celebrate a team achievement and provide instructions to transition to their next program or activity

References

Kuypers, L. (2011). *The zones of regulation*. Think Social Publishing.

Losh, M., & Capps, L. (2006). Understanding of emotional experience in autism: Insights from the personal accounts of high-functioning children with autism. *Developmental Psychology*, *42*(5), 809–818.

Resources for Stage C

In this section you will find photocopiable versions of the following resources:

- the *Team reflection chart* template; and
- the *3-2-1 chart* template.
- **Please note:** The *Goal and skill performance sticker chart* template and *Target Skills icons* stickers can be found in Chapter 4 resources section.

Team Reflection Chart: thinking about our strengths and next steps

✓ Skills we used well during Stage B (playing the game):

↻ Skills we can focus on next time:

3-2-1 Chart

3 skills I used: what are three skills you used well during play?		

2 skills I didn't use: what are two skills you didn't use during play?	

1 next step: what skill do you want to focus on next session?

7 Introducing 15 Target Skills

Introduction

In each of the three stages of this intervention you will have seen references to the Target Skills, a set of 15 high-priority collaborative social skills. This chapter introduces the 15 Target Skills and provides practical advice through which interventionists can scaffold, nurture and support the development of these skills. Interventionists need to know not just what these skills involve and what they look like during cooperative play, but also how to create the conditions in which children will recognise independently when to use each of the Target Skills. For children to be able to do this, they must be able to recall the underlying purpose of each of the skills. To help interventionists to think about how they will work towards developing independence, the 15 Target Skills are grouped into six overarching categories, describing how these individual skills can be used together:

- Encouraging participation in group activity
- Supporting participants to consider others' perspectives on fairness
- Recognising when to give instructions and share information
- Creating an environment for constructive communication
- Drawing on individual and collective expertise
- Providing encouragement and performance feedback

For each of these categories, I provide a series of recommendations for how interventionists can support and nurture the performance of these skills as children work towards independence.

Why should you focus on these 15 skills?

A range of possible collaborative social skills was considered and evaluated using three different perspectives, which can be thought of as three different sources of evidence to be compared and contrasted in deciding which skills matter the most:

DOI: 10.4324/9781003025917-7

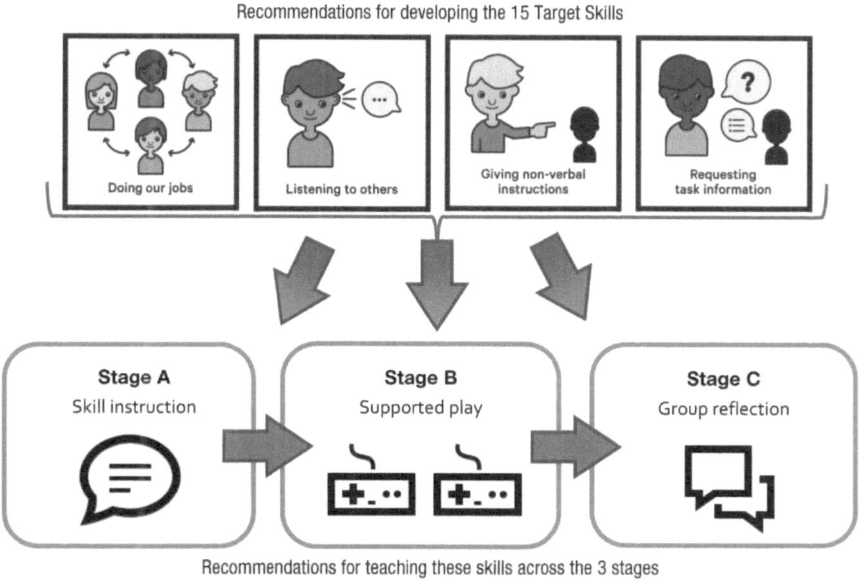

Figure 7.1 Recommendations for developing and teaching Target Skills across the three stages.

- Skills identified through consultations with the **team around the child.** Collating the professional and personal expertise of speech and language pathologists, teachers, teaching assistants, parents and, where possible, children with lived experiences of neurodiversity illustrated areas of commonality between all of these stakeholders.
- Skills identified through my own **professional observations** of working with children, including scrutiny of the most common areas of challenge for my students when completing group tasks that require a high degree of collaborative problem-solving.
- Skills identified through the analysis of areas of commonality in the **learning progressions**. As detailed in Chapter 8, these 'pathways' for children developing the skills required to collaborate with others in a more sophisticated way each highlight a range of requisite social skills.

Collating and sorting these skills to identify which skills were essential was no easy task, but it was important. Interventionists often have limited time to implement a social capacity–building intervention, so identifying a manageable number of high-priority Target Skills was necessary. To do this, I compared and contrasted the lists of skills from each source of evidence with patterns of priority soon emerging. As shown below, a process of triangulation then

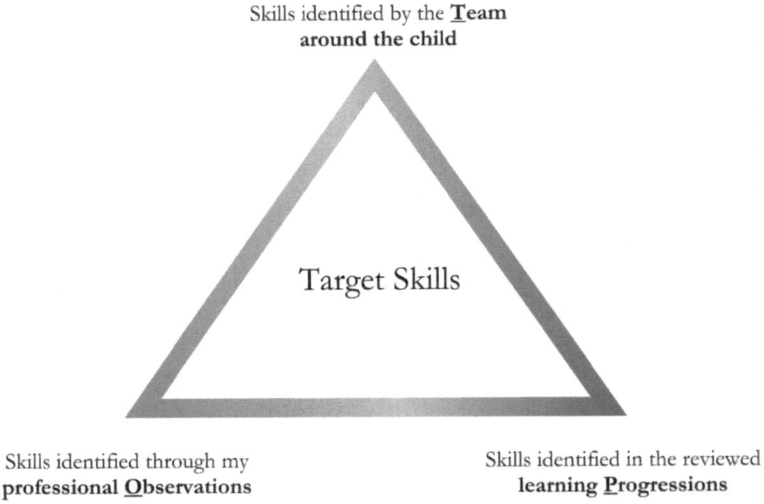

Figure 7.2 The three sources of evidence informing the final list of Target Skills.

occurred, with the skills identified on multiple lists given priority for inclusion in the final list of Target Skills.

Starting with these 15 Target Skills should allow your participants to develop the foundational skills required for engaging in collaborative play and problem-solving, without requiring them to change who they are as individuals. This final point is increasingly important for our neurodiverse communities, as conditions such as autism or ADHD are discussed more frequently as *differences* rather than deficits. By concentrating on these 15 skills, your focus can remain on developing leadership and team-based skills instead of fixing 'broken' individuals.

Overview of all 15 Target Skills

Keeping this context in mind, below are the 15 Target Skills, including a *grounded definition* for each skill. Defining a skill through providing an illustration of what a skill might look or sound like can assist you in communicating the importance of these skills to the participants. Contextualisation makes these skills meaningful. Some of these grounded definitions provide more sophisticated performances of the skill, with these denoted using an ⇧ icon. It is also important to note that some of the provided examples are interactions in the shared physical space (in the room), while others are interactions that occur in the virtual game environment.

Skill name	*What does this look/sound like during play?*	*Example during play*
Encouraging participation in group activity		
1. Doing our jobs 	• Playing the game while attempting to accomplish the team goal.	• A player using their avatar in the game to flick a switch so the other players' avatars can go through a door.
Supporting participants to consider others' perspectives on fairness		
2. Taking turns 	• Voluntarily offering, either verbally or physically, to relinquish control to another player. • Verbally communicating that other players can make decisions.	• A player passes their controller to another participant once the timer indicates that their turn is finished.
Recognising when to give instructions and share information		
3. Giving verbal instructions 	• Verbally communicating instructions to another player or the group. • More sophisticated communicators can adjust their language when another person does not understand their instructions.	• A player directs another participant to move their avatar next to a specific door and then to wait for them.

4. Giving non-verbal instruction 	• Pointing at the screen or to the controller with a hand, head or foot gesture. • A more sophisticated communicator can adjust their gestures when another person does not understand their instructions.	• Pointing to a hidden object in the background of a level to tell the other players to try to collect it.
5. Offering help 	• Asking another player or the group if they need assistance with the mechanics of the game. • Physically communicating to another player that they can help them.	• A player turning to a person who is finding it difficult to control their avatar and asking, 'Do you need me to show you the controls?'
6. Sharing task information 	• Verbally informing another player about the rules or mechanics of the game or the team goal. • A more sophisticated communicator can simplify and distil the information into smaller parts if another person does not understand them.	• A player explaining that the team needs to collect three parts of a key to open a door blocking their progress through the level.
Creating an environment for constructive communication		
7. Listening to others 	• Verbally or physically acknowledging that they heard their peer. • Changing actions in the game to comply with their peers' instructions.	• Giving a 'thumbs up' when another player asks them to move their avatar closer to an object in the level.

8. Checking for understanding  	• Asking whether someone understands after giving an instruction or sharing information. • A more sophisticated communicator will monitor the actions of their peers to check for understanding, and then check again if required.	• After giving another play an instruction to jump onto a particular platform, the participant follows by asking, 'So do you know where to go now?'
9. Quiet voices  	• Using a volume that allows other children to be heard. • A more sophisticated communicator can monitor and adjust their volume independently when they recognise they are being too loud.	• A player lowers the volume of their voice when they hear another player begin to talk to a peer.
Drawing on individual and collective expertise		
10. Asking for help  	• Verbally communicating to another player or the group that they need help with the mechanics of the game. • Picking up the *Help* card.	• A player is unsure of the jump button, so they pick up the *Help* card and pass it to another participant (at which point they can communicate their needs by *requesting task information*).
11. Requesting task information  	• A question directed from one player to another player or the group about the rules of the game, the mechanics (such as controls) or the team goal.	• A player asks another player which button on the controller will make their avatar jump.

12. Asking your friends for ideas

- Verbally requesting from an individual or the group possible solutions to a puzzle or challenge within the game.

- After failing to defeat an end-of-level 'boss' enemy, a player asks their team for ways they could possibly do more damage to this enemy.

13. Requesting performance feedback

- One player verbally asking another player or the group for feedback on performance (for example, 'How am I going?').
- A more sophisticated communicator will identify the area they want feedback on, guiding the attention of the feedback provider.

- Following an unsuccessful attempt at a flying level, a player asks another player how they can be better at piloting the spaceship.

Providing appropriate encouragement and performance feedback

14. Encouraging others

- Making a positive comment about the performance of a player.
- Verbally reassuring a player when they make a mistake.
- A more sophisticated collaborator will monitor the emotional state of their teammates and will provide encouragement when needed to keep the team engaged.

- A player telling another player who has crashed their spaceship that 'It is okay because we can always try again'.

15. Providing performance feedback 	• One player verbally communicating to another player or the group their perceptions of an individual or the team's level of performance, either within the game or in using the social skills. • A more sophisticated collaborator will monitor the emotional state of their teammates and provide feedback during breaks in play or lulls in action.	• A player telling another participant that they are 'Really good at the jumping levels but need to practice flying the spaceship'.

While these individual skills are important to learn in isolation, the collaborative capabilities of the participants really begin to develop when they combine these skills to work together in increasingly sophisticated ways. The following sections of this chapter focus on how participants could use these skills in combination and on ways that you, as an interventionist, can support participants to experiment and consolidate their understandings of these skills during play.

Combining skills: Encouraging participation in group activity

ENCOURAGING PARTICIPATION IN GROUP ACTIVITY

Target Skill(s):

1. Doing our jobs

Participation is a prerequisite for the use of all other focus social skills, as every social interaction requires at least two people (All et al., 2016; Griffin et al., 2012). Engaging with a peer is the foundational step on which performance of all the other skills depends. In this intervention, video games are positioned as a shared area of interest, providing sufficient motivation for sometimes socially isolated children to sit with their peers and play together. This intervention describes participating in play to work towards a shared goal as '**Doing our jobs**'. In the context of this intervention, we consider how they participate in cooperative gameplay. At a foundational level, individuals need to recognise that they are part of a team and have a role within that team. Providing meaningful contexts through the use of well-designed games is key to getting everyone actively engaged with their peers.

Getting everyone involved: The importance of selecting the right games to encourage participation

Effective game design can guide players towards working with their peers to complete team goals without participants having to make a conscious choice. Constraining player agency might seem to be in conflict with the principles of agency espoused by games-based learning advocates such as Gee (2007b) and Squire (2005), but my own research has found some clear benefits of 'manufactured' social interactions when working with neurodiverse players. While at first glance withholding the choice of whether to participate in working with peers to be successful in the game might seem undemocratic, in my experience, removing the choice to work independently results in near-universal team play. If a child wants to play the game, they have to play with other children.

EXAMPLE OF A GAME THAT ASSIGNS EVERYONE AN IMPORTANT JOB

The rules of **Rayman Legends** provide a perfect example of encouraging team participation. These dictate that both players must fulfil their roles within the team to complete the level, with no one player being able to complete the required tasks as an individual. One section of the first level requires Player One to rotate a wheel that manipulates the physics of a maze, while the other players have to navigate through this perilous labyrinth avoiding spikes. Through coordinating their movements with the person rotating their environment, players can safely reach the end point of the level.

While games will not *teach* the Target Skills, they can play a big role in providing as many opportunities as possible for practising these skills under the guidance of the interventionists. Strategic game selection is therefore vital in ensuring that all players are active participants. Chapter 9 explores the role of game design in creating the conditions for collaboration in more detail.

Organising jobs within the team

Children do have a large degree of agency in self-organising roles, or 'jobs', within the team. Discussions about who will perform which job can occur in the lead-up to play, during play and in the guided reflection post play. My research has found that interventionists need to facilitate these discussions, ideally during time-out breaks in Stage B or during video review in Stage A. As players regularly rotate through various roles, new vocabulary is often required. Here is some role-defining vocabulary that I have found useful:

VOCABULARY FOR DEFINING ROLES WITHIN A TEAM

- **Guardian**: a player fulfilling this role ensures that all players can safely traverse a particularly challenging section of a level, such as jumping over a lava pit. Guardians can either provide verbal instructions to their teammates while letting them go first or they can show them how to cross an obstacle by modelling the required steps in the game.
- **Shield**: this involves a more experienced player clearing enemies and obstacles for a novice player so that they have a smoother run through the level.
- **The Glue**: due to the name, this is a personal favourite of mine. This role involves one player ensuring that the group stays together and that no one is left behind. **Please note**: Some games require that the group stay on the same screen while others will allow people to run ahead of their peers.

Cognitive load theory provides a lens for explaining the necessity of rehearsing this language. As explored in Chapter 2, cognitive load theory emphasises that steps should be taken to ensure that learners can draw upon their long-term memory as much as possible to reduce the burden on their working memory (Sweller et al., 2011). The interventionist should model specialised terminology for each role in a game in the context of its use. Vocabulary also needs to be rehearsed prior to play to avoid the participants' over-reliance on their working memories and becoming overloaded during these discussions of roles within the team. This is another excellent benefit of video review during Stage A.

RECOMMENDATIONS FOR SUPPORTING PARTICIPATION

1. As a prerequisite for the use of all social skills, interventionists should be strategic in selecting games that guide players towards working together to complete the team goals *(planning prior to session)*.
2. Interventionists should guide players to discuss their role and the roles of their peers within the team during video review or during time-out breaks *(Stage A and Stage B)*.
3. Interventionists should practice and model specialised terminology for each role prior to every session of play *(Stage A)*.

Combining skills: Considering others' perspectives on fairness

SUPPORTING PARTICIPANTS TO CONSIDER OTHERS' PERSPECTIVES ON FAIRNESS

Target Skill(s):

2 Taking turns

Once participants are working towards a common team goal, they require systems for organising transitions between roles within the game. As explored further in Chapter 9, some games will assign specific responsibilities and tasks to certain playable characters. Additionally, many games have limited items that grant the player who picks them up with a special perk, like a health bonus, and these present wonderful opportunities to discuss taking turns in relation to concepts of fairness and perspective-taking to achieve the team goals. Interventionists need to guide discussions around what constitutes fairness and implement strategies for supporting the participants in considering the perspectives of their peers.

Perspective-taking is a complex skill that some researchers argue can be challenging for children with neurological differences, such as autism, to develop (Baron-Cohen, 2017; Baron-Cohen et al., 1985). The first step in helping children to understand the importance of turn-taking is ensuring that everyone understands the language used to describe this skill. Teaching the key phrases listed below, alongside the examples of this skill being used during gameplay, will provide a solid foundation for children to begin talking about how and when they should 'take turns'.

Phrases for discussing 'turn taking'	
• Changing roles	Rather than saying to a child that their turn has finished, I tell them they are changing roles. This subtle shift in language is useful in reminding them that they still have an important and active role in helping to achieve the team goal(s).
• Monitoring time	When talking about turn-taking, I always emphasise that we need to be monitoring, or keeping track of, the remaining time before we change roles. If children are aware of how long they have left, it helps minimise 'surprises' when they are asked to change roles.
• Fairness	'That's not fair!' is a phrase I've heard more than once in my teaching career. As a subjective and abstract concept, reaching a common understanding of fairness can be very challenging for any group of children. It is important to explore understandings of what a 'fair turn' means and to facilitate a negotiated definition on which all your participants agree. If they are finding this challenging, they can be prompted by asking the group 'Why do we use a timer?'

While the idea of 'taking turns' might be familiar to many children, it is not always easy for them to know when it is appropriate. Contextually specific rules for understanding what a person might be thinking often need to be taught explicitly. Once they recognise that another participant might also want to play the game, they just need to know the steps for offering a turn. Interventionists can use a scripted video to teach which indicators to look for and to reinforce the reasons why it is important to share roles and opportunities. Presented below is an example of a script that I have found to be effective:

Script for a video model: 'We take turns when playing together'	
Script for voice over	*Video footage*
Everyone in our team loves playing video games together.	[show children playing together and looking happy or excited]
We all want to have a turn playing the game. Sometimes I get to play the game.	[show children playing]
Other times I have to wait for my turn. While we are waiting, our role is to help the players by sharing advice and encouraging our teammates.	[show children waiting and supporting their peers]
To make sure everyone has a fair amount of playing time, we use a timer to keep track of how long until we change roles within our team.	[show child checking the timer]
When the timer is up, we need to swap roles within the team.	[show players swapping]
This way we can all have a fair turn at playing the games.	[show happy children playing together]

Interventionists can use the functional limitations of games, such as the possible number of simultaneous players, to provide a context for having participants consider fairness from multiple peoples' perspectives. From the very first lesson, some children I work with will recognise the importance of an impartial means for allocating turns of playing the game, underpinned by their perceptions of fairness. The use of a visual timer provides one way for children to self-monitor and evaluate their play time but, importantly, this requires an understanding of the concept of time.

Beyond managing resources such as controllers in the physical environment, some games include mechanics that demand players take turns in the virtual environment. This could be a puzzle with an ordinal solution, where one avatar has to hit a switch before the other avatars can proceed, or it might be a platform that can carry only two avatars at a time. Both examples require an element of delayed gratification for some players, with some temporarily taking on passive roles within the team.

When players are forced to wait for a turn in the game, more skilful players will often ensure that they go first and then guide their less skilful team member through the challenge. This guiding of less skilled players can actually represent a powerful opportunity for players to model in-game solutions and strategies, and then perform more sophisticated communication and perspective-taking skills in coaching those less skilful players. The use of video review provides a fertile space for children to assess their actions and for the interventionist to guide them in identifying opportunities for peer coaching.

RECOMMENDATIONS FOR SUPPORTING PARTICIPANTS TO CONSIDER FAIRNESS AND MULTIPLE PERSPECTIVES

4 Children need to be taught the contextual rules for recognising when another child might want a turn *(Stage A)*.

5 Interventionists should use the functional limitations of games, such as a limited number of players or power-ups, as a context for discussions of fairness from multiple peoples' perspectives *(Stage A and Stage C)*.

6 When children are required to take turns within the game, interventionists can support waiting expert players in coaching novice players and highlight the importance of all players in achieving the team goal *(Stage B)*.

Combining skills: Recognising when to give instructions and share information

RECOGNISING WHEN TO GIVE INSTRUCTIONS AND SHARE INFORMATION

Target Skill(s):

3 Giving verbal instructions
4 Giving non-verbal instruction
5 Offering help
6 Sharing task information

These four skills are central in the process of providing instructions and sharing information with others so that the coordination of actions is possible. Central to all four of these skills is children learning to be aware of their peers' levels of understanding, and then learning how to respond appropriately. Although motivated players will monitor the performance of their peers regularly to make progress in the game, when a player is not fulfilling their role in the team, the interventionist should support the team in communicating this constructively. Once participants develop the skills to check for understanding, the interventionist can support them in tailoring their language and provide instructions or share information in a way that the intended audience can understand.

A number of potential supports can nurture the development of the skills participants require to monitor the degree of understanding of their peers and to evaluate and respond to their contributions. Once again, as an interventionist, you need to teach these steps for communication explicitly in the context in which participants will perform them. Many modern games offer some form of mechanical tutorial in their early levels. If a game does feature a tutorial level, you can use these slower-paced sections to coach players. This will help participants recognise the signs that a player might not know what to do, identify what the challenge is for that particular player and understand the language required to share instructions or information on how to address that challenge. These early instructional levels also direct players on how to combine the individual strengths of each player to solve a problem, modelling instructional language with supporting visual cues. The explicit, visual instructions provided in the tutorial levels of many modern games align well with the principles for effective video modelling (Green et al., 2017; Mechling & Swindle, 2013; Reichow & Volkmar, 2010). Interventionists can use the language provided by the game to model communication between the players.

While instructions provided by the game can be useful for you and some of your participants, some individuals might have difficulty in interpreting them. On the surface, this might seem like a barrier, but it actually presents an opportunity for peer-mediated instruction. Interventionists can assign the mentor roles to specific expert players and then provide prompts, reminding them that they have this role. Even when playing unfamiliar games, this can be an opportunity for 'gamers' to use their knowledge of genre conventions to practise communicating and checking for understanding with their peers. Many neurodiverse individuals prefer visual instructions (Rao & Gagie, 2006), with many of the children in my research initially attempting to communicate through pointing or physical modelling. Through the interventionist-led reflection provided by video review, some participants who prefer non-verbal communication can begin, independently, to supplement their physical cues with verbal instructions.

Through the analysis of the use of these skills in one of my research projects, I developed the model presented below. This model outlines the steps that interventionists need to teach explicitly so that participants can work towards independently monitoring and evaluating whether the intended audience has understood them. You can model these steps during the video review of a section of a gameplay, such as when a player attempts to explain how to navigate over a crevasse. By verbalising their internal cognitive processes explicitly,

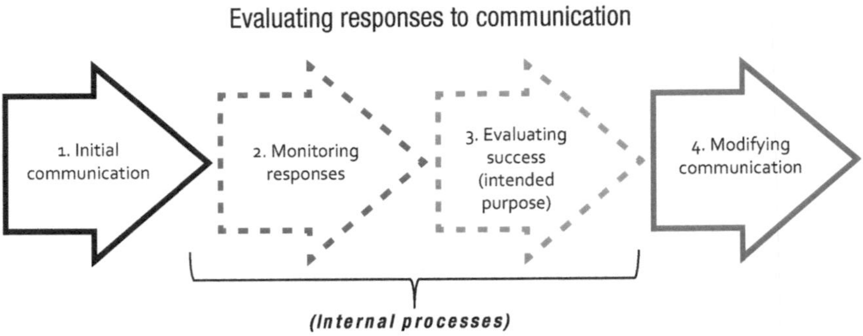

Figure 7.3 Evaluating responses to communication.

interventionists can guide participants through the processes required for evaluating responses to communication. You can structure this process as the 'initial communication', 'monitoring responses' from the intended recipients, 'evaluating success' in terms of achieving the intended purpose and then 'modifying communication' depending on this evaluation.

The use of video footage of past gameplay during Stage A provides opportunities to show the performance of these steps. When using games that create interdependence between players, interventionists can subsequently review gameplay footage with their children to highlight how offering help and sharing task information can be mutually beneficial in achieving the team goal. As long as they have the required language, the use of explicit examples drawn from recent play allows participants to practise verbalising their internal thought processes. You can support the development of this language through the use of prompts and by modelling the language when they describe their own internal processes during gameplay.

RECOMMENDATIONS FOR SUPPORTING CHILDREN TO RECOGNISE WHEN TO GIVE INSTRUCTIONS AND SHARE INFORMATION

7 Interventionists should use slower-paced tutorial levels to coach children in recognising when and how to provide instructions and share information with peers *(Stage B)*.

8 Interventionists can introduce peer-mediated instruction to position expert players as mentors, providing close support to the mentor in checking for understanding and modifying their language *(Stage B)*.

9 Interventionists should model their internal cognitive processes aloud, guiding children through the steps for checking for understanding *(Stage A and Stage B)*.

Combining skills: Creating an environment for constructive communication

CREATING AN ENVIRONMENT FOR CONSTRUCTIVE COMMUNICATION

Target Skill(s):

7 Listening to others
8 Checking for understanding
9 Quiet voices

These three social skills are important for creating an environment of constructive communication. As interventionists working with often reluctant communicators, we need to place a high value on participants considering the perspectives of other people within a group. To consider other perspectives, children must be able to listen actively and process what is being said to them. This presents a challenge for interventionists as 'listening to others' is amongst the most difficult skills to identify and measure during sometimes chaotic play, yet it is a foundational skill in communication. It is particularly hard to capture individual instances of listening, especially when players' eyes are directed towards the action occurring on the screen. This is further complicated by the preferences some children have for not making eye contact, either as a manifestation of the differences of autism, differences in cultural expectations or a combination of the two. Despite these challenges, listening is essential in communication between team members. As such, interventionists need to know how to identify when participants are listening and how to reinforce the performance of this skill positively.

One way of identifying individual instances of a child listening to another child is in the observation of verbal acknowledgements. These acknowledgements can be either direct, such as an answer to a question, or indirect, such as saying something that continues the conversation that another child has begun. Increasing the frequency of acknowledgements should be an early priority in your intervention, as this will allow the other players and the intervention staff to recognise that attempts at verbal communication are being processed by the intended recipients. Interventionists should prompt children to provide an acknowledgement if they have recognised that someone is attempting to communicate with them.

Another method for identification of listening is when a player changes their behaviour in the game as a result of a verbal instruction, comment or request from a peer. This requires a degree of interpretation, but when children are trained to look for such changes, they can recognise that team members are listening to them. This final point needs to be highlighted explicitly to some children with socio-emotional differences; 'listening to others' is not just about the message receiver, it also involves the sender knowing how to check that the message has been received and interpreted in the intended manner.

This is why I have also introduced 'checking for understanding' as a Target Skill. Recognising when instructions or feedback have been understood can be a complex process, as often children and young adults will want to please their peers and not agitate the person giving the instructions. I have found that they will often say they understand and then suffer in silence. It is therefore important not only to teach our participants that they should check for understanding, but also for interventionists to model for them that it is socially acceptable to admit a lack of clarity. We must create a safe environment so that everyone feels comfortable asking for more information or for information in another form.

Finally, to be able to listen easily to their peers and check for understanding, participants need to be able to hear them. The use of 'quiet voices' is relatively easy to measure but amongst the most difficult skills to teach. This is because the appropriate application of these skills changes depending on cultural context. My research has found that volume is contingent upon the emotional investment the child has in the verbal interaction, their recognition of acoustic environments and their ability to plan their responses to prompts ahead of time. One of the primary reasons for using video games is to harness the excitement created by this medium to motivate participation in collaborative play and problem-solving. By its nature, excitement naturally leads to heightened emotional states, which, in turn, makes controlling the volume of voice neither a priority nor a reasonable expectation for the participants.

So, given that exciting games can make regulating volume so difficult, when is it important for participants to use a quiet voice? My research has found that this should be emphasised when they are not playing or during lulls in action. Opportune times for interventionists to highlight 'using a quiet voice' include during the post-play feedback and when planning the scheduled time-out breaks.

Please note: Also remember that regular emotional breaks during play are vitally important to allow time for children to plan their communication in advance and to mentally rehearse how they will deliver their instructions.

RECOMMENDATIONS FOR CREATING ENVIRONMENTS FOR CONSTRUCTIVE COMMUNICATION

10 Interventionists should prompt children to provide a verbal acknowledgement if they have recognised that someone is attempting to communicate with them *(Stage B)*.

11 Interventionists should focus on modelling and encouraging 'quiet voices' during skill instruction, time-out breaks, the group reflection and when there are lulls in action during gameplay *(Stage A and Stage B)*.

12 Regular time-out breaks allow interventionists to support children in regulating their emotional states and planning their verbal communication in advance *(Stage B)*.

Combining skills: Drawing on individual and collective expertise

> **DRAWING ON INDIVIDUAL AND COLLECTIVE EXPERTISE**
>
> Target Skill(s):
>
> 10 Asking for help
> 11 Requesting task information
> 12 Asking your friends for ideas
> 13 Requesting performance feedback

A primary goal of this intervention is to use an area of interest and relative strength for the participants playing video games to help them develop the 15 Target Skills. Building from this area of strength presents real opportunities for peer-mediated instruction and coaching. When team members use the four skills shown above, they can draw upon their collective expertise, benefiting both individual players and assisting the entire team in achieving common goals in games featuring designed interdependence.

Pride as a barrier

In relation to cultural considerations, a questionable suggestion has been raised that the differences inherent in autism might impact upon the recognition of knowledge in others (Baron-Cohen et al., 2001), but these children, like every child, also want to feel that they have the respect of their peers. In my experience, players who identify as 'gamers' have a sense of pride in their self-perceived expertise. For many children with whom I have worked, knowing things about their favourite video games that their school mates do not is a badge of honour. Rather than not recognising the abilities of others, my research has found that there can be a reluctance to turn to others for any form of assistance as they think it can diminish their 'gamer cred'. A useful example involves looking at the use of the skill 'asking for help'. In my study, children who acknowledged being inexperienced gamers asked for help regularly, but this skill was much less frequently used by players who saw gaming as integral to their sense of identity. When investigated, the barrier to asking for assistance seemed to be pride. These experienced gamers might have recognised that they required either knowledge of the game mechanics or assistance within the virtual environment to overcome an obstacle but, to protect their social capital within the group, they would rather experience failure than admit to not knowing what to do.

The use of video review in this context provides a powerful tool for addressing the challenges of social capital. Footage of situations in which the players appear stuck can be replayed to highlight the indicators that, individually, players might not have the solution to a problem. Ideally, these contexts involve all players demonstrating through their in-game actions that they do not understand how to progress towards the collective goal. Examples of such indicators observed in my research include players repeating the same failed strategy multiple time, or the lack of movement from the players' in-game avatars. To develop the ability of participants to recognise when they are 'stuck', interventionists can model their own processes. They can facilitate this by 'thinking aloud', modelling how even adults identify situations in which they have insufficient knowledge, and then using first-person language to obtain this knowledge from other children.

Script for a video model: 'Asking other players is a good idea'	
Script for voice over	*Video footage*
Everyone in our team loves playing video games together.	[show children playing together and looking happy or excited]
Sometimes we get to a puzzle or an area and do not know what to do.	[Show an example of a puzzle in a popular game using gameplay footage]
That is when it is a good idea to ask our team members for ideas.	[Show one player asking, 'What do you think we should we do?']
We might not know what to do by ourselves, but if we ask each other for ideas, we can work out what we need to do.	[Show footage of participants communicating verbally and non-verbally as a group]
When we ask, we should then listen to everyone's ideas and then try them out.	[Show footage of participants taking turns to speak and giving each other a 'thumbs up' to show they have listened]
Asking other players for ideas helps us to find out what to do.	[Show game footage of the players' avatars completing the puzzle and making progress]

Changing social perceptions around what it means to ask for help is important and emphasises the primacy of the team goal in measuring success in the game. A game that values collective achievement rather than individual success is vitally important here.

RECOMMENDATIONS FOR DRAWING UPON INDIVIDUAL AND COLLECTIVE EXPERTISE

13 Interventionists need to make explicit connections between the collective knowledge of the team and group success during video review and during breaks in play *(Stage A and Stage B).*

14 During video review, interventionists should show footage of contexts in which the players appear to be stuck to highlight indicators that, individually, players might not have the solution to a problem *(Stage A).*

15 Interventionists should model their own processes by 'thinking aloud' about having insufficient knowledge to solve a problem, and then modelling the language used to obtain this knowledge from other players *(Stage A and Stage B).*

Combining skills: Providing appropriate encouragement and performance feedback

PROVIDING ENCOURAGEMENT AND PERFORMANCE FEEDBACK

Target Skill(s):

14 Encouraging others
15 Providing performance feedback

At a superficial level, providing encouragement and performance feedback can be the most intuitive approach for participants with socio-emotional differences. Usually, positive performance feedback, or the idea of acknowledging the successes of others, is taught across contexts from a young age. Many of the children with whom I have worked had already been coached in the socially expected phrasing and tone used to do this. My research has found that children who rely on social scripts appear to be reasonably proficient in identifying the right time to put these scripts into action when the commentary is simplistic and positive. Reflecting on their own experiences of social scripting, a number of autistic authors over the years have noted that scripting was an important strategy for ensuring they adhered to social expectations, even when they did not fully comprehend the reasons for acting in a certain way (Grandin, 2006; Jackson, 2002).

Reflecting on scripting in my own research, the effectiveness (and limitations) of a scripted approach when providing encouragement and feedback during cooperative play was evident after analysis of hours of video footage. I observed a high number of instances of children congratulating successful members of their team, particularly when the game provided visible cues that this player had done something worthy of praise, such as finding a hidden path or landing the final blow on a significant enemy. Interventionists should positively reinforce instances of children acknowledging the successes of others, as this is a desirable social behaviour.

Beyond providing superficial positive feedback following prompts from interventionists, these skills seem to become much more challenging for some participants as they do not understand the purpose and value of them. This reflects the challenges some children experience in displaying cognitive empathy, or knowing what someone else might be thinking, and recognising when to initiate communication. Another common challenge is identifying an appropriate time and form to give constructive feedback. To address these challenges, interventionists can have a very 'hands on' role during play. By encouraging participants to maintain a positive motivational state through helpful rephrasing of feedback, children can see a 'worked example' or model of effective feedback.

Helping children to rephrase their feedback

Original feedback (all genuine quotes):	*Rephrased feedback:*
'You made me die!'	'When you pushed me off the bridge that caused me to die, which made me feel angry and slowed our team down'.
'It's your fault we missed the coin'.	'Next time we should try to get the coin because it will give us more lives. We can do this by [replacement actions for next time]'.
'You didn't get many points'.	'I can see that you are trying hard. Did you know that if you pick up more items you will get more points?'
'Why can't you hold the controller properly?'	'Do you need help holding the controller? It might be easier if you hold it like this' [model for peer].

Teaching the power of positivity

When modelling this feedback, as an interventionist, you need to make clear connections to the expected impact of positive phrasing. Such phrasing will ensure other team members persist and work to improve their individual performance. When playing cooperative games with elements of interdependence, this benefits the entire team. It can be rare for the person providing encouragement to connect their positive performance feedback explicitly to the specific actions of their peers. Even after this has been modelled through video review, the speed at which most games progress means that players can find few opportunities to provide this level of detail. This is problematic because it then places the burden on the receiver to interpret this encouragement, exacerbating the challenges some neurodiverse children experience integrating verbal and non-verbal communication. Whether the player receiving the praise understands the relationship between their play and this feedback is entirely dependent on their understanding of the goals of the game and their cognitive capability and interest in analysing the context in which the words were stated. You need to model praising specific positive actions and encourage children to do the same.

You also need to position encouragement and performance feedback as essential and complementary tools for effective teamwork and achieving success in the game. Children should learn to provide constructive feedback that identifies the problem and the next steps for the player to address this problem while minimising emotive language. While this must be taught and modelled explicitly, the results of my research also highlight the need for regular breaks so that children can provide timely encouragement and feedback without the pressure of having to continue playing the game. This is particularly true for providing performance feedback when an individual is not fulfilling their role within the team. Interventionists might need to take the initiative, call a time-out at the point of need and guide children through discussing the context in which the players find themselves and the appropriate language to use to ensure the constructive phrasing of the message.

RECOMMENDATIONS FOR ENCOURAGING EFFECTIVE FEEDBACK

16 Interventionists should positively reinforce instances of children acknowledging the successes of others, encouraging them to link their positive performance feedback to the specific actions of their peers *(Stage A, Stage B and Stage C).*

17 Interventionists need to teach and model the language for providing constructive feedback explicitly, with regular breaks during play for rehearsing the required language to express and receive feedback *(Stage A, Stage B and Stage C).*

18 Interventionists should highlight examples of more complex forms of feedback during video review, with this feedback being positioned as essential for effective teamwork and achieving success in the game *(Stage A).*

Summary of key ideas in Chapter 7

The recommendations presented in this chapter provide interventionists with an overview of the 15 Target Skills and a set of strategies and supports they can use to help children learn how to combine the focus social skills with increasing levels of sophistication. You can refer to the single page summary of the 18 recommended strategies in the resources section of this chapter.

The following chapter focuses on how you can assess your participants as they work together, with a mapping of the 15 Target Skills to each of the social dimensions and levels of the *Collaborative Problem-Solving Progressions.* You can use this chapter as a guide to the language and strategies you should be using to teach the 15 Target Skills. Chapter 9 will help you identify the sequence in which you can teach these skills independently and in combination.

References

All, A., Castellar, E. P. N., & Van Looy, J. (2016). Assessing the effectiveness of digital game-based learning: Best practices. *Computers & Education, 92*, 90–103.

Baron-Cohen, S., Leslie, A. M., & Frith, U. (1985). Does the autistic child have a 'theory of mind'? *Cognition, 21*(1), 37–46.

Baron-Cohen, S., Wheelwright, S., Skinner, R., Martin, J., & Clubley, E. (2001). The autism-spectrum quotient (AQ): Evidence from Asperger syndrome/high-functioning autism, males and females, scientists and mathematicians. *Journal of Autism and Developmental Disorders, 31*(1), 5–17.

Baron-Cohen, S. (2017). Editorial perspective: Neurodiversity – A revolutionary concept for autism and psychiatry. *Journal of Child Psychology and Psychiatry, 58*(6), 744–747.

Gee, J. P. (2007). *What video games have to teach us about learning and literacy*. Palgrave Macmillan.

Grandin, T. (2006). *Thinking in pictures: My life with autism* (2nd ed.). Vintage Books.

Green, V. A., Prior, T., Smart, E., Boelema, T., Drysdale, H., Harcourt, S., Roche, L., & Waddington, H. (2017). The use of individualized video modeling to enhance positive peer interactions in three preschool children. *Education and Treatment of Children, 40*(3), 353–378.

Griffin, P., Care, E., & McGaw, B. (2012). The changing role of education and schools. In P. Griffin, B. McGaw, & E. Care (Eds.), *Assessment and teaching of 21st century skills* (pp. 1–15). Springer.

Hesse, F., Care, E., Buder, J., Sassenberg, K., & Griffin, P. (2015). A framework for teachable collaborative problem solving skills. In P. Griffin & E. Care (Eds.), *Assessment and teaching of 21st century skills: Methods and approach* (pp. 37–56). Springer.

Jackson, L. (2002). *Freaks, geeks, and Asperger syndrome*. Jessica Kingsley Publishers.

Mechling, L. C., & Swindle, C. O. (2013). Fine and gross motor task performance when using computer-based video models by students with autism and moderate intellectual disability. *Journal of Special Education, 47*(3), 135–147.

Rao, S. M., & Gagie, B. (2006). Learning through seeing and doing: Visual supports for children with autism. *Teaching Exceptional Children, 38*(6), 26–33.

Reichow, B., & Volkmar, F. R. (2010). Social skills interventions for individuals with autism: Evaluation for evidence-based practices within a best evidence synthesis framework. *Journal of Autism and Developmental Disorders, 40*(2), 149–166.

Squire, K. (2005). Changing the game: What happens when video games enter the classroom? *Innovate: Journal of Online Education, 1*(6), 1–8.

Sweller, J., Ayres, P., & Kalyuga, S. (2011). *Cognitive load theory*. Springer-Verlag.

Resources

In this section you will find photocopiable versions of the following resources:

- the *Summary of the* 18 *recommendations.*
- **Please note:** The *Target skills icons* stickers can be found in the resources section of Chapter 4.

Encouraging participation in group activity	Creating an environment for constructive communication

1 As a prerequisite for the use of all social skills, interventionists should be strategic in selecting games that guide players towards working together to complete the team goals *(planning prior to session)*. 2 Interventionists should guide players to discuss their role and the roles of their peers within the team during video review or during time-out breaks *(Stage A and Stage B)*. 3 Interventionists should practice and model specialised terminology for each role prior to every session of play *(Stage A)*.	10. Interventionists should prompt children to provide a verbal acknowledgement if they have recognised that someone is attempting to communicate with them *(Stage B)*. 11. Interventionists should focus on modelling and encouraging 'quiet voices' during skill instruction, time-out breaks, the group reflection and when there are lulls in action during gameplay *(Stage A and Stage B)*. 12. Regular time-out breaks allow interventionists to support children in regulating their emotional states and planning their verbal communication in advance *(Stage B)*.

<table>
<tr><th>Supporting participants to consider others' perspectives on fairness</th><th colspan="4">Drawing on individual and collective expertise</th></tr>
<tr><td>
</td><td>
</td><td>
</td><td>
</td><td>
</td></tr>
<tr><td>4 Children need to be taught the contextual rules for recognising when another child might want a turn (Stage A).
5 Interventionists should use the functional limitations of games, such as a limited number of players or power-ups, as a context for discussions of fairness from multiple peoples' perspectives (Stage A and Stage C).
6 When children are required to take turns within the game, interventionists can support waiting expert players in coaching novice players and highlight the importance of all players in achieving the team goal (Stage B).</td><td colspan="4">13 Interventionists need to make explicit connections between the collective knowledge of the team and group success during video review and during breaks in play (Stage A and Stage B).
14 During video review, interventionists should show footage of contexts in which the players appear stuck to highlight indicators that, individually, players might not have the solution to a problem (Stage A).
15 Interventionists should model their own processes by 'thinking aloud' about having insufficient knowledge to solve a problem, and then modelling the language used to obtain this knowledge from other players (Stage A and Stage B).</td></tr>
</table>

Recognising when to give instructions and share information	Providing appropriate encouragement and performance feedback

7 Interventionists should use slower-paced tutorial levels to coach children in recognising when and how to provide instructions and share information with peers *(Stage B)*. 8 Interventionists can introduce peer-mediated instruction to position expert players as mentors, providing close support to the mentor in checking for understanding and modifying their language *(Stage B)*. 9 Interventionists should model their internal cognitive processes aloud, guiding children through the steps for checking for understanding *(Stage A and Stage B)*.	16 Interventionists should positively reinforce instances of children acknowledging the successes of others, encouraging them to link their positive performance feedback to the specific actions of their peers *(Stage A, Stage B and Stage C)*. 17 Interventionists need to teach and model the language for providing constructive feedback explicitly, with regular breaks during play for rehearsing the required language to express and receive feedback *(Stage A, Stage B and Stage C)*. 18 Interventionists should highlight examples of more complex forms of feedback during video review, with this feedback being positioned as essential for effective teamwork and achieving success in the game *(Stage A)*.

8 Assessing collaboration during play

Introduction

Moving beyond the implementation of the three stages, this chapter examines how interventionists can assess the use of the Target Skills at increasing levels of sophistication. While collaboration is inherently a group activity, we need to be able to measure the impact of this intervention on individual children and young adults. The first step in assessment is generating data. This chapter provides practical advice for conducting frequency counts and making field notes as well as recommendations on how to streamline these processes using the specifically designed ***Data generation sheet***.

Once we have generated our data, as interventionists we need to know how to analyse and interpret the material to make decisions about what each child is ready to learn. This is where an assessment tool called the *Collaborative problem-solving empirical progressions* (Hesse et al., 2015) is particularly useful, with its specific focus on measuring the collaborative sophistication of individuals. A useful way to think of these progressions is as a 'learning map' for us to know where our children and young adults are in their present capabilities and to identify the next steps in becoming more effective collaborators. Developed by the Melbourne Graduate School of Education's Assessment Research Centre, these carefully designed rubrics are particularly well suited to identifying what children can do when playing team-based video games with peers.

These developmental progressions are also useful for interventionists in providing an overview of the different levels of collaboration, with detailed descriptions of what skills should look like when used together in increasingly complex ways. This chapter presents an overview of the three social dimensions found within the progressions: participation, perspective taking and social regulation. For each level, indicators are given of what performance at that level looks like when performed at increasing levels of sophistication.

Assessment as part of the intervention cycle

Well-designed assessment is a vital part of the teaching and learning cycle as it tells us as interventionists what we have got right in terms of how we are

DOI: 10.4324/9781003025917-8

supporting our participants. As such, it should not be a simple case of 'teach, test and move on' but rather:

- Initially assessing to find out what the child is ready to learn, with the ongoing cycles of:
  a) **planning** how best to teach the child the targeted knowledge/skill;
  b) **teaching** the child at the point of readiness;
  c) **assessing** to identify what the child has learnt at the end of session.

These cycles of plan-teach-assess inform interventionists which of the Target Skills should be the focus for each individual in the intervention group. Key to this cycle is generating and analysing data during Stage B to ensure that these decisions are based on evidence rather than well-meaning, but often misguided, assumptions.

Generating data during Stage B

Building on my own professional experiences in high demands classrooms, I developed the *Data generation sheet* as a tool to ensure that generating data during an intervention allows for an accurate measure of the use of Target Skills and the conditions in which they were being used. I also streamlined the process so that I could focus on supporting my learners. Through my research, I experimented with which types of data were the most useful in guiding my intervention so that the children could achieve their goals during Stage B. After experimenting with numerous options, two types of data stood out as being the most useful for understanding what was happening in my intervention:

- **Skill performance frequency counts:** a measure of how often each participant performed one or more of the Target Skills. These data provide a numerical count.
- **Field notes:** brief handwritten 'battle notes' on the key events during Stage B and the conditions in which the children used the Target Skills. These notes provide the context for the frequency count.

Using the Data generation sheet

Interventionists are busy individuals and require assessment tools that provide the information they need in the most efficient way possible. This is the overarching purpose of the *Data generation sheet*. Below you can view a completed example of how a completed sheet might look, followed by instructions on how to complete the main sections of the sheet. This tool uses a simple layout to assist interventionists in recording field notes and keeping track of the Target Skills the participants are using. Each sheet provides spaces for data for three

Data generation sheet

Participant names + goal Target Skills	Field notes	Skill performance frequency counts				
Name: *Link*	**Asking Samus a lot more than Mario about what the team needs to do. *Really enjoyed Level 6. *Pointing to Help card but not picking it up to give to peers or us, so no one is helping him.*	1. Doing our jobs III	2. Taking turns ~~IIII~~ I	3. Using our voice to give instructions ~~IIII~~ II	4. Giving non-verbal instruction	5. Offering help I
Goal: *Requesting task info.*		6. Sharing task information ~~IIII~~ ~~IIII~~ II	7. Listening to others III	8. Checking for understanding II	9. Quiet voices II	10. Asking for help *See note*
		11. Requesting task information ~~IIII~~ III	12. Asking your friends for ideas	13. Requesting performance feedback IIII	14. Encouraging others III	15. Providing performance feedback I
Name: *Samus*	**Video model seems to have worked – now using language from the video to ask for help verbally.*	1. Doing our jobs ~~IIII~~ ~~IIII~~	2. Taking turns II	3. Using our voice to give instructions	4. Giving non-verbal instruction ~~IIII~~ IIII	5. Offering help
Goal: *Asking for help*		6. Sharing task information III	7. Listening to others	8. Checking for understanding	9. Quiet voices II	10. Asking for help ~~IIII~~ III
		11. Requesting task information IIII	12. Asking your friends for ideas II	13. Requesting performance feedback III	14. Encouraging others I	15. Providing performance feedback
Name: *Mario*	**Improved waiting for his turn to play as the main character. *Visual timer seems to be particularly effective.*	1. Doing our jobs IIII	2. Taking turns III	3. Using our voice to give instructions IIII	4. Giving non-verbal instruction	5. Offering help
Goal: *Taking turns*		6. Sharing task information ~~IIII~~ I	7. Listening to others IIII	8. Checking for understanding	9. Quiet voices IIII	10. Asking for help
		11. Requesting task information	12. Asking your friends for ideas	13. Requesting performance feedback	14. Encouraging others	15. Providing performance feedback II

Figure 8.1 Example of a completed *Data generation sheet.*

participants, so if you are working with four or more participants you will need multiple sheets.

Please note: You should use this tool in conjunction with the tracking of skill use through the *Goal and skill performance sticker chart* introduced in Chapter 4 (setting goals) and Chapter 5 (recording skill performance). These two tools have two completely different audiences, with the *Goal and skill performance sticker chart* designed to provide real-time information to the participants, while the *Data generation sheet* captures information for the interventionists. If I am taking on the interventionist role of 'data collector' during Stage B, I use a clipboard to ensure that my field notes and counts remain largely private.

How often should I generate data?

Ideally, you should be generating data every session. Data help inform which skills we focus on in our intervention by noting how participants are responding to the coaching provided by the interventionists and tracking the degree to which children are independently using the Target Skills. That said, from my own experiences I recognise that this can be difficult for interventionists, particularly if only one adult is implementing the intervention. You do not need to generate data for the *entirety* of Stage B; you can focus on a ten-minute sample of play. If you are selecting a sample, I would suggest doing this in the second half of your allocated time in Stage B so that, ideally, the children are settled and familiar with the mechanics of the game (in the event you have introduced a new title). Any less than ten minutes and you might not have sufficient data to make informed decisions about what your participants can do independently.

Recording skill performance frequency counts

The primary objective of this intervention is to improve the collaborative capabilities of the participants. To do this, individuals need to develop an understanding of each of the Target Skills and then practise combining these skills while working as part of a team during gameplay. One indicator that children are improving their ability to collaborate with their peers is an increase in the number of times they use each Target Skill. While different game and social contexts will, of course, impact whether a skill is used or not, counts of how frequently a skill is used will help interventionists gauge whether participants can apply what they have been taught in Stage A.

Below is an example of a frequency count data set, showing the number of times Target Skills 1–5 were used by a group of five participants. It is worth noting that this frequency count was completed by myself after the session had finished, using the available video footage. As explored in a later section of this

Table 8.1 Example of a frequency count for Target Skills

	Doing our jobs	*Taking turns*	*Listening to others*	*Encouraging*	*Quiet voices*
Child A	Full participation	5	2	8	1
Child B	Full participation	2	3	2	
Child C	1 outside break (5 minutes)	4	6	7	5
Child D	Full participation	9	3	2	0
Child E	Full participation	9	4	2	5
Child F	Full participation	1	4	2	5

chapter, there are benefits and challenges to either taking frequency counts in real time or using the recorded video to do this after the fact.

Rather than just comparing results in the short term, say two weeks, interventionists should look at longer-term trends over successive sessions and then analyse the patterns in skill use. When reviewing the counts for each session, the field notes will provide important context that should help to explain why the children are using, or not using, each of the Target Skills.

Recording field notes

While frequency counts can be useful in understanding whether children can recall the steps in performing a skill, they tell us very little about whether a child understands when that skill is being used in a way that is conducive to collaboration. Interventionists also need to understand why children use these skills in particular contexts but not others, as there could be barriers created by other children, the interventionists or the game that is preventing a Target Skill from being utilised effectively.

It is important to be strategic in what you record during the session, as it is almost impossible to record every detail and extraneous information rarely adds to an interventionist's understanding of their children. Video recording and subsequent analysis can be helpful in allowing interventionists to reflect on their field notes without the pressures of implementing the intervention. Field notes can help remind you of key events or patterns of behaviour you have noticed, which you can then revisit through reviewing the footage to allow for a more in-depth analysis.

In addition to being strategic, it is important to attempt to remove personal bias from these observations. To do this, Griffin (2018) suggests using directly observable forms of evidence. He argues that rather than relying on general assumptions as to what a child can and cannot do, interventionists need to rely on judgement-free notes on what an individual can do, say, make or write. Beginning with these categories, I have adjusted the language to be most useful for interventionists in the context of cooperative gaming, as shown below.

Directly observable forms of evidence during cooperative gameplay

Form of evidence	*Examples in the physical environment*	*Examples in the virtual (game) environment*
What can the child **do**? (actions)	Voluntarily passing their controller to another player when their turn has finished.	Having their avatar pick up an item box and bring it to another player's avatar so they can use it.
What can the child **say**? (verbally or through *augmentative and alternative communication*, such as a text-to-speech device)	Passing the *Help* card to another player asking them to assist with learning how to move their character in a new game.	Making their avatar jump up and down on the spot to attract the attention of other players to a particular item or object (such as a doorway).
What can the child **create**? (artefacts/products)	Drawing a 'plan of attack' to defeat a troublesome enemy.	Using an on-screen 'paint brush' to draw a way through a difficult section of a level.

Juggling data generation and other roles

In explaining the role of field notes, I discussed the opportunity to use the video footage to supplement real-time observations. It is, however, possible to generate your data completely after the conclusion of your session. Interventionists need to decide whether to generate data while conducting Stage B, or to wait until after the session is complete and review the video footage. Each approach has its own benefits, but ultimately you should make this decision by considering:

- the levels of support required by the children during play;
- whether you and any co-interventionists have the time to review the footage of Stage B following the completion of the session; and
- the mental well-being of staff (including teaching assistants and volunteer parents) when trying to do many things simultaneously with a high degree of care and fidelity.

It is useful to consider these matters while keeping in mind the benefits of each approach, as outlined below.

Benefits of real-time data generation	*Benefits of deferred video data generation*
• **A more complete view of the room**: As the interventionists are physically located in the room, they can look around the space and see what else might be impacting on the children (e.g., other children walking past the room).	• **Ability to review footage:** Interventionists can rewatch the footage multiple times, increasing the accuracy of their observations.
• **Accounts for sensory factors:** Smells and subtle sounds that might have a large impact on some individuals with sensory differences but can be noted only by being physically present.	• **Focusing on subtle movements:** Sometimes the interactions of participants can be very subtle, and video footage allows for pausing and zooming in on hand gestures or other indicators of attempted communication.
• **Optimal use of time:** Generating data during Stage B means that it is not necessary to rewatch closely all of the footage after the session concludes.	• **A record of context:** When interventionists are busy, they sometimes notice only the behaviour, not the antecedents or consequences of that behaviour. Video footage can provide a context for these behaviours.

It is worth taking the time to discuss with your professional team which approach to use. There is no 'right' approach, only the approach that is right for your children and young adults, colleagues and yourself at this point in time. Both are valid and both will lead to important insights. If you are the sole interventionist, I strongly recommend using the video footage to complete the *Data generation sheet.*

Using the *Collaborative problem-solving empirical progressions* to assess learning

When I set out to design this intervention, I required a specialised tool that described in detail the different social components of collaboration, and then what each developmental level of these components should look like when being used in my intervention. Fortunately, I did not need to look very far. The University of Melbourne Assessment Research Centre had just completed the 'Assessment and Teaching of 21st Century Skills' (ATC21S) project. One product of this project was the previously mentioned set of developmental progressions, the *Collaborative problem-solving empirical progressions*, which unpack the social dimensions required for effective collaborative problem-solving. This is a valuable assessment and planning tool as it provides a particular social context in which a specific set of social skills are required (Hesse et al., 2015). As indicated by their name, these progressions focus on collaborative problem-solving and the performance of collaborative social skills. Augmented versions of the *Collaborative problem-solving empirical progressions* have been adapted for this book, presented as a series of rubrics contextualised for assessing collaboration during digital games–based social skills interventions.

Understanding the social dimensions of collaboration

To measure the level of collaborative sophistication of individuals during a group task, the ATC21S project used task analysis to identify three essential social dimensions required for collaborative problem-solving (Hesse et al., 2015). These social dimensions present a hierarchy of social skills and behaviours that children use to work together to solve a problem. These dimensions are:

Participation: the degree and quality of engagement of participants in completing the group task, which is conceptualised as independent work (or play) as the lowest form and progressing to increasingly sophisticated involvement in the group activity (Hesse et al., 2015).

Social regulation: the degree to which participants can recognise and manage the sharing of different tasks and activities within the group (Hesse et al., 2015).

Perspective-taking: the degree to which participants understand that others do not always see what they can see, and the degree to which they can adapt their communication to account for this (Hesse et al., 2015).

These social dimensions are added to two identified cognitive dimensions that involve the ways in which children learn and develop in those skills (Hesse et al., 2015): task regulation and knowledge building. However, as this book is focused on developing collaborative social skills, the emphasis in this chapter remains on the three social dimensions. The organisation of these skills is shown in the diagram below (adapted from Griffin et al., 2010), with the social dimensions shown on the left-hand side.

A developmental staircase for our participants to climb

When training interventionists how to use learning progressions to assess their children, I often use the metaphor of a staircase. The rubrics for participation, social regulation and perspective-taking are organised in order of performance sophistication (from Level A: Independent working, making progress or 'climbing' towards Level F: Cooperation and shared goals).

Before moving to the next level or step, a child must have demonstrated that they can independently and consistently perform the described behaviours of their current level. Given the profiles of the potential participants in this intervention, it is important to highlight that these progressions are designed for *all* learners, regardless of age or label of disability.

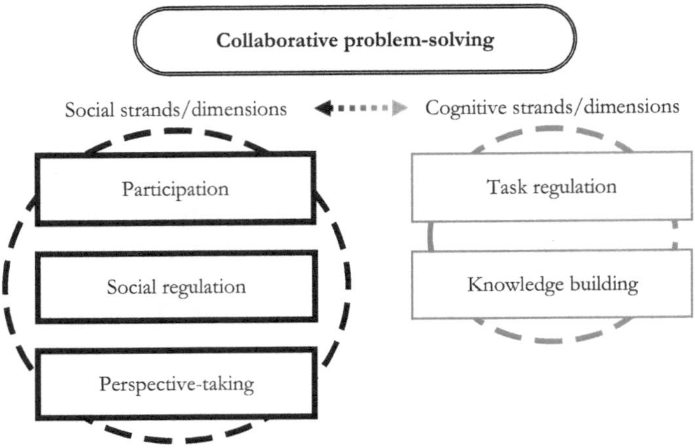

Figure 8.2 The dimensions of collaborative problem-solving.

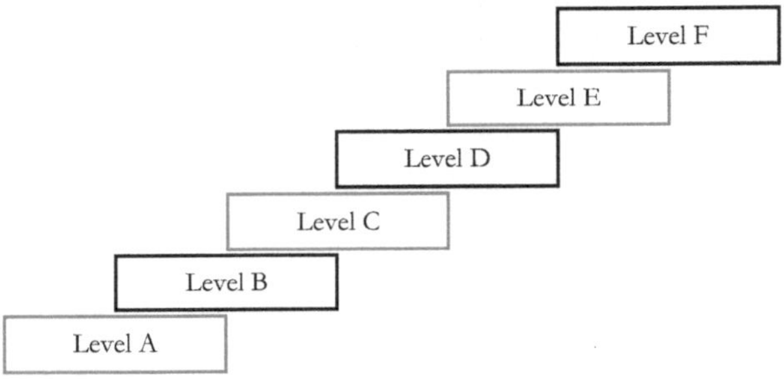

Figure 8.3 The developmental 'staircase'.

Assessing participation

In these progressions, participation involves examining the degree and quality of individual participation in completing the group task (Hesse et al., 2015). This dimension requires opportunities for children to work with others to complete a task. As has been the case with many children with whom I have worked over the years, individuals often first attempt to complete tasks independent of their peers. Needless to say, this is not collaboration. As children develop a more sophisticated level of participation, they begin to interact with their peers, prompting and responding to the contributions of others (Griffin et al., 2010; Hesse et al., 2015). The table below provides an overview of the indicative behaviours required for assessing levels of participation. Each includes a description of what this might look like in practice and is presented as a 'staircase' progression.

Assessing perspective-taking

In broad terms, perspective-taking is the degree to which children understand that others do not always see what they can see, and the degree to which they can adapt their communication to account for this (Hesse et al., 2015). When discussing contextually adjusting communication, Rehfeldt et al. (2007) emphasised an awareness of the potential for differences between an individual and their peers, defining perspective-taking as an individual's 'awareness of informational states in oneself and in others' (p. 24). This can be thought of as 'audience awareness', with more sophisticated levels of awareness resulting in an individual being able to adapt their own behaviour to increase the suitability for others. As previously provided for participation, the following table provides an overview of the indicative behaviours required for assessing levels of perspective-taking as children work from Level B (Supported working) towards Level F (Cooperation and shared goals).

Assessing social regulation

Social regulation is the third dimension within these progressions. Assessing the ability of a child to influence the actions of others might sound difficult

Table 8.2 Levels of participation and corresponding indicative behaviours

	Level	*Description of participation*
	E – Appreciated & valued partnership	• The child is able to participate actively in unfamiliar tasks. • The child initiates and promotes interaction with their partner often before entering their own answer.
	D – Mutual commitment	• The child perseveres to solve the task by repeating attempts and/or multiple strategies.
	C – Awareness of partnership	• The child demonstrates effort towards solving the problem. • The child discusses the task with their partner by responding to communication cues and requests.
	B – Supported working	• The child participates in the task when it is familiar. • Interaction between partners occurs more frequently but it is limited to only when it is necessary for completing the task.
	A – Independent working	• The child commences the task independently focusing on the instructions provided. • Interaction with their partner is limited to the beginning of a task and only in those situations where the instructions are clear.

Source: Adapted from Hesse et al., 2015.

Table 8.3 Levels of perspective-taking and corresponding indicative behaviours

	Level	*Perspective-taking*
	F – Cooperation & shared goals	• The child can tailor communication with their partner based on their awareness of their partner's understanding from the start of the task. • The child incorporates the contributions from their partner to suggest new solution paths or modify incorrect ones. • The child uses solutions provided by their partner and works more collaboratively through the problem-solving process.
	E – Appreciated & valued partnership	• The child acknowledges and responds to contributions from their partner but does not make changes to their original plan.
	D – Mutual commitment	• The child modifies communication with their partner to improve common understanding and share resources and information.
	C – Awareness of partnership	• The child makes contributions to their partner's understanding.
	B – Supported working	• The child is not overtly responsive to their partner, often taking a long time to respond or not responding at all and tends to ignore their partner's contributions.
		(Requires social interaction – **Participation Level B**)

Source: Adapted from Hesse et al., 2015.

to do, but in the context of this intervention we can think of social regulation as the degree to which individuals can recognise and manage the sharing of different tasks within a group (Hesse et al., 2015). Gesthuizen, Harrison and Latheef (2018) argue that self-evaluation of one's own performance is central to recognising when to control the actions of others. The following table provides an overview of the indicative behaviours required for assessing levels of social regulation as children increase their sophistication in their social interactions. Once again, participants are working towards Level F (Cooperation and shared goals).

These progressions offer a means for identifying the levels of proficiency that the children demonstrated in collaborative problem-solving. They also serve as a point of reference for sequencing goals. Once you have assessed what each participant is ready to learn, it is important to plan how to make progress towards the next developmental level. By reviewing the strategies noted in the previous chapter for promoting the use of the 15 Target Skills, you can plan how to encourage your participants to combine these skills in increasingly sophisticated ways as described in the three progressions.

Table 8.4 Levels of social regulation and corresponding indicative behaviours

Level	*Social regulation*
F – Cooperation & shared goals	• The child assumes group responsibility for the success of the task. • The child can manage conflicts with partners successfully, resolving differences before proceeding on a possible solution path. • The child is able to evaluate their overall performance in the task. • The child is able to evaluate the strengths and/or weaknesses of their partner based on their performance during the task.
E – Appreciated & valued partnership	• The child attempts to resolve differences in understanding with their partner but resolution of differences is not reached. • The child is able to comment on their partner's performance during the task.
D – Mutual commitment	• The child comments on or shares information with their partner regarding their own performance while attempting the task. • The child is aware of their partner's performance on the task.
C – Awareness of partnership	• The child has a common understanding with their partners of the problem. • The child reports to their partner regarding their own activities on the task.
B – Supported working	• The child still works largely independently, taking responsibility for their own actions during the task. • The child is aware of their own level of performance during the task.
	(Requires social interaction – **Participation Level B**)

Source: Adapted from Hesse et al., 2015.

Sharing assessment data with colleagues, families and caregivers

Using the *Collaborative problem-solving empirical progressions* can be useful for communicating with a range of audiences what a child is ready to learn. Co-analysing where a child sits in relation to each of the three domains can be helpful in providing a common language and vocabulary between team members for sharing their observations of the learner. Likewise, reviewing these rubrics with families and caregivers can allow for an exchange of understandings about what the participants in this intervention should be working on during the sessions. We just need to acknowledge the limitations of using this instrument in making judgements about an individual child. These progressions provide an informal, non-normed assessment that interventionists can use without any specialised training. This means that while they are accessible for anyone to use, they are not clinical and should not be used in isolation for reporting in legal documents, such as individual education plans, or in applications for government funding.

Assessment data from other sources can help to 'fill in the gaps' for areas not covered in the *Collaborative problem-solving empirical progressions*. If you are running an intervention in conjunction with other specialist allied health programs, such as speech and language pathology sessions, it is important to share information and assessment data where feasible. As interventionists working with the same child, you can incorporate their assessment data into your own decision-making processes and share ideas for goal setting and prioritisation. As a professional, I strongly encourage you to ask families and caregivers to share their lived expertise and knowledge about their child, including what they think the participant is ready to learn. Collaboration is key to ensuring that we are all working with each other, rather than against each other, to improve outcomes for our children.

Summary of key ideas in Chapter 8

- Data help inform which skills we focus on in our intervention and should be generated in every session. We use these data to analyse how participants are responding to our instruction and coaching and to track the degree to which children are using the Target Skills independently.
- One indicator that children are improving their ability to collaborate with their peers is an increase in the number of times they use each Target Skill *(frequency counts)*.
- We also need to understand why children use these skills in particular contexts but not others. There could be barriers created by other children, interventionists or the game that prevent children from using a Target Skill effectively. To add this texture to our frequency counts, we also create *field notes*.
- The *Data generation sheet* is a tool for conducting frequency counts and creating field notes. This simplifies and streamlines the processes of data generation while simultaneously implementing the intervention.
- The *Collaborative problem-solving empirical progressions* (Hesse et al., 2015) specifically measure the collaborative sophistication of individuals and can serve as a 'learning map' for interventionists. These progressions highlight different levels of participation, perspective-taking and social regulation.

References

Gesthuizen, R., Harrison, M., & Latheef, I. (2018). Exploring social regulation in minecraft. *Australian Council for computers in education 2018 conference proceedings*, Sydney, Australia, pp. 17–37.

Grau, V., & Whitebread, D. (2012). Self and social regulation of learning during collaborative activities in the classroom: The interplay of individual and group cognition. *Learning and Instruction, 22*(6), 401–412.

Griffin, P. (2018). *Assessment for teaching* (2nd ed.). Cambridge University Press.

Griffin, P., Murray, L., Care, E., Thomas, A., & Perri, P. (2010). Developmental assessment: Lifting literacy through professional learning teams. *Assessment in Education: Principles, Policy & Practice, 17*(4), 383–397.

Hesse, F., Care, E., Buder, J., Sassenberg, K., & Griffin, P. (2015). A framework for teachable collaborative problem solving skills. In P. Griffin & E. Care (Eds.), *Assessment and teaching of 21st century skills: Methods and approach* (pp. 37–56). Springer.

Rehfeldt, R. A., Dillen, J. E., Ziomek, M. M., & Kowalchuk, R. K. (2007). Assessing relational learning deficits in perspective-taking in children with high-functioning autism spectrum disorder. *The Psychological Record, 57*(1), 23–47.

Volet, S., Vauras, M., & Salonen, P. (2009). Self-and social regulation in learning contexts: An integrative perspective. *Educational Psychologist, 44*(4), 215–226.

Resources

In this section you will find photocopiable versions of the following resources:

- the *Data generation sheet*; and
- a printable copy of the *Collaborative problem-solving empirical progressions.*

Data generation sheet

			Field notes	Skill performance frequency counts				
Participant names + goal Target Skills	Name:	Goal:		1. Doing our jobs	2. Taking turns	3. Using our voice to give instructions	4. Giving non-verbal instruction	5. Offering help
				6. Sharing task information	7. Listening to others	8. Check for understanding	9. Quiet voices	10. Asking for help
				11. Requesting task information	12. Asking your friends for ideas	13. Requesting performance feedback	14. Encouraging others	15. Providing performance feedback
	Name:	Goal:		1. Doing our jobs	2. Taking turns	3. Using our voice to give instructions	4. Giving non-verbal instruction	5. Offering help
				6. Sharing task information	7. Listening to others	8. Check for understanding	9. Quiet voices	10. Asking for help
				11. Requesting task information	12. Asking your friends for ideas	13. Requesting performance feedback	14. Encouraging others	15. Providing performance feedback
	Name:	Goal:		1. Doing our jobs	2. Taking turns	3. Using our voice to give instructions	4. Giving non-verbal instruction	5. Offering help
				6. Sharing task information	7. Listening to others	8. Check for understanding	9. Quiet voices	10. Asking for help
				11. Requesting task information	12. Asking your friends for ideas	13. Requesting performance feedback	14. Encouraging others	15. Providing performance feedback

Level	*Participation*	*Perspective-taking*	*Social regulation*
F – Cooperation & shared goals		• The child can tailor communication with their partner based on their awareness of their partner's understanding from the start of the task. • The child incorporates the contributions from their partner to suggest new solution paths or modify incorrect ones. • The child uses solutions provided by their partner and works more collaboratively through the problem-solving process.	• The child assumes group responsibility for the success of the task. • The child can manage conflicts with partners successfully, resolving differences before proceeding on a possible solution path. • The child is able to evaluate their overall performance in the task. • The child is able to evaluate the strengths and/or weaknesses of their partner based on their performance during the task.
E – Appreciated & valued partnership	• The child is able to participate actively in unfamiliar tasks. • The child initiates and promotes interaction with their partner often before entering their own answer.	• The child acknowledges and responds to contributions from their partner but does not make changes to their original plan.	• The child attempts to resolve differences in understanding with their partner but resolution of differences is not reached. • The child is able to comment on their partner's performance during the task.
D – Mutual commitment	• The child perseveres to solve the task by repeating attempts and/or multiple strategies.	• The child modifies communication with their partner to improve common understanding and share resources and information.	• The child comments on or shares information with their partner regarding their own performance while attempting the task. • The child is aware of their partner's performance on the task.

Source: Adapted from Hesse et al. (2015).

C – Awareness of partnership	• The child demonstrates effort towards solving the problem. • The child discusses the task with their partner by responding to communication cues and requests.	• The child makes contributions to their partner's understanding.	• The child has a common understanding with their partner of the problem. • The child reports to their partner regarding their own activities on the task.
B – Supported working	• The child participates in the task when it is familiar. • Interaction between partners occurs more frequently but it is limited to only when it is necessary for completing the task.	• The child is not overtly responsive to their partner, often taking a long time to respond or not responding at all and tends to ignore their partner's contributions.	• The child still works largely independently taking responsibility for their own actions during the task. • The child is aware of their own level of performance during the task.
A – Independent working	• The child commences the task independently focusing on the instructions provided. • Interaction with their partner is limited to the beginning of a task and only in those situations where the instructions are clear.		

Source: Adapted from Hesse et al. (2015).

9 Game design that creates the conditions for collaboration

Introduction

Game design plays an important part in creating the conditions for collaboration. But not all games are created equal. While interventionists explicitly teach and coach children to perform the Target Skills at the point of need, games create the opportunities to *use* these skills. Depending on the design of a game, players might be less likely or more likely to perform certain skills as a result of what the game demands of them. The ways in which games guide players to interact with each other are so important for the effectiveness of this intervention. Chapter 9 shares 39 recommendations for game design identified through my research that can help you, as interventionists, analyse and make informed decisions about which games to use within your settings. As depicted in the diagram below, these 39 recommendations have been grouped within four overarching themes.

To arrive at these recommendations, I coded hours upon hours of footage at the University of Melbourne International Centre for Classroom Research. Through this process, it was possible to analyse the behaviours of players across a range of games and to identify connections between how the games positioned the players in the virtual (game) world and the interactions taking place between the players. While these 39 recommendations will be useful for interventionists when evaluating existing games, this innovative analysis also offers game designers insights into developing more effective and inclusive games in the future.

Using example games to illustrate these recommendations

Some interventionists reading this book might not be familiar with games or gaming, but the wonderful thing about this intervention is that you do not need to be an expert gamer. To assist in getting your head around the 39 recommendations for what to look for when selecting a game, I introduce four games in this chapter as described below to illustrate why each recommendation is important. These four games are Rayman Legends, Kirby and the Rainbow Paintbrush, Super Mario 3D World and Star Fox Zero.

DOI: 10.4324/9781003025917-9

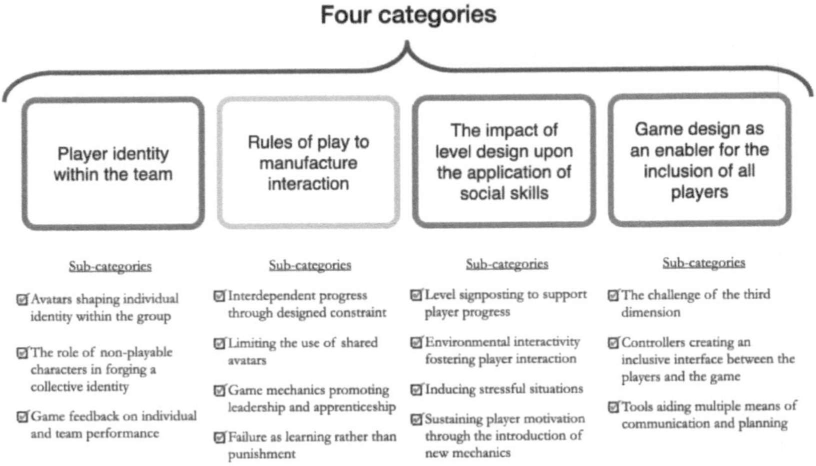

Figure 9.1 Four overarching themes capturing 39 recommendations.

Rayman Legends

Rayman Legends (Ubisoft, 2013), referred to as **Rayman**, is a cooperative 2D platform game (similar in style to the classic Super Mario Bros.). Players work together to navigate their protagonists through the levels, adhering to the established genre conventions. However, there is a twist! These players receive assistance from another player using the Wii U Gamepad's touch screen to control the character *Murfy*.

- This character can move around the screen much like a mouse cursor and can manipulate the environment to assist the progress of the other players.
- Unlike the other characters, *Murfy* is not constrained by gravity and cannot lose life or hit points, but the successful completion of a section requires the other characters to scroll the screen and get to a designated checkpoint intact.
- The effect of these design choices fosters situations in which players have to coordinate their actions with the player controlling *Murfy* in order to solve puzzles to move through the game.

Kirby and the Rainbow Paintbrush

Kirby and the Rainbow Paintbrush (Nintendo, 2015), referred to as **Kirby**, is another cooperative 2D platform game. Unlike **Rayman**, the protagonist *Kirby* is indirectly controlled by using the stylus and touch screen to draw a line from the character to where they want him to go, using the *Rainbow Paintbrush*.

- In this game the player has a limited supply of energy to draw this line, and they cannot move *Kirby* while this supply is depleted and slowly recharging. This has the effect of leaving *Kirby* prone and vulnerable to attack, which is where the other players have an important role.
- These other players control *Waddle Dees* and serve as protectors of *Kirby*. If these characters run out of life, they are temporarily out of the game but soon restored to full health. Think of it as a small time-out from play.
- On the other hand, if *Kirby* loses all of his health, it is game over for everyone.
- Only *Kirby* can progress the screen, so other players have to ensure that *Kirby* can move forward safely.
- The player controlling *Kirby* can also use the *Rainbow Paintbrush* to paint temporary lines to shield other players from falling projectiles or to serve as platforms for them to jump on and reach higher ground.

Super Mario 3D World

Super Mario 3D World (Nintendo, 2013), referred to as **Mario**, is a semi-cooperative 3D platform game. Much like the previous two games, **Mario** tasks players with working together to defeat enemies, solve puzzles and reach the endpoint of the game.

- Certain sections of the game require the coordination of movement and activity, such as the concurrent flicking of switches. However, unlike the previous two games, the players are mostly free to run ahead and leave their peers behind.
- To a certain extent, the game even encourages this via a 'king of the hill' mechanic. This mechanic involves awarding the first person to reach the end of level flag with a crown for their avatar to wear in the subsequent level, denoting them as the current 'king' of the game.
- These game design decisions create a tension, requiring players to cooperate in order to progress, but also encouraging them to maintain a degree of competitive independence from their peers.
- **Mario** is also a more complex game when compared with **Rayman** and **Kirby** due to the game requiring players to navigate levels on a three-dimensional plane. Players have to solve more complex puzzles, particularly because of the more sophisticated physics engine underpinning this game in comparison to two-dimensional platform games.
- This game also delights in playing with user expectations by defying long-established genre conventions, such as which platforms are safe to stand on and which items should be collected.

Star Fox Zero

Star Fox Zero (Nintendo, 2016) or **Star Fox**, is a cooperative action game and falls within the subgenre of 'on-rails shooter'. This game has two co-pilots sharing a common *Arwing* aircraft. One player serves as the pilot steering the spacecraft, and the other player serves as the gunner, shooting at enemy targets.

- There are two key differences between **Star Fox** and the previous three example games. The first is the shared control of a common avatar, the *Arwing*, creating a level of co-dependence not available in the other games, and there is no allowance for individual action within the game.
- The second difference is the genre of the game and the implications its conventions have for participants. **Star Fox** is a 3D action game, which alternates between sections of the game being on-rails, where the pilot's field of movement is restricted, and sections where the pilot has the freedom to fly anywhere.
- This genre is known for the speed of the action occurring on-screen and allows little time for processing or hesitation in communication between the pilot and the gunner.

While discussing the 39 recommendations below, I refer to these games to help explain what their design considerations look like in action and to help you think about other games you might consider using as part of your intervention.

Player identity within the team

One of the most interesting game design considerations is the way that aesthetic components interact with the game rules, the mechanics of play and the narrative to produce a sense of player identity. This is evident in the design and 'feel' of the playable avatars used in a game, and what this means for individual identity within a group. The degree to which these avatars serve as utilitarian tools or in-game projections of the player in the physical world is central to understanding this relationship. Furthermore, how each game uses non-playable characters to manipulate and shape the relationships between players is important in considering how the game positions each player as a member of a collective team.

Avatars shaping individual identity within the group

While not true of every game, many games use playable 'avatars', or characters, who represent the player in the virtual world. For example, in the game **Rayman**, the players can play as *Rayman* or his friends. Familiar character designs are useful in allowing players to identify themselves and their allies in the virtual environment. My research has found that children often have an 'instrumental view' of their avatars, with players needing to recognise their avatars as the tools through which they interact with the game world and their peers. Players knowing which avatars they are controlling is an essential first step in virtual world collaboration, but, as interventionists, you need to be mindful of the role of familiarity in creating expectations about these avatars. Some avatars are immediately familiar to participants as they appear in a whole series of games. This makes the task of self-identification and peer identification much easier and creates a wave of excitement and anticipation for the players. A classic example of this is *Mario* in **Super Mario 3D World**. Other avatars will be new to most of the participants and it will take time for children to become familiar with them.

As avatars serve as tools of agency, players need to differentiate between their peers and other characters and objects in the virtual world. While **Mario** provides a distinct virtual appearance for every player's avatar, **Kirby** provides different colour variations of the same model for players in the secondary roles. Using visually similar models can be problematic, as players can forget which of their physical world allies is controlling which avatar in the virtual world. This is less likely to be an issue in **Mario**, as players often know the names of popular characters. This can actually increase verbal communication as players can confirm with their peers who is using which avatar by name. Also important is the ability to recognise friend from foe, with the use of different colour palettes and distinctive designs providing useful visual cues for players who might have trouble recalling the cast of characters within a game universe.

When given the choice to select an avatar, the primary aesthetic concern for the children with whom I have worked is that their avatar reflects how they want others in the group to see them. Everyone wants to fit in and perception matters to all children. When given the choice to select their characters, players should be allowed some degree of freedom to select how they want to be represented in the virtual world. Although in a perfect world this would not be the case, in many of the settings in which I have run this intervention, issues around gender representation have emerged. The reasons for this are complex, but many games still present a very binary and stereotypical representation of female characters. The character *Princess Peach* provides an excellent example of dated representation. When playing **Mario**, children who strongly identify as male often argue that they do not want to play as the sole female protagonist, *Princess Peach*, yet the game requires one of the players to play as this character in the four-player mode. The caution here is that character design needs to be thoughtful to avoid perpetuating negative stereotypes. You should look for games that provide players with choices as to how they are represented.

RECOMMENDATIONS

1 Familiar character designs are useful in allowing players to identify themselves and their allies in the virtual environment.
2 There needs to be a distinct visual difference between player avatars and enemies.
3 When players select their avatars, they should have a choice on how they are represented aesthetically in the game.

The role of non-playable characters in forging a collective identity

Video games often include a cast of non-playable characters who serve a number of roles and with whom players can interact. Non-playable characters in cooperative multiplayer games usually adhere to one of three roles, with each role having a different impact on social interactions between the players. The first role is providing advice on the mechanics of the game, including introducing the rules of play and explaining the value of new capabilities to players. These characters are tools designed to establish the goals and norms of the game. This, in turn, shapes the collective identity. For interventionists, directly referring to the advice provided by these characters, particularly through spoken dialogue, is useful in modelling the language that players can use in providing instruction to their peers. The second role is to help advance the narrative or to build a sense of a 'lived in' world for the players to explore. Narratives can help provide meaning and emotional investment in the goals, functioning as a way of keeping players engaged in the cooperative play. The third role is to assist the players by becoming an active participant in the gameplay, using artificial intelligence (AI) to play alongside the other players. To promote an environment conducive to collaboration between players, non-playable characters should provide players with advice and build the narrative but should leave the actual gameplay to the humans.

The idea of requiring a coordinated approach to defeating enemies is epitomised in the way games often use end of level 'bosses' as the penultimate test of player skill. Larger enemies, such as *Whispy Woods* in **Kirby** and *Bowser* in **Super Mario 3D World**, are more complex, creating lengthier events involving players having to combine their individual capabilities. When the game requires players to coordinate their actions by distributing abilities between different characters, this creates a sense of positive interdependence between the players (González-González & Blanco-Izquierdo, 2012; Zea et al., 2009). This provides fertile ground for teaching social skills at the point of need during these interactions. To facilitate the performance of the Target Skills, boss battles should require a high degree of group planning, problem-solving and coordination. Rather than introducing new concepts or character moves, the focus should be on the simultaneous application of previously rehearsed player capabilities.

RECOMMENDATIONS

4 Non-playable computer-controlled allies should provide players with advice and build the narrative but should have limited impact on the actual gameplay.

5 Defeating some enemies should require multiple steps from multiple players.

6 Boss battles should require group planning, problem-solving and coordination through the simultaneous application of previously rehearsed skills.

Game feedback on individual and team performance

In this intervention, players receive feedback in the virtual world from the game and in the physical world from both interventionists and peers. Feedback systems employed by the game can provide important information on the performance of individual players and, more importantly, the degree to which the team is working as a cohesive unit. Findings from my research reinforce the importance of feedback in increasing the frequency and sophistication of performing the Target Skills. While we might argue that the feedback systems in commercial games focus on improving skill in the game, and not the performance of social skills, feedback systems have an important part to play. My research has confirmed that immediate feedback is essential for ensuring that players are continuously monitoring and evaluating their individual contributions to the team. Feedback on individual performance within the game can help in providing metrics through which the players can evaluate their own play and that of their peers. Game-based feedback should focus on player performance in working towards the goals of the game. When used in conjunction with feedback systems in the physical environment (discussed earlier in this book), we can use this task-level information to improve individual performance in fulfilling each player's role in the collective team. As such, games designed to promote social interaction should focus on providing individual-level feedback important for achieving the goals of the team, with feedback on the performance of Target Skills provided by interventionists.

While considering what is emphasised in game feedback, we also need to consider how games convey information to players. As this information is a key consideration for all players in improving their role performance, it is important that everyone can access and interpret it. Feedback can include a numerical score, but it should also include supporting visual, audio and haptic cues so that a wide range of players can interpret this information. Delaying the quantification of performance until a period of non-play can allow the children space to practise social skills without the added pressure of hearing how they are doing in comparison to their peers. From a learning perspective, providing more detailed feedback when the player is not being asked to do anything else reduces the cognitive load. This allows players sufficient time for processing and evaluating their play in light of this information.

RECOMMENDATIONS

7 Players should receive individual-level feedback. This is important to them in fulfilling their individual roles within the team during gameplay.

8 Feedback related to progress towards the collective goal should emphasise team-level feedback over individual-level feedback.

9 Feedback should be accessible to all players using multiple modes of representation and allow for sufficient processing time.

Rules of play to manufacture interaction

Beyond building player identity, games can also use targeted mechanics or rules of play to manufacture social interactions between players. Within cooperative multiplayer games, a spectrum of individual limitations and co-dependence exists, with the introduction of some form of constraint upon individual players, creating a degree of interdependence between individuals.

Interdependent progress through designed constraint

Co-located gaming often uses one of two techniques to ensure that all players can view themselves in the virtual environment: a subdivided portion of the screen for each player, known as a 'split screen'; or a 'shared screen' that keeps all players locked to a common space. All four example games presented in this chapter use shared screens, although some of the games listed in *Chapter 10* use split windows where every player has their own 'mini screen'. Interestingly, shared-screen games often have diverging rules to determine when the shared perspective 'scrolls' to a new scene in the level. For example, **Kirby** locks the camera to its titular protagonist, with the responsible player controlling what all players can see and the direction the team travels through the level. This creates a form of 'asymmetrical interdependence' with the privileging of one player over the other players. If a player who is not playing as the primary character moves too far out of frame, they are teleported back to *Kirby*. **Rayman** and **Mario** are more democratic, with the camera following the majority of players. In the event a player moves too far away from the pack, this lone player is placed in a 'bubble' and returned to the other players.

Designed constraint also has a role in ensuring regular participation from all players regardless of skill. Overcoming obstacles or puzzles to progress provides a means through which the game can achieve regular participation of all players. The strategic distribution of required capabilities amongst the players is important as this manufactures a need for everyone to have a role. Ideally the game should provide every player with a clearly defined purpose. In **Rayman** this is evident in the relationship between the characters *Rayman* and *Murfy* in a level titled *Dungeon Dash*. To progress, *Rayman* must reach the end of the level safely, but this is not possible without *Murfy* lowering and raising an intricate set of bridges, gates and platforms. To complete the level, both players must be involved, using their distinct but complementary capabilities. While the addition of more player-controlled avatars does dilute the role of *Rayman* in this level, *Murfy* remains centrally important. As group participation is a prerequisite for developing other social skills, active engagement in the group activity is vitally important. It is essential to minimise the amount of time a player is passive within the game by presenting puzzles or obstacles requiring the involvement of all players.

RECOMMENDATIONS

10 Screen scrolling should require all avatars to be in close proximity to ensure more skilful players remain with less skilful players, and to provide opportunities for democratic decision making.

11 Active participation should be manufactured through the use of puzzles or obstacles requiring the involvement of all players.

12 Specific capabilities should be distributed amongst the avatars so that they need to be combined with the capabilities of other avatars in order to progress.

Limiting the use of shared avatars

Sharing a common avatar forces the most intimate forms of coordination but can cause high levels of frustration. Some children need more auditory processing time, particularly when processing a quick succession of verbal instructions from their peers, so a near-constant requirement for verbal communication can present a significant barrier. In **Star Fox** the capabilities of the *Arwing* fighter are distributed between two players. My research into the use of these mechanics in an intervention found that, regardless of whether all players have access to the same capabilities, a significant challenge exists when players share the same resources. These shared resources include power-up items, scoring items and, most notably, a health bar. Should the shared avatar crash or be destroyed, every player has to restart the mission. Such design decisions stand in contrast to the individual agency that a number of digital games researchers believe underpin video games as effective spaces for learning (Bidarra et al., 2013; Gee, 2007; Squire, 2005). Instead, **Star Fox** creates complete co-dependency, with the action or inaction of one player possibly causing the failure of all players. Complete co-dependency invokes high-stakes cooperative gaming, providing very little accommodation for less skilful players. As we want to ensure our children are in an emotional state conducive to collaborative problem-solving and constructive social interactions, this can present a big problem. If you select a game using shared avatars, it should provide differentiated roles for different skill levels. An example of this would be if the pilot role in **Star Fox** had an option for a simplified control scheme to allow a proficient player to work with an expert controlling the weapons systems (unfortunately, it does not have this option).

RECOMMENDATIONS

13 Ideally games with shared avatars should allow players to progress through the level at their own pace without forced movement.

14 Games using shared avatars should provide differentiated roles for different skill levels.

Game mechanics promoting leadership and apprenticeship

An interesting finding from my research has been that certain game mechanics can encourage players to take on leadership roles within the group. This is particularly the case when players are learning how to play the game and/or determining the most effective strategies for overcoming challenging segments of a level. Over the years I have found that drawing on the wealth of knowledge of the experienced gamers in my groups has provided clear opportunities for peer mentoring and coaching. Peer mentoring requires expert gamers to be familiar with the rules and strategies of the games being played, but they do not need to be experts in the first session. In one of my studies, the metagame became part of this project as the participating children went home to research the games that were unfamiliar to them. Researchers such Gee (2018) and Hayes and Duncan (2012) have long highlighted the inherently social nature of knowledge generation in gaming 'affinity spaces', such as conversations in Twitch and YouTube comments. Expertise can be generated by players refining their understandings through these online discussions. As interventionists I strongly believe we should cherish and build on these positive online social interactions.

Games such as **Kirby** feature a primary protagonist controlled by a single player, with the other players serving in support roles. This places the weight of responsibility and agency on the person in this primary role, positioning the person using this character as the de facto leader of the group. My research has found that if the person in the primary role is considered by the playing group to be an expert, this can actually be detrimental to the performance of some Target Skills. However, if the player placed in the primary role is viewed as requiring assistance, this can provide fertile opportunities for the more experienced players in secondary roles to coach and support this player. This, in turn, supports their team members in achieving the common goal. This means that if a game does adopt a designed imbalance in agency between playable characters, either the design of the game or the interventionist needs to ensure that players switch between these primary and secondary roles within the team. This ensures that every player experiences some level of agency and provides peer coaching opportunities through the sharing of experiences.

When a game uses characters with largely similar or identical capabilities and roles within the team play, game mechanics must ensure that less skilful players still have a required and regular role in achieving the team goal. This can be achieved through a number of designed mechanics, such as requiring a certain number of players to move an obstacle or a number of players standing together on a switch to open a door. When less knowledgeable players are required to do something in the virtual world, this provides an opportunity for experienced players to offer instructions and clarify understanding.

RECOMMENDATIONS

15 The game should support peer coaching by adopting established genre conventions, allowing experienced players to utilise their knowledge to coach novice players.
16 Players should have opportunities to switch between primary and secondary roles in the team.
17 The play mechanics should allow less skilful players to have a required and regular role in achieving the team goal.

Failure as learning rather than punishment

Failure in video games can play an important part in players developing their knowledge and skills of the game (Gee, 2013). However, in my experience, this is true only when the players reflect actively upon what went wrong and how they could approach a problem or event differently in the next attempt. My research reaffirmed that for this to be possible, players need to be in an emotional state that is conducive to such honest self and peer analysis. While, of course, interventionists and participating children have important roles in the regulation of individual and collective emotional states, game design also has a role. Part of this role is ensuring that players feel that failure is fair. While common goals are important, players should have independent, individual health bars to ensure that more skilled players are not penalised by less skilled players. When games require active participation to progress but also reward individual skill, a playing environment is set that allows for emotionally devised peer coaching. Notably, it is through this peer coaching that I have observed some of the most sophisticated uses of the Target Skills.

Building upon this idea of 'fair failure', when individual players are unsuccessful, they need to be able to reflect on the reasons why and reattempt the challenge in a timely manner. This is a delicate balancing act for interventionists and game designers to manage, as reinstating a player in the game too quickly can often deny them the opportunity to reflect adequately on their performance and reduce the sense of risk and challenge. In my experience, interventionists can support self-reflection by giving players a short period of time as observers of the action, allowing them to view how other players approach challenges. However, if players are removed from the game for too long, there is a risk of disengagement (Garzotto, 2007). To ensure that games remain 'pleasantly frustrating', getting this difficulty curve right is essential. When a player's avatar dies and those of their peers are still alive, that player should be able to 'respawn' relatively quickly so they do not feel disengaged from the game.

In terms of determining the relative consequences of collective failure, once again there needs to be a balance between motivating players in trying to be successful and ensuring that players are not discouraged by disproportionately harsh punishments. Games should have multiple checkpoints within a level, so when all of the players' avatars are killed, they can return to an area close to where they died. Using a shared bank of 'lives' can be detrimental in promoting positive social interactions among the players. The limited nature of this resource can result in more skilful players becoming frustrated when the team receives the dreaded 'Game Over' screen as a result of the disproportionate number of deaths from less skilful players.

RECOMMENDATIONS

18 Players should have independent, individual health bars to ensure that more skilled players are not penalised by less skilled players.
19 When a player's avatar dies while those of their peers are still alive, this player should be able to 'respawn' relatively quickly, and there should be an element of player interactivity in this waiting time.
20 Games need to have multiple checkpoints within a level so that when all players' avatars are killed, they can return to an area close to where they died.

The impact of level design upon the performance of social skills

In addition to the designed capabilities of the avatars and the rules of the game world, level design has a significant impact on the way players interact within the virtual and the physical environments. This includes the impact of different forms of level signposting on decision making, promoting interactions between players, inducing tension and stressful situations and sustaining player motivation and investment in achieving the team goal.

Level signposting to support player progress

Signposting the ways in which levels support and guide the players towards achieving their team goal influences how players can understand that goal. I have found that sharing a common understanding of the team goal is vitally important in coordinating actions between team members. Confirming my earlier observations as a teacher implementing games-based interventions, my research has found that, for children with cognitive challenges, this clarity is of the utmost importance. This is especially true when discussing clarity of directional movement, in other words, knowing where to go in the game. While in other contexts games that require exploration and freedom of navigation in large open worlds might be beneficial, games being used to facilitate interactions between the players need to maintain some form of linearity to focus the attention of players. As noted earlier, the use of a shared-screen mechanic, by necessity, also results in limiting independent exploration. Levels should follow a largely linear path so that all players have a general understanding of the direction in which they need to move. The emphasis must be placed on how players can work together to progress towards the shared destination.

Signposting is also important in highlighting to players the safe areas of a level and which areas to avoid. Aesthetic cues, such as glowing red lava accompanied by the sounds of fire burning, are examples of visual and auditory warnings to players to stay away from these hazards within the level. Obvious cues are important when a hazard will result in instant failure, ensuring that every player understands the risk. Other environmental hazards, such as the swinging axes in the background of a level in **Rayman**, provide subtler visual cues to signal that these objects will injure the player's avatar, but they will not cause instant death. In this example, the blades of the axes have an animated glint of light reflecting from them. While this sounds like an obscure warning, this cue is used throughout the game to signify when environmental objects are 'active' (rather than decorative) and will have some positive or negative impact upon the player. These little signs can help players with cognitive challenges to recognise where they need to go and how they can navigate the game environment successfully.

RECOMMENDATIONS

21 Levels should follow a largely linear path so that all players have a general understanding of the direction in which they need to move.

22 Hidden paths leading to special items or bonuses can be included, but players should always be able to return to the more linear sections of the level.

23 High-stakes hazards, such as bottomless pits, should have a clear visual cue that these will cause instant failure and should be avoided.

Environmental interactivity fostering player interaction

One means by which designers engage players through level design is environmental interactivity. This refers to non-sentient elements of a level that the player can manipulate in some way through an action. Interactivity can be categorised into two broad types. 'Optional interaction' gives players the choice to manipulate the environment to gain some sort of benefit; 'mandatory interaction' requires players to manipulate the environment before they can progress.

Optional interactivity can be a clever design mechanic, providing a means for more skilful or knowledgeable players to reduce the difficulty barrier for their peers through indirect forms of assistance. For example, in **Rayman** there are sections of levels that include switches that provide temporary bridges. While not required to complete the level, these bridges allow players to traverse this section of the level, avoiding more challenging enemies directly below them. The use of such optional interactive devices provides a means for proficient players, who might not necessarily have the language to assist their peers, to still find a way to support and nurture these players. In my analysis of skill performance during play, some of the highest frequencies of interaction between players were recorded in the sections of **Rayman** that included these devices, particularly with players providing evaluative feedback on collective performance. These sections proved to be particularly effective in motivating those expert players who were otherwise hesitant to communicate verbally, as these sections required a clear understanding by all players of their respective roles. The expert gamers clarified not only the role of the less experienced players in these scenarios, but also their own role within the team. Interventionists can build on such opportunities to highlight the importance of providing clear explanations and checking for understanding.

Frequent use of optional interactivity is ideal for providing players some agency in terms of how often they decide to take these options. However, 'optionality' can also present challenges when working with players with social-emotional differences. Inherently, some children might not be concerned about the welfare or success of their peers, so for an intervention focusing on social skills performance they require some impetus to interact with their peers. Level design that uses mandatory interactivity is one means of encouraging these players to consider the role of their teammates. Obstacles in a level might require multiple players to interact in a coordinated fashion in order to proceed, such as the coordinated detonation of bomb blocks to destroy an impeding boulder in **Kirby**. On first thought, this might seem like an opportunity for players to 'check out', but, in my research and teaching, in every instance of players encountering such obstacles they attempted to work with their teammates. These experiences serve as a significant illustration of the power of game design in provoking social interaction where there might otherwise be none.

RECOMMENDATIONS

24 Levels should include optional interactive objects that can assist the progress of another player, such as switches that provide a temporary bridge.

25 Obstacles in some levels may mandate the interaction of multiple players before they are allowed to proceed, such as the synchronised detonation of bomb blocks to destroy an impeding boulder.

26 There should be minimal pressure on players when new interactive objects and obstacles are first introduced, allowing them room for error and time to coordinate their actions correctly until they are familiar with how they work.

Inducing 'stressful situations'

One of the most powerful benefits of well-designed video games is their ability to motivate through adherence to the 'Goldilocks principle', namely, providing the appropriate level of challenge by not being too easy or too hard. This is more difficult when games involve multiple players with varying levels of skill. One way for games to gradually increase the level of challenge is by having players use well-rehearsed skills in scenarios designed to create a sense of stress (Gee, 2013; Squire, 2005). Stressful situations can be induced by mechanics such as a giant wall of fire chasing the players in the *Dungeon Dash* level in **Rayman**. In this level, players use skills they have been practising over the previous levels, but now they have to execute these skills in a timely fashion. Visual and audio cues build the sense of tension, from the more obvious effect of the large-scale wall of fire to the change in colour tones around the players' avatars as the wall gets closer to them. Findings from my research suggest that all players should have sufficient 'safe' time to practice using such mechanics and, in stressful situations, use only mechanics with which they are familiar.

To ensure that these situations encourage a collective approach to planning and problem-solving, these designed situations should require input from all players. However, ways should be available for more skilful players to offer in-game assistance to their peers. This can involve these skilful players being able to use objects or items to temporarily reduce the pressure on the team, removing the immediate risk to less skilful players. When these mechanics are combined with sections of a level that require all players to complete an action in order to progress, optional in-game assistance can help in shaping a peer-mentoring relationship between the players. Through this relationship, players will have the opportunity to rehearse and perform a range of Target Skills.

RECOMMENDATIONS

27 In stressful situations, players should use only mechanics with which they are familiar, with sufficient 'safe' time allowed for practice.

28 The game should communicate to players when stressful situations will end.

29 Designed stressful situations should require input from all players and should allow players to offer in-game assistance to each other to reduce the immediacy of failure.

Sustaining player motivation through the introduction of new mechanics

As an overarching goal of this intervention is to use video games to encourage active participation, it is essential that the game designs motivate players. One way to do this is through the introduction of new mechanics at regular intervals, helping to maintain a sense of constant discovery. Each introduction of a new mechanic is also important in providing additional opportunities for interactions between the players. Level design has an important role to play in ensuring that these interactions around a new mechanic can occur in a way that is conducive to players using the Target Skills. Key to this is the principle that levels should offer safe spaces for players to explore new gameplay mechanics (Anthropy & Clark, 2014; Shute et al., 2011). This affords players the opportunity to explore these new capabilities collectively, without the risk of failure and all of the associated tension and anxiety that comes with that risk.

Once players have been given the opportunity to work out how a new move or game object operates, levels should then introduce situations in which the players are required to use these mechanics through experimentation. When levels have players apply their previously rehearsed knowledge of an avatar's special move or a power-up in novel situations, the group members are likely to discuss the possibilities and limitations of a new capability. An example of this is the introduction of the *Cat Suit* power-up in **Mario**, which allows avatars to climb vertical walls within the level. The introduction of power-ups and novel mechanics is most effective when all players have a foundational knowledge of the capability, so these new situations for application should first require the use of a move or object in isolation.

As players develop a deeper understanding of the benefits offered by this new move or power-up, new mechanics can be used and integrated with previously introduced mechanics. For example, in **Mario**, players soon learn to use the *Cat Suit*'s wall climb with their standard jump capability to bounce from wall to wall. At this point, another new mechanic can be introduced, forming a cyclical process that maintains the sense of constant discovery and helps prevent boredom through excessive repetition. This cycle is not dissimilar to the

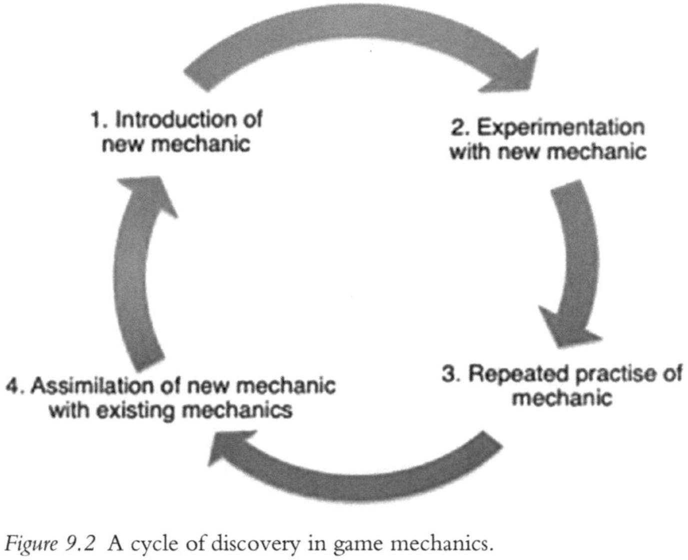

Figure 9.2 A cycle of discovery in game mechanics.

pedagogical concept of 'spaced practice', discussed in *Chapter 2*, with players being provided multiple exposures to a game mechanic. The four stages in the cycle are presented in the diagram below.

This cycle can be used in deciding the points at which new mechanics should be introduced during the initial planning of the scope and sequence of a game. New mechanics are important in maintaining interest in the game and in facilitating discussion as players explore these new capabilities together.

RECOMMENDATIONS

30 New mechanics should be introduced regularly to maintain the sense of discovery, experimentation, assimilation and mastery.
31 Levels should begin with safe spaces for players to explore new gameplay mechanics so that they can practice these without the risk of failure.
32 Situations should be introduced in which the players are required to use new mechanics in isolation and then in combination with previously introduced mechanics.

Game design as an enabler or a barrier to inclusion of all players

Great care needs to be given to ensure that the games are accessible to all players, particularly in identifying specific enablers and barriers to participation. Considerations of great importance include the challenges presented by three-dimensional virtual environments, the way that games controllers should be configured for use within the games and the benefits of in-game tools for alternative means of communication.

Challenges presented by the third dimension

My research identified that game designers need to prioritise accessibility over complexity for games to be used as part of this intervention, especially when it comes to the axis of movement within these virtual worlds. In most instances, I found that children controlling characters within a two-dimensional field of play presents no issues, but significant issues with control were observed in games that required avatars to navigate through complex three-dimensional environments. Whether these issues were a result of the increased visual processing demands placed on the players or the more complicated control schemes required by three-dimensional games varied from child to child, but the take-home message is that three dimensions can create barriers.

RECOMMENDATIONS

33 Games can contain elements of three-dimensional gameplay, but players should be restricted to moving on a two-dimensional axis.
34 Bonus levels and limited sections of a level can use three-dimensional movement, but these should be low risk in nature and optional to completing the primary goals.

Controllers creating an inclusive interface between the players and the game

A player's ability to participate in a game can be determined by the technology used to access that game, such as the affordances offered by the controller. Accessibility can mean different things to different players, with the most important thing in terms of game control being choice. Multiple control options should be made available to players to accommodate different levels of fine motor control and preferences for physical or touch-based inputs. As shown below, Nintendo's Wii U Gamepad provides an excellent example of the different ways that players can control their avatars and interface with the virtual environment.

Certain players will prefer the use of the touch screen, either through a direct interface via their finger or through using the stylus. While using their fingers would be a more familiar experience for children who use a tablet or smartphone regularly, fingers can also block the screen. Using a stylus might address this issue, but children with fine motor control difficulties can find this much more challenging than using direct touch. Traditional buttons and an analogue joystick have been popular with the more experienced gamers with

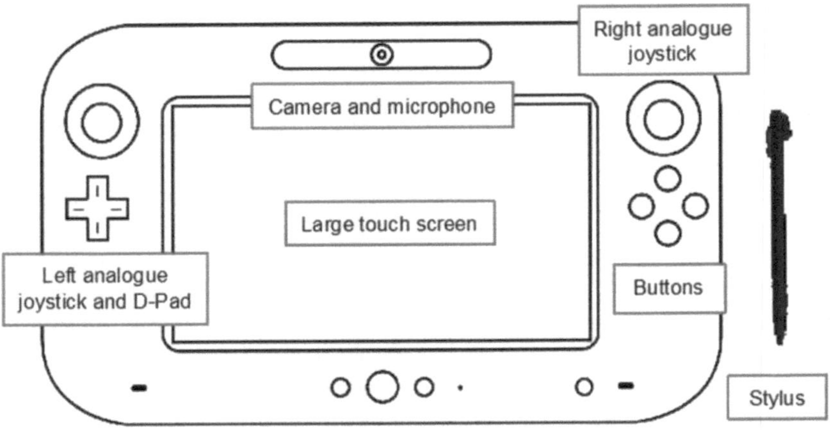

Figure 9.3 Image of Nintendo's Wii U Gamepad.

whom I have worked and, surprisingly, also with some children with fine motor control difficulties. This could be due to the tactile feeling when they press a button, a feature not possible with touch-based controls. The use of 'rumble' or force feedback is popular with most children and, when used strategically, it can provide haptic cues to players with visual processing challenges.

RECOMMENDATIONS

35 Multiple control options should be available to accommodate players with different levels of fine motor control and preferences for physical or touch-based inputs.
36 'Rumble' or force feedback can be used strategically to provide haptic cues to players with visual processing challenges.
37 To reduce the barrier to learning a new game, the default control configurations should be similar to those of popular commercial games.

Tools aiding multiple means of communication and planning

Over the years I have worked with hundreds of different children and have learnt that there can be radically different preferred means of communication in a single group. Rather than ignoring these preferences, interventionists and game designers should find ways to accommodate them, as they can augment verbal communication and help facilitate increased communication sophistication. *Murfy* in **Rayman** is one game-based tool that could be used as a form of digital laser pointer, allowing the player to virtually point to things on the screen. Including digital pointer tools are important in supporting players who preference visual communication over verbal communication.

Opportunities for children to call time-outs when additional planning or processing time is required is an important feature of this intervention. While *Chapter 5* explored the facilitation of time-out breaks through the introduction of a system in the physical world, games also have a role in allowing for pauses in the action. An in-game break card feature should be present in the design of games to promote social interaction. This feature should allow any player to pause the game but still view the screen and use the pointer tool.

RECOMMENDATIONS

38 A digital pointer tool is important in supporting players who preference visual communication over verbal communication.
39 An in-game break card feature should be present to allow players to pause the game but still use the pointer tool.

Summary of recommendations: A checklist for evaluating games

Now you are familiar with all 39 recommendations, you need to know how to evaluate any games you might want to use as part of your intervention. To help you in making an evidence-informed decision, we suggest you use the following checklist as a starting point. This checklist frames these recommendations as things to think about and provides a scoring system to help you keep track of how well a certain game aligns with these evidence-informed recommendations.

While the checklist score can serve as one point of reference in helping your decision making, it should not be the only consideration in choosing a game. Other factors to consider include:

- **Suggestions by the participating children**: We know how important participant voice is in successful interventions, and ideally many of your targeted children will have a strong interest in gaming. Build from this interest and use their knowledge of games to help you decide an appropriate title to play.
- **Age ratings**: All games have age ratings much like films, so it is important as an act of duty of care that we introduce games that contain appropriate language and depictions of action. Choose carefully and follow the ratings despite the predictable pressure you will receive from some of your participating children. To help you with this, I provide reviews of appropriate games in the next chapter.
- **Representation**: Beyond appropriate language and depictions of action, it is important to select games that avoid overly sexualised content or stereotypical depictions of race or religion. Even if a game is non-violent, it is important that everyone feels safe and welcome in the group. Unfortunately, even some games rated as being family friendly can include insensitive portrayals of minorities or outright sexism.

Weighing these factors in conjunction with your analysis of the game through the checklist can help ensure that your intervention will use the right game for the children in your group. Your chosen game(s) should not only be enjoyable for participants, but also provide them with every opportunity to be successful social learners.

Instructions for using this checklist to select the right game

- Play the new game with a critical friend, ideally someone who has also had experience implementing or plans on implementing this intervention.
- After playing the new game for 30 minutes, work with your critical friend using this checklist to systematically check ☑ whether you have found each recommendation in the game.
- Calculate the score and record your thoughts on the second page of this checklist.
- Remember this checklist should only be one point of reference when selecting a cooperative multiplayer game to use in this intervention.

Game name:	
System:	
Age rating:	

Player identity within the team		
	Avatars shaping individual identity within the group	
	1	Familiar character designs are useful in allowing players to identify themselves and their allies in the virtual environment. ☐
	2	There needs to be a distinct visual difference between player avatars and enemies. ☐
	3	When players select their avatars, they should have a choice on how they are represented aesthetically in the game. ☐
	The role of non-playable characters in forging a collective identity	
	4	Non-playable computer-controlled allies should provide players with advice and build the narrative but should have limited impact on the actual gameplay. ☐
	5	Defeating some enemies should require multiple steps from multiple players. ☐
	6	Boss battles should require group planning, problem-solving and coordination through the simultaneous application of previously rehearsed skills. ☐
	Game feedback on individual and team performance	
	7	Players should receive individual-level feedback. This is important to them in fulfilling their individual roles within the team during gameplay. ☐
	8	Feedback related to progress towards the collective goal should emphasise team-level feedback over individual-level feedback. ☐
	9	Feedback should be accessible to all players using multiple modes of representation and allow for sufficient processing time. ☐

Rules of play to manufacture interaction		Interdependent progress through designed constraint
	10	Screen scrolling should require all avatars to be in close proximity to ensure more skilful players remain with less skilful players, and to provide opportunities for democratic decision making. ☐
	11	Active participation should be manufactured through the use of puzzles or obstacles requiring the involvement of all players. ☐
	12	Specific capabilities should be distributed amongst the avatars so that they need to be combined with the capabilities of other avatars in order to progress.☐
		Limiting the use of shared avatars
	13	Ideally games with shared avatars should allow players to progress through the level at their own pace without forced movement. ☐
	14	Games using shared avatars should provide differentiated roles for different skill levels. ☐
		Game mechanics promoting leadership and apprenticeship
	1	The game should support peer coaching by adopting established genre conventions, allowing experienced players to utilise their knowledge to coach novice players. ☐
	16	Players should have opportunities to switch between primary and secondary roles in the team. ☐
	17	The play mechanics should allow less skilful players to have a required and regular role in achieving the team goal. ☐
		Failure as learning rather than punishment
	18	Players should have independent, individual health bars to ensure that more skilled players are not penalised by less skilled players. ☐
	19	When a player's avatar dies while those of their peers are still alive, this player should be able to 'respawn' relatively quickly, and there should be an element of player interactivity in this waiting time. ☐
	20	Games need to have multiple checkpoints within a level, so that when all players' avatars are killed, they can return to an area close to where they died. ☐

Level design that is conducive to social skills performance		Level signposting to support player progress
	21	Levels should follow a largely linear path so that all players have a general understanding of the direction in which they need to move. ☐
	22	Hidden paths leading to special items or bonuses can be included, but players should always be able to return to the more linear sections of the level. ☐
	23	High-stakes hazards, such as bottomless pits, should have a clear visual cue that these will cause instant failure and should be avoided. ☐
		Environmental interactivity fostering player interaction
	24	Levels should include optional interactive objects that can assist the progress of another player, such as switches that provide a temporary bridge. ☐
	25	Obstacles in some levels may mandate the interaction of multiple players before they are allowed to proceed, such as the synchronised detonation of bomb blocks to destroy an impeding boulder. ☐
	26	There should be minimal pressure on players when new interactive objects and obstacles are first introduced, allowing them room for error and time to coordinate their actions correctly until they are familiar with how they work. ☐
		Inducing stressful situations
	27	In stressful situations, players should use only mechanics with which they are familiar, with sufficient 'safe' time allowed for practice. ☐
	28	The game should communicate to players when stressful situations will end. ☐
	29	Designed stressful situations should require input from all players and should allow players to offer in-game assistance to each other to reduce the immediacy of failure. ☐
		Sustaining player motivation through introducing new mechanics
	30	New mechanics should be introduced regularly to maintain the sense of discovery, experimentation, assimilation and mastery. ☐
	31	Levels should begin with safe spaces for players to explore new gameplay mechanics so that they can practice these without the risk of failure. ☐
	32	Situations should be introduced in which the players are required to use new mechanics in isolation and then in combination with previously introduced mechanics. ☐

Game design as an enabler for including all players

The challenge of the third dimension
33 Games can contain elements of three-dimensional gameplay, but players should be restricted to moving on a two-dimensional axis. ☐
34 Bonus levels and limited sections of a level can use three-dimensional movement, but these should be low risk in nature and optional to completing the primary goals. ☐
Controllers creating an inclusive interface between the players and the game
35 Multiple control options should be available to consider players with different levels of fine motor control and preferences for physical or touch-based inputs. ☐
36 Rumble' or force feedback can be used strategically to provide haptic cues to players with visual processing challenges. ☐
37 To reduce the barrier to learning a new game, the default control configurations should be similar to those of popular commercial games. ☐
Tools aiding multiple means of communication and planning
38 A digital pointer tool is important in supporting players who preference visual communication over verbal communication. ☐
39 An in-game break card feature should be present to allow players to pause the game but still use the pointer tool. ☐

Final score (out of 39): _____ (each ☑ is one point)		
0-10: This game is unlikely to create enough opportunities for interactions	**11-25**: This game offers sufficient opportunities for collaborative play so is appropriate for use.	**26-40**: This game is ideal for this intervention and should be prioritised for use.
Your final evaluation of this game (one sentence)		

References

Anthropy, A., & Clark, N. (2014). *A game design vocabulary*. Pearson Education.

Bidarra, J., Rothschild, M., Squire, K., & Figueiredo, M. (2013). The AIDLET model: A framework for selecting games, simulations and augmented reality environments in mobile learning. *International Journal of Web-Based Learning and Teaching Technologies*, *8*(4), 50–71.

Burgers, C., Eden, A., van Engelenburg, M. D., & Buningh, S. (2015). How feedback boosts motivation and play in a brain-training game. *Computers in Human Behavior*, *48*, 94–103.

Chen, M. (2012). *Leet noobs: The life and death of an expert player group in World of Warcraft*. Peter Lang.

Crawford, G. (2011). *Video gamers*. Routledge.

Garzotto, F. (2007). Investigating the educational effectiveness of multiplayer online games for children. In *Proceedings of the 6th international conference on interaction design and children* [Conference proceedings] (pp. 29–36). New York. ACM.

Gee, J. P. (2007). *What video games have to teach us about learning and literacy*. Palgrave Macmillan.

Gee, J. P. (2013). *Good video games + good learning: Collected essays on video games, learning and literacy* (2nd ed.). Peter Lang.

Gee, J. P. (2018). Affinity spaces: How young people live and learn online and out of school. *Phi Delta Kappan*, *99*(6), 8–13.

González-González, C., & Blanco-Izquierdo, F. (2012). Designing social videogames for educational uses. *Computers & Education*, *58*(1), 250–262.

Hayes, E. R., & Duncan, S. C. (2012). *Learning in video game affinity spaces (new literacies and digital epistemologies)*. Peter Lang.

Nintendo. (2013). *Super Mario 3D World* [Videogame]. Retrieved from https://www.nintendo.com.au/catalogue/super-mario-3d-world

Nintendo. (2015). *Kirby and the Rainbow Paintbrush* [Videogame]. Retrieved from https://www.nintendo.com.au/catalogue/kirby-and-the-rainbow-paintbrush

Nintendo. (2016). *Star Fox Zero* [Videogame]. Retrieved from https://www.nintendo.com.au/catalogue/star-fox-zero

Shaw, A. (2012). Do you identify as a gamer? Gender, race, sexuality, and gamer identity. *New Media & Society*, *14*(1), 28–44.

Shute, V. J., Rieber, L., & van Eck, R. (2011). Games ... and ... learning. In R. Reiser & J. Dempsey (Eds.), *Trends and issues in instructional design and technology* (3rd ed., pp. 321–332). Pearson Education.

Squire, K. (2005). Changing the game: What happens when video games enter the classroom? *Innovate: Journal of Online Education*, *1*(6), 1–8.

Sweller, J., Ayres, P., & Kalyuga, S. (2011). *Cognitive load theory*. Springer-Verlag.

Ubisoft. (2013). *Rayman legends* [Videogame]. Retrieved from https://www.nintendo.com/games/detail/rayman-legends-wii-u

Zea, N. P., Sánchez, J. L. G., Gutiérrez, F. L., Cabrera, M. J., & Paderewski, P. (2009). Design of educational multiplayer videogames: A vision from collaborative learning. *Advances in Engineering Software*, *40*(12), 1251–1260.

10 A guide to cooperative video games

Introduction

To help you in getting started with digital games–based intervention, this final chapter provides a concise list of existing video game consoles and software titles that are viable options for use in your program. Technical capabilities for each respective video game system are presented alongside my anecdotal experiences of using these consoles in my own programs. Likewise, reviews of each game included perceived areas of strength and challenge in regard to the game design principles outlined in the previous chapters as well important practical considerations such as the maximum number of players and the game genre.

Overview of gaming systems

Video games consoles are more pervasive now than ever. The gross annual global revenue generated from video games during 2020 is estimated at a staggering US$179 billion, which is almost double the total annual earnings of the film industry (Gilbert, 2020). This is not a COVID-19 induced flash in the pan but rather the continuation of a long-term trend (Takahashi, 2016). Gaming consoles will be key to your intervention. It is therefore important to understand the differences between each system, as game libraries will vary between machines as will accessibility options. While the children and young adults you work with will no doubt request the latest and greatest consoles (such as the PlayStation 5 or Xbox Series X both released in late 2020), you do not need to spend a lot of money to find a console with games well suited for use in this intervention. In this section, a series of newer current generation and previous generation consoles are detailed, presenting interventionists with relevant technical details (such as the supported number of players) and my own subjective evaluation of the suitability of the respective game libraries. Review the below tables, find out what you might already have access to in your school and setting and explore what is financially feasible. There is no single correct answer, but it is important to be aware of your options.

Playing with power: current generation consoles

As of the time of writing, these gaming systems can be considered the current generation of systems, although the Sony PlayStation 4 and the Xbox One

DOI: 10.4324/9781003025917-10

have been usurped by the arrival of their respective replacements. That said, both systems should still be receiving new titles for at least several more years due to their high numbers of existing users and shortages of the new consoles (Wiseman, 2021). I have also included Windows PCs here because these are already in many schools, and this platform has received versions of many of the games I recommend that you consider for your intervention.

	Nintendo Switch (released 2017)	*Sony PlayStation 4/5 (released 2014/2020)*	*Microsoft Xbox One/Series X (released 2014/2020)*	*Windows PC (constant revisions)*
Cost(s)	Mid-tier system cost with games spanning from free to expensive	Mid-tier system costs/Expensive system cost with games spanning from free to expensive	Mid-tier system costs/Expensive system cost with games spanning from free to expensive	Expensive system cost with games spanning from free to expensive
Controller options	Joy-Cons are small controllers that offer button inputs, motion controls and haptic (vibration) feedback. Can be difficult to use for players with fine motor skill challenges or larger hands. Players can also use a Switch Pro controller that provides a more traditional input option.	The PlayStation 4 uses the DualShock4, a traditional controller with two analogue sticks, button and trigger inputs and a small track pad. The PlayStation 5 uses the DualSense, with a similar layout to previous controllers but provides sophisticated haptic (vibration) feedback.	The Xbox One/Series X supports a range of controllers. While the default controllers use a traditional layout (dual analogue sticks, buttons and triggers), the Microsoft Adaptive Controller is a game changer for players with fine and gross motor challenges. It allows for play using switches and buttons and is a wonderful example of co-design.	Windows PCs offer the most controller options. Beyond using a keyboard and mouse, PCs are compatible with most Bluetooth gamepads, adaptive controllers and specialised assistive gaming technology. One example of this latter category is eye gaze technology allowing players to control their characters without using their hands.
Personal preference	1st choice due to the range of age-appropriate local multiplayer games	3rd choice due to having less age-appropriate local multiplayer games	2nd choice due to the accessibility options	4th choice due to the relatively high entry costs and need to upgrade

Oldies but goldies: previous generation gaming consoles

As any gamer born in the 1980s will tell you, new does not necessarily mean better. These four older consoles offer plenty of options, with hardware and games often found in second-hand stores for very reasonable prices. Someone in your school or setting might even have one or more of these systems in storage that they could donate for your program. Ask around, as it might surprise you who has one of these devices lying around their house!

	Nintendo Wii U (released 2012)	*Sony PlayStation 3 (released 2014/2020)*	*Nintendo Wii (released 2006)*	*Microsoft Xbox360 (released 2005)*
Cost(s)	Low cost (system and most games) but rising in price as a collectible	Low cost (system and most games)	Low cost (system and most games) but rising in price as a collectible	Low cost (system and most games)
Controller options	One of the most controversial designs ever, the Wii U gamepad is a wonderful tool for inclusive play despite its appearance. It allows touch controls and traditional analogue stick and button inputs. It also includes a camera and a microphone, with some games providing a choice of how people play.	The PlayStation 3 uses the DualShock 3, a traditional controller with dual analogue sticks, buttons, triggers and limited motion controls. The PlayStation Move motion controllers are also supported by a small number of games.	A revolution at the time, the Wii uses rudimentary motion controls, allowing for more accessible game experiences. Designed to be used by a wider audience, the controller is designed to look like a traditional TV remote control.	The Xbox360 uses a traditional controller with dual analogue sticks, buttons and triggers. A number of games support the Kinect sensor that allows full-body controls of specifically designed games, rather than using traditional controller inputs.
Personal preference	1st choice due to diverse control options and the range of age-appropriate local multiplayer games.	Tied 3rd choice due to having less age-appropriate local multiplayer games.	2nd choice due to the motion controls and range of age-appropriate games.	Tied 3rd choice due to having less age-appropriate local multiplayer games.

Game reviews

Use these game reviews in conjunction with the local knowledge within your school or setting to decide on which games you will use in your program. Each game is rated out of five in the four areas that my research found to be the most important in creating the conditions for collaboration: (1) team identity, (2) rules of play, (3) level design and (4) inclusive design. While these reviews are well informed by the hours upon hours I have spent using these titles with hordes of children and young adults, you might have different experiences based on the individuals with whom you are working. All of these games have been enjoyed by the majority of my participants. Begin here but do not be afraid to experiment. This list contains a variety of games for a diverse range of audiences, but all of these games are suitable for play in a school or therapy setting.

2D platform games

Rayman Legends

<table>
<tr><th colspan="2">Gaming system(s)</th><th>Game genre</th><th colspan="2">Possible simultaneous players</th></tr>
<tr><td colspan="2">Wii U, Switch, PS3, PS4, Xbox360, Xbox One</td><td>2D platform</td><td colspan="2">4 simultaneous players (5 players on Wii U)</td></tr>
<tr><td colspan="5">An outstanding multiplayer game that exemplifies the principles of interdependent design in a creative take on the classic 2D platform genre. Rayman Legends requires close coordination between the player controlling the green fly character Murfy and the players using the other protagonists. As players work their way towards the finish line of each level, the game demands a high frequency of interactions through clever obstacles and multi-staged enemies. While the high-quality animation is often humorous, it can be a little visually overwhelming and the design of the characters can make it slightly difficult for some children to remember who they are controlling. That said, touch screen controls for Murfy are a wonderful option for players with fine motor skills challenges. If you are looking for a game to begin your program, Rayman Legends has a lot to recommend.</td></tr>
<tr><td>Team identity (/5)</td><td colspan="2">Rules of play (/5)</td><td>Level design (/5)</td><td>Inclusive design (/5)</td></tr>
<tr><td>🎮🎮🎮🎮</td><td colspan="2">🎮🎮🎮🎮🎮</td><td>🎮🎮🎮🎮🎮</td><td>🎮🎮🎮🎮</td></tr>
</table>

Ms. Splosion Man

Gaming system(s)	Game genre	Possible simultaneous players
Xbox360, Switch, Windows PC	2D platform	4 simultaneous players

A sequel to the immensely popular 'Splosion Man, this multiplayer physics-based platform game has a wickedly dark sense of humour (which very occasionally crosses into adult-targeted territory). Hidden behind the vibrant graphics is a clever design that requires players to 'explode' themselves and their teammates to reach new heights, requiring a high degree of coordinate planning and action. The levels serve as a form of obstacle course with players engaging in often hilarious 'productive failure', experimenting with 'exploding' different objects in their environment and learning what does and does not work in this world. This game has a wonderful atmosphere although some players with low levels of patience, differences in sensory processing or who experience challenges with fine motor control might find this game too much. A good choice if you are working with older and more experienced gamers.

Team identity (/5)	**Rules of play (/5)**	**Level design (/5)**	**Inclusive design (/5)**
🎮🎮🎮	🎮🎮🎮	🎮🎮🎮	🎮🎮

Kirby and the Rainbow Paintbrush

Gaming system(s)	*Game genre*	*Possible simultaneous players*
Wii U	*2D platform*	*4 simultaneous players*

So what is Kirby? In this game, *Kirby* is a pink ball of clay that players must safely steer (and escort) through a series of levels and boss character encounters. The game requires the players to coordinate between *Kirby* and his friendly assistant *Waddle-Dees* to make progress, with *Kirby* being controlled using a stylus (representing the titular Rainbow Paintbrush). Player 1 draws lines of where they want *Kirby* to move on the Wii U gamepad, while the other players control *Waddle-Dees* using traditional gamepad inputs. While *Waddle-Dees* have less life than *Kirby*, they quickly respawn if they run out of health. If *Kirby* dies, then all of the players need to restart the level. The use of the stylus with the high stakes of controlling *Kirby* can create frustrations for players who have difficulties with fine motor control as it relies on coordination between the player's drawing and the continual natural movement of *Kirby*. Presenting multiple team roles with multiple control inputs is commendable, although it can leave some players feeling secondary if they are unable to control *Kirby*. Cute visuals and a very forgiving level of difficulty make this game ideal for younger players as long as they can come to grips with controlling the protagonist.

Team identity (/5)	**Rules of play (/5)**	**Level design (/5)**	**Inclusive design (/5)**
🎮🎮🎮½	🎮🎮🎮	🎮🎮🎮½	🎮🎮🎮

Donkey Kong Country Tropical Freeze

Gaming system(s)	Game genre	Possible simultaneous players
Switch, Wii U	2D platform	2 simultaneous players

A revitalisation of the classic Super Nintendo series, Donkey Kong Country Tropical Freeze maintains the whimsical charm, iconic characters and unforgiving level of difficulty of the originals. Controlling one of four distinct members of the *Kong* family, players combine their unique abilities to make progress through levels. Visually interesting and with one of the greatest video game soundtracks of all time, this game is hard. If you are working with expert gamers with a high degree of patience, Donkey Kong Country Tropical Freeze provides varied levels and ample opportunities for players to support each other. That said, it can be difficult to even keep both characters on screen and many levels force you to make decisions quickly, creating a high degree of stress.

Team identity (/5)	**Rules of play (/5)**	**Level design (/5)**	**Inclusive design (/5)**
🎮🎮🎮	🎮🎮	🎮🎮🎮	🎮

The Lost Vikings (part of the Blizzard Arcade Collection)

Gaming system(s)	Game genre	Possible simultaneous players
Switch, PlayStation 4, Xbox One, Windows PC	2D platform	3 simultaneous players

A rerelease of the Blizzard Entertainment classic, the Lost Vikings was one of the first collaborative platform games to feature dispersed abilities, requiring players to work together and synchronise their actions to complete the puzzle-like levels. Each visually distinctive *Viking* has clearly defined unique abilities, such as being able to attack or to jump. Careful planning and experimentation are required to test how these abilities can be combined to be able to progress past obstacles and to complete the increasingly complex levels. Two players can play simultaneously but the screen will always follow player one, which can potentially cause tensions and make it difficult for player two. It should also be noted that as this game was designed prior to the widespread use of voiceovers in games, the Lost Vikings can be very text heavy, which can present a barrier to the inclusion of players' cognitive processing difficulties.

Team identity (/5)	**Rules of play (/5)**	**Level design (/5)**	**Inclusive design (/5)**
🎮🎮🎮🎮	🎮🎮🎮	🎮🎮🎮🎮	🎮🎮

3D platform games

Super Mario 3D World

Gaming system(s)	Game genre	Possible simultaneous players
Switch, Wii U	3D platform	4 simultaneous players

Building on the mechanics and characters of the iconic Nintendo series, Super Mario 3D World is an easy crowd-pleaser although it requires less teamwork than other games. Designed primarily for provoking a sense of fun without taking itself too seriously, each level seemingly introduces something new. This could be a new item or a level design that challenges the established conventions of the series. While the use of familiar characters makes this a game that almost anyone wants to pick up and play, some players with cognitive challenges have found it difficult to judge where they are in the 3D space, particularly when other players and enemies are running around. Navigating the additional plane combined with constantly changing expectations and mechanics can become frustrating for these players. In terms of collaborative play, this game emphasises individual achievements over team play, with the first player to reach the end of level flagpole awarded a crown to wear for the next level. A little bit of competition can be fun, but this needs to be carefully managed by the interventionists.

Team identity (/5)	**Rules of play (/5)**	**Level design (/5)**	**Inclusive design (/5)**

Sackboy: A Big Adventure

Gaming system(s)	Game genre	Possible simultaneous players
PS4, PS5	3D platform	4 simultaneous players

Featuring an endearing cast of characters, Sackboy is a traditional 3D platform game that has an accessible entry level of difficulty that gradually increases as the game progresses. Players will rarely get lost as the design is mostly linear, with clear signposting in almost every instance. While the mechanics of play encourage largely parallel exploration, the game features several specifically designed levels demanding player coordination and collaborative problem-solving. If you are supporting a new group of players who want more agency in how they interact with the world, the lack of reliance on other players can make this game a solid initial choice. The tried and tested gameplay is complemented by well-designed visuals, and the soundtrack is catchy without becoming annoying.

Team identity (/5)	**Rules of play (/5)**	**Level design (/5)**	**Inclusive design (/5)**

Cooperative puzzle games

Overcooked 1 and 2

Gaming system(s)	Game genre	Possible simultaneous players
Switch, PS4, PS5, Xbox One, Xbox Series X, Windows PC	Action/puzzle	4 simultaneous players

Fancy a bit of frantic kitchen action? This acclaimed four-player game series sees a team of chefs working together to fulfil order dockets whilst navigating increasingly bizarre and dangerous kitchen environments. Players must cut, mix, cook and plate ingredients while their kitchen fills with lava, floorboards fall away or other obstacles suddenly appear out of nowhere. Both games present an increasing series of challenges from an overhead view, with players needing to synchronise and communicate what they are doing and will do next, as the game applies pressure. Simple controls and mechanics make this an easy game to pick up and play, although it is not for everyone. For some players, particularly those with cognitive processing difficulties or heightened levels of anxiety, the time pressure can become too stressful. The visual presentation is colourful but simple, making it easy for players to find their avatar, with a rather nondescript soundtrack that doesn't distract from the action.

Team identity (/5)	**Rules of play (/5)**	**Level design (/5)**	**Inclusive design (/5)**

Catastronauts

Gaming system(s)	Game genre	
Switch, Windows PC, PS4, PS5, Xbox One, Xbox Series X	Action/puzzle	4 players (simultaneous play)

How hard can it be to maintain a spaceship? Catastronauts (a portmanteau of catastrophe and astronaut, with unfortunately no cats involved) attempts to answer that very question. This game requires players to delegate tasks and to synchronise their actions repairing broken equipment, putting out fires and firing laser cannons and an assortment of other space-aged weapons at alien attackers. Things can quickly get out of hand, with the interior layout of your spaceship changing level to level, creating barriers and frustrations to your ease of navigation. Presented in a simplistic single-screen field of action, this game encourages a high degree of interaction. While the first few levels can be completed with relative ease, the stress soon increases and near constant communication is required. Some players with auditory processing challenges will find this too much, but most children with whom I have played this enjoy this intensity when supported with regular breaks for review and planning. Although it uses only three buttons, some players will find the different buttons for picking up items and putting them down overwhelming when faced with increased pressure.

Team identity (/5)	**Rules of play (/5)**	**Level design (/5)**	**Inclusive design (/5)**

Lovers in a Dangerous Spacetime

Gaming system(s)	Game genre	Possible simultaneous players
Windows PC, Switch, Xbox One, Xbox Series X, PS4, PS5	Action/platform/puzzler	4 simultaneous players

As far as genre-defying games go, Lovers in a Dangerous Spacetime is wonderfully frantic and surreal. In this unique action platform puzzler (or perhaps genre defying?), players work together to pilot their spaceship through the universe trying to restore 'love' wherever they venture (and rescuing trapped 'Lovers' along the way from the evil anti-love robots). I assure you this is a family friendly game. Throughout the game players can collect different types of gems that they can use to upgrade components of their ship, giving this game a real sense of progression. Coordinated actions and decision making are requisites for success, as players move around their ship, which is presented using a two-dimensional 'side on' perspective. While the action is often tense, the use of the side on perspective results in this game being more accessible for some players compared to the overhead perspective found in Overcooked or Catastronauts. Cute character designs and a spacey soundtrack afford a wonderful sense of surreal adventure that will appeal to most players.

Team identity (/5)	**Rules of play (/5)**	**Level design (/5)**	**Inclusive design (/5)**
🎮🎮🎮	🎮🎮🎮🎮	🎮🎮🎮🎮	🎮🎮

Affordable Space Adventures

Gaming system(s)	Game genre	Possible simultaneous players
Wii U	2D flight adventure	3 simultaneous players

Exploring space is a popular theme for multiplayer games, with Affordable Space Adventures offering a unique take on collaborative navigation and resource management. Working as a team to control a single craft, each player is responsible for certain systems (directional steering, engine power, weapons and headlights) in order to find their way home on a hostile alien planet. Using a side on, two-dimensional perspective, spectacular landscapes and set pieces forge an interesting game world. The team will need to work together to solve puzzles and manage their available resources, with all three players being important in solving most puzzles. In comparison to other games reviewed in this chapter, Affordable Space Adventures usually allows players to slow down and to work at their own pace, which is a welcome change for individuals with cognitive processing challenges.

Team identity (/5)	**Rules of play (/5)**	**Level design (/5)**	**Inclusive design (/5)**
🎮🎮🎮	🎮🎮🎮🎮	🎮🎮🎮	🎮🎮🎮½

Moving Out

Gaming system(s)	Game genre	Possible simultaneous players
Switch, PS4, PS5, Xbox One, Xbox Series X, Windows PC	Action/puzzle	4 simultaneous players

Not normally considered an exciting premise for a game, this moving simulator requires players to work together to move awkwardly shaped objects out of a house into a waiting moving van. Heavier items such as beds and fridges require two or more players to lift, with everyone racing the clock to complete the move. Just like in a real move, objects of different sizes and shapes need to be prioritised and moved in a sequence that will allow everything to fit. This requires a lot of team-level planning, sharing of ideas and critical debate. While the time pressure and the complexity of the house layout increase as the game progresses, it has never become too overwhelming for most of the participants with whom I have worked playing Moving Out. That's not to say this is an easy game; rather, it feels less stressful than Overcooked or Catastronauts. This is due partly to the clean visual design, making the action easy to comprehend for players of all levels of skill.

Team identity (/5)	Rules of play (/5)	Level design (/5)	Inclusive design (/5)

Untitled Goose Game

Gaming system(s)	Game genre	Possible simultaneous players
Windows PC, Switch, PS4, PS5, Xbox One, Xbox Series X	Action/puzzle	2 simultaneous players

Honk! The award-winning Australian-designed goose simulator offers a fun two-player cooperative mode. The goal of this game is for players to complete a series of tasks any way they can to cause as much chaos as possible to the non-playable inhabitants of the world. Players will be stealing keys, spraying hapless bystanders with water and generally being annoying. Two players can each pilot their own goose, with the largely locked overhead perspective requiring players to plan and negotiate where they are going next. Some tasks require coordinated actions, suck as one person luring an unsuspecting farmer close to a sprinkler and the other player turning on the tap when the unfortunate non-playable character gets close enough to be soaked. Beyond the officially designed cooperative mode, some of my participants have enjoyed 'co-piloting' the goose on the Windows PC, with one player using the keyboard to steer the said bird, while the other player uses the mouse to control the goose's beak. The game is slower paced with little punishment for failing a task, which makes it ideally suited for students with cognitive processing challenges, although some players may be frustrated with the careful timing required for some of the tasks (for example, having to wait for a non-playable to be standing in a certain spot).

Team identity (/5)	Rules of play (/5)	Level design (/5)	Inclusive design (/5)

Role-playing and adventure games

Secret of Mana

Gaming system(s)	Game genre	Possible simultaneous players
Switch, PS4, PS5, Windows PC	Real-time role playing	3 simultaneous players

The classic Squaresoft role-playing game from the 1990s has been rereleased on a number of systems, although I would argue that the best way to experience it is still on the original Super Nintendo (or the Super Nintendo Mini released in 2017). Yes, I am showing my age! In terms of coordinating actions there is a high degree of freedom and limited mandated interaction, although as the game becomes more difficult players will need to support each other. Enemies can be tough and players benefit from equipping complementary items, planning their attacks and healing each other. Beyond screen scrolling following player one, the incentive for playing as a team comes from the difficulty met by those who try to 'go it alone'. Thinking about the inclusion of all players, the timed attacking system may be a little confusing for some children who have never played this style of role-playing game before, as button mashing (hitting the attack button repeatedly) is ineffective. The pixel art is spectacular but can become visually overwhelming for some children with cognitive processing challenges. Where this game really shines is in the story that it tells, but again all of the dialogue is text-based, which can present further barriers for younger children or those with emerging literacy skills.

Team identity (/5)	Rules of play (/5)	Level design (/5)	Inclusive design (/5)
🎮🎮🎮	🎮🎮🎮	🎮🎮	🎮🎮

Don't Starve Together

Gaming system(s)	Game genre	Possible simultaneous players
Switch	Role-playing game	4 simultaneous players

If you are working with some fans of Minecraft this could be a great choice for your group! Players work together to collect resources and build up a civilisation during the daytime to survive the nighttime creepers. As day and night cycles alternate, players must plan their actions and ensure they are back safely in their base by the time the sun sets. Once enough basic resources have been collected, tools can be crafted and crops can be planted to ease the burden of running out of food, but the biggest obstacle is often overconfidence in how far players can move away from the safety of their base and still make it home in time before the sun goes down. Coordination of actions and sharing of responsibilities is the only way for teams to be successful during the limited safe time within each day-night cycle. Beautifully hand-drawn cartoon graphics and humorous sound effects help to make this more an exercise in comedy than horror, but the stress of a ticking clock can create tensions within a group. The overhead view, in combination with relatively simple controls, makes this a more accessible experience than Minecraft, although it can become easy for players to become disorientated if they rotate the camera.

Team identity (/5)	Rules of play (/5)	Level design (/5)	Inclusive design (/5)
🎮🎮🎮	🎮🎮🎮	🎮🎮🎮🎮	🎮🎮🎮

3D action games

Luigi's Mansion 3

Gaming system(s)	Game genre	Possible simultaneous players
Switch	3D adventure	2 simultaneous players

An interesting adventure game that sticks closely to the formula of the previous two games in the series, *Luigi* and *Gooigi* (a translucent gooey *Luigi* doppelganger) work together to hunt ghosts, solve puzzles and explore a haunted hotel. Using their ghost-hunting vacuums, players move through a linear series of themed hotel floors collecting elevator buttons to make progress. The difficulty level is very accessible, although this is very much *Luigi*'s game with the second player serving in a supporting role. The two playable characters do have some differences, with *Gooigi* able to change his shape to squeeze through grates and bars, but vulnerable to any water lying around. In classic Nintendo fashion, the visuals are more 'cute' rather than horrifying, with a dry sense of humour throughout. However, the music is markedly chilling, creating a wonderful atmosphere through the approximately ten hours of gameplay. Pacing is slower than other games, which will benefit players with information processing challenges, and the control scheme is relatively intuitive. If your children or young adults are interested in an age-appropriate take on the classic series Resident Evil, this could be the game for them.

Team identity (/5)	**Rules of play (/5)**	**Level design (/5)**	**Inclusive design (/5)**

Star Fox Zero

Gaming system(s)	Game genre	Possible simultaneous players
Wii U	On rails shooter	2 simultaneous players

Based on the classic Nintendo on rails shooter series, players work together to co-pilot a shared *Arwing* through intense action set pieces. This game is best compared to a virtual rollercoaster of non-stop shooting and explosions. One pilot steers the spaceship using a traditional controller, while the other player uses the Wii U controller to precisely aim the weapons systems. Near constant waves of enemies and numerous obstacles can create a great deal of stress, so this is a game best enjoyed by players of a similar skill level. For the player aiming the weapons, it can be a little disconcerting having to look at the larger TV to gauge a large video, and then looking down at the Wii U gamepad to aim more precisely. Players who have cognitive processing or fine motor challenges will find this an exercise in frustration. That said, the memorable characters, the bountiful explosions and the tense soundtrack all help to create an atmosphere of exhilaration and a sense of achievement at the end of every level.

Team identity (/5)	**Rules of play (/5)**	**Level design (/5)**	**Inclusive design (/5)**

Next steps for you as a digital games–based interventionist

Now that you have explored some time-possible cooperative games that you can use as a starting point, it is time to begin planning to put the Level Up Collaboration intervention into action in your school or setting. The emphasis throughout this book has been that experimentation guided by the research evidence, your team's collective professional judgement and the voices of participants will be key in a successful implementation. This of course extends to the games that you select for use during Stage B. There will be hundreds of other possible titles for you to choose from, including games released after the publication of this book. Use the recommendations outlined in Chapter 9 in conjunction with the local knowledge of your staff and participants to make informed choices about what is most likely to be effective for your intervention. Finally, don't be afraid of productive failure. I have tried some software titles with one group and found them to be highly effective, only to try them with a different cohort to find that the same title just does not work with this other group. When this happens in your intervention, work with your team to identify the variables that might be causing this difference in outcome and learn from this to inform your decision making in the future. If you find a game that you think everyone should know about, please do share it far and wide.

Digital games–based intervention is fun because the participants are usually excited to be involved, and this enthusiasm is contagious. Enjoy your time with your participants and celebrate the successes of your group, big or small. Many of my most memorable and emotionally powerful moments have been implementing the Level Up Collaboration intervention with the passionate gamers with whom I have had the privilege of working throughout my career. I hope this program brings you and your community the same joy that it has brought to me.

References

Gilbert, B. (2020, December). *Video-game industry revenues grew so much during the pandemic that they reportedly exceeded sports and film combined*. Retrieved from https://www.businessinsider.com.au/video-game-industry-revenues-exceed-sports-and-film-combined

Takahashi, D. (2016, June). PwC: Game industry to grow nearly 5% annually through 2020. Retrieved from https://venturebeat.com/2016/06/08/the-u-s-and-global-game-industries-will-grow-a-healthy-amount-by-2020-pwc-forecasts/

Wiseman, L. (2021, May 10). *Sony now expecting PS5 shortages to continue into next year*. Retrieved from https://www.kotaku.com.au/2021/05/sony-expects-ps5-shortages-to-continue-into-next-year

Index

Page numbers in *italics* represent figures while page numbers in **bold** mark the location of tables.